FOSS Next Generation

Science
Resources

Full Option Science System
Developed at
The Lawrence Hall of Science,
University of California, Berkeley
Published and distributed by
Delta Education,
a member of the School Specialty Family

1511921
978-1-62571-448-0
Printing 11 — 6/2021
Webcrafters, Madison, WI

FOSS Science Resources

FOSS Science Resources

Mixtures and Solutions

Table of Contents

Mixtures

Sand is a mixture.

The next time you are at the beach, pick up a handful of sand. Look at it closely. You will see that each grain of sand is really a tiny rock. Not only that, but the grains are different colors. And some of the grains are not rocks at all. They are little pieces of seashells.

Sand is a **mixture**. A mixture is two or more materials put together, or combined. This sand is a mixture of black, white, tan, and gray rocks, and bits of shell. A handful of sand is a mixture of several different things.

Mixtures are everywhere. But if you are not looking for them, you could miss them. The sidewalk is a mixture you can walk on. It is several sizes of rock mixed with cement. A bowl of mixed nuts is a mixture you can eat. So are fruit salad, vegetable soup, and carrot-and-raisin salad. And if you ate some mixed nuts, vegetable soup, and salad, just think about the mixture in your stomach!

A mixture of nuts

A mixture of vegetables and water (soup)

A mixture of carrots and raisins (salad)

5

A ball stays the same size and shape in any container.

Making Mixtures

Mixtures like sand or mixed nuts are made when two or more solid materials are combined. **Solid** is one of the three common states of **matter**. Solid objects have **mass**, take up space, and have a definite shape and **volume**. A ball, for instance, stays the same size and shape in your hand, on a tabletop, or in a cup.

Chocolate syrup poured into milk is a mixture. Lemon juice and water is a mixture. So is oil and vinegar. These are examples of mixtures made of two **liquid** materials. Liquid is the second common state of matter. Liquids have mass, take up space, and have a definite volume. But liquids do not have a definite shape. A volume of water can have a different shape depending on whether it is in your hand, on a tabletop, or in a cup. Liquids take the shape of the container they are in.

Your breath is a mixture. The exhaust coming out of a car is a mixture. The air that surrounds Earth is a mixture. These are examples of mixtures made of **gaseous** materials. **Gas** is the third common state of matter, but we can't always see gases. Most gases are colorless and **transparent**. Some gases, however, have color, like those that make smog. We can see air on a smoggy day.

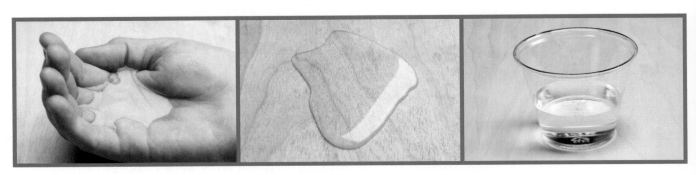

Water changes shape depending on the container you put it in.

A smoggy day in New York City

Gases have mass and take up space, but they do not have definite volume or shape. A mass of air will not stay in your hand, on a tabletop, or in a cup. Gases are shapeless and expand to fill any closed container they are in.

Solids and liquids are often mixed. **Salt** and pepper are mixed with oil and vinegar to add flavor to salad dressing. Flour and water are mixed to make bread. Cereal and milk are mixed for breakfast. Rice is mixed with water to cook it.

Gases and liquids are mixed sometimes, but often the gas separates from the liquid as bubbles. That's what happens when you pour root beer into a glass. The **carbon dioxide** (CO_2) gas that was mixed with the liquid root beer forms bubbles. The bubbles rise to the surface and pop. Then the carbon dioxide in the bubbles mixes with the air. But for a while, the root beer is a lively mixture of liquid and gas.

What ingredients make up this breakfast mixture?

What is the liquid and what is the gas in this mixture?

7

Mixtures of solid and gas aren't often made on purpose. But they happen all the time by accident. If you fill a glass with marbles, you have a mixture of marbles and air. The spaces between the marbles are filled with air. The same is true of any solid object in a container. When it snows, the air (gas) is mixed with frozen water (solid). Dust floating around in the air is also a mixture of solid and gas.

Can you have a mixture of solid, liquid, and gas? Yes. Remember that glass of root beer? Just add a few ice cubes. The glass of ice-cold root beer is a mixture of solid, liquid, and gas.

Mixing Solids and Liquids

Mixtures of solids and liquids are interesting. Several things can happen. When gravel and water are mixed, the gravel sinks to the bottom of the container. If you stir the mixture, things move around, but that's about it.

Mixing gravel and water

Mixing powdered milk and water

Mixing salt and water

Gravel mixture after 5 minutes

Powdered milk mixture after 5 minutes

Salt mixture after 5 minutes

When you mix powdered milk and water, the powder makes the mixture cloudy white. The mixture remains cloudy.

When you mix salt and water, the salt disappears. The mixture is transparent and colorless.

Gravel, powdered milk, and salt all make mixtures with water. After stirring, you can still see the gravel and milk, but the salt is gone. Salt is different in some way.

A mixture of salt and water forms a **solution**. When solid salt and liquid water are mixed, the solid disappears into the liquid, and the mixture is transparent. This mixture is a solution. A solution is a special kind of mixture.

When a solid material disappears in a liquid, it is not gone. It has **dissolved**. When the solid material dissolves, it breaks into pieces so tiny that they are invisible. The solid material that dissolves is called the **solute**. The liquid in which the solute dissolves is called the **solvent**. Every solution is made of a solute dissolved in a solvent. Salt (solute) dissolves in water (solvent) to make a saltwater solution.

Salt (solute) dissolves in water (solvent).

The Universal Solvent

Water dissolves thousands of **substances**. For this reason, it is called the universal solvent. Countless substances are dissolved in the oceans. The fluids in living organisms, such as blood and sap, contain water with thousands of substances dissolved in the water. Look around. Does everything dissolve in water?

Water Properties
Boiling point = 100° Celsius (C)
Freezing point = 0° Celsius (C)
Density = 1 gram per milliliter (g/mL)

Taking Mixtures Apart

You made a mixture of gravel and water in class. You put 50 milliliters (mL) of water and a spoonful of gravel in a cup, and the job was done. Then you separated the mixture of gravel and water. You poured the mixture through a screen. The gravel stayed on the screen, and the water passed through.

All mixtures can be separated. But not all mixtures can be separated in the same way. The **physical properties** of the materials in the mixture can be used to separate the mixture.

Particle size is a physical property of gravel. Particle size is a physical property of water. The particles of gravel are larger than the holes in the screen. The particles of water are smaller than the holes in the screen. The screen can be used to separate the mixture.

In class, the mixture of **diatomaceous earth** and water passed through the screen. The particles of the powder and water are both smaller than the holes in the screen. What property will separate powder from water? The answer is size again. Powder particles are larger than the holes in filter paper. Water particles are smaller. Filter paper will separate a mixture of powder and water.

A screen can separate gravel and water.

Other Ways to Separate Mixtures

Imagine you open a drawer to get a rubber band. Oops, the rubber bands spill. So do a box of toothpicks and some nails. The drawer has an accidental mixture of nails, toothpicks, and rubber bands. How can you separate the mixture?

You can use the property of shape. You can pick out each piece one at a time. But it might take 10 minutes to separate the mixture.

Nails are made of steel. Steel has a useful property. Steel sticks to magnets. If you have a magnet, you can separate the steel nails from the mixture in a few seconds. **Magnetism** is a property that can help separate mixtures.

A mixture of nails, toothpicks, and rubber bands

What about the toothpicks and rubber bands? Wood floats in water. Rubber sinks in water. The property of **density** (sinking and floating) can be used to separate the wood toothpicks and rubber bands. Drop the mixture into a cup of water. Then scoop up the toothpicks from the surface of the water. Pour the water and rubber bands through a screen. The water will pass through the screen, but the rubber bands won't. Now the job is done.

Magnetism is a property that helps separate mixtures.

Density is a property that helps separate mixtures.

Separating Solutions

A mixture of salt and water is a solution. The dissolved salt particles and the water particles are both smaller than the holes in filter paper. The property of size is not useful for separating a solution of salt and water. But **evaporation** will work.

Salt crystals

Evaporation is the **change** of state from liquid to gas. Water **evaporates**, but salt does not. When a salt solution is left in an open container, the water slowly turns to gas and goes into the air. The salt is left behind. Solutions can be separated by evaporating the liquid.

The salt left behind after evaporation doesn't look like the salt that dissolved in the water. Is it still salt? Yes, it is. When the water evaporates, the salt reappears as salt **crystals**. Salt crystals always look square. Salt crystals often have lines going from corner to corner, forming an X.

Many solid materials dissolve in water to make solutions. When the water evaporates, the materials reappear as crystals. Each different material has its own crystal shape. Some crystals are needle shaped. Other crystals are six sided. Others are like tiny fans.

Crystal shape is a physical property. Crystal shape can be used to identify materials. Whenever you observe square shaped crystals in an evaporation dish, you will know that salt might be one of the ingredients in the solution.

Three different crystal forms

Conservation of Matter

There's one more thing to think about when you make a mixture. All matter has mass. Anything that has mass is matter. If you have 200 milliliters (mL) of water in a cup and add 30 grams (g) of sand to the cup of water, what will the mass of the mixture be? The mass of the 200 mL of water is 200 g, so the mass of the mixture will be 200 g (water) + 30 g (sand) = 230 g (mixture). That seems pretty easy to understand.

200 g water +  **30 g sand** =  **230 g mixture**

But the mixture of salt and water is a little trickier to think about. When you mix 30 g of salt with 200 g of water, what do you think the mass of the mixture will be? The salt disappears in the water, so what happens to its mass? Did you conduct this investigation? The mass of the clear solution is 230 g. That is the sum of the mass of the water (200 g) and the mass of the salt (30 g). The mass of a substance like salt does not change when it dissolves. Even if you can't see it, the salt is still there, and its mass has not changed. In fact, mass never goes away. Mass is **conserved**, therefore matter is conserved. That means matter can change shape, state, or location, but it can never be lost or destroyed.

200 g water +  **30 g salt** =  **230 g salt mixture**

Matter is never destroyed, but it can change. Wood (matter) changes to ash when it burns.

Sometimes it is hard to understand how matter is conserved. For instance, when you have a campfire, a large mass of wood burns and all that is left at the end of the evening is a small pile of ash.

If matter is conserved, where did the mass of the wood go? The fire produced several things. It produced smoke, light, and heat. Light and heat are **energy**. Energy is not matter. Smoke is gas and tiny particles of soot. Gas and soot are matter. That's where the wood went. The fire changed most of the mass of the wood into gas and tiny particles. The particles drifted off into the air. Gases and tiny particles have mass.

If you could capture all the smoke and dust coming up from the fire, and gather up all the ashes, what would you find? You would find that the mass of the gas and ash would add up to the mass of the wood you put on the fire earlier. Conservation of matter is just one of the great truths of nature. Matter can never be destroyed, but it can be changed.

As you continue your investigations of mixtures, you might find an instance where your observations suggest that matter is not conserved. But matter is always conserved. You will have to do some deep thinking to explain why your evidence suggests that matter is conserved.

The Story of Salt

Most people don't notice it, but salt is everywhere. It is in most of the foods we eat. It is in ocean water and used in cooking. There are places on land where great deposits of salt are found. The salt flats near Salt Lake City, Utah, are one example. That salt was left behind when seawater evaporated a very long time ago.

Salt (**sodium chloride**) has been important to people since early times. It was often used to keep food from spoiling. Heavily salted food could be preserved for a long time. When sailors spent months at sea, the foods they carried on their ships were heavily salted.

Salt is the oldest-known food additive. The earliest reference to salt was written in China around 2700 BCE. It described how salt made food taste better and helped people stay healthy.

The value of salt led to the development of the salt industry. Salt was first mined from salt deposits on land. It was packaged and sold or traded in marketplaces. In Europe, some monarchs placed heavy taxes on salt. In France, the salt tax was one of the reasons for the French Revolution in 1789.

Salt was important in United States history, too. Salt became one of the main products shipped along the Erie Canal in the 1800s. During the Civil War (1861–1865), Union forces attempted to destroy the South's salt industry. They did not want the South to be able to preserve food for its soldiers.

Today, more uses have been found for salt. It is added to the diets of livestock to improve their health. It is used to soften hard water and to **melt** ice on slippery roads. Salt is also used to make other chemicals, such as chlorine and sodium.

Science Practices

1. **Asking questions.** Scientists ask questions to guide their investigations. This helps them learn more about how the world works.

2. **Developing and using models.** Scientists develop models to represent how things work and to test their explanations.

3. **Planning and carrying out investigations.** Scientists plan and conduct investigations in the field and in laboratories. Their goal is to collect data that test their explanations.

4. **Analyzing and interpreting data.** Patterns and trends in data are not always obvious. Scientists make tables and graphs. They use statistical analysis to look for patterns.

5. **Using mathematics and computational thinking.** Scientists measure physical properties. They use computation and math to analyze data. They use mathematics to construct simulations, solve equations, and represent different variables.

6. **Constructing explanations.** Scientists construct explanations based on observations and data. An explanation becomes an accepted theory when there are many pieces of evidence to support it.

7. **Engaging in argument from evidence.** Scientists use argumentation to listen to, compare, and evaluate all possible explanations. Then they decide which best explains natural phenomena.

8. **Obtaining, evaluating, and communicating information.** Scientists must be able to communicate clearly. They must evaluate others' ideas. They must convince others to agree with their theories.

Scientists ask questions and communicate information. Are you a scientist?

Engineering Practices

1. **Defining problems.** Engineers ask questions to make sure they understand problems they are trying to solve. They need to understand the constraints that are placed on their designs.

2. **Developing and using models.** Engineers develop and use models to represent systems they are designing. Then they test their models before building the actual object or structure.

3. **Planning and carrying out investigations.** Engineers plan and conduct investigations. They need to make sure that their designed systems are durable, effective, and efficient.

4. **Analyzing and interpreting data.** Engineers collect and analyze data when they test their designs. They compare different solutions. They use the data to make sure that they match the given criteria and constraints.

5. **Using mathematics and computational thinking.** Engineers measure physical properties. They use computation and math to analyze data. They use mathematics to construct simulations, solve equations, and represent different variables.

6. **Designing solutions.** Engineers find solutions. They propose solutions based on desired function, cost, safety, how good it looks, and meeting legal requirements.

7. **Engaging in argument from evidence.** Engineers use argumentation to listen to, compare, and evaluate all possible ideas and methods to solve a problem.

8. **Obtaining, evaluating, and communicating information.** Engineers must be able to communicate clearly. They must evaluate other's ideas. They must convince others of the merits of their designs.

Engineers use models.

17

Extracts

One of the most popular beverages in the world is tea. Tea is a plant grown all over Asia. The leaves are picked by hand, dried, and shipped around the world. Tea is prepared for drinking by soaking tea leaves in boiling water.

Another beverage enjoyed all over the world is coffee. Coffee is the seed of the coffee tree fruit. The seeds, called beans, are removed from the fruit, dried, and then roasted. The roasted beans are ground into a coarse powder. Boiling water is poured over the ground beans to prepare the coffee.

Tea and coffee are both **extracts**. An extract is a solution. To make an extract, plant material (leaves, bark, roots, seeds, flowers, and so on) is put into a solvent. The solvent dissolves *some* of the substances out of the plant material. The plant material doesn't dissolve completely. Only a tiny part of it dissolves. Often the only evidence that anything has dissolved is a change to a solvent. Extracts contain dissolved substances that have color, odor, and taste.

You probably know of some other extracts. Vanilla is an extract made by soaking vanilla beans (a seedpod) in a solvent. The flavor of root beer is an extract made by soaking the bark from the roots of sassafras trees in a solvent. Peppermint, wintergreen, almond, and many other flavors are used to prepare foods and drinks. Extracts allow us to enjoy the special flavors of these plants without having to work with the plants that produce them.

Many of our favorite tastes are oils. Cinnamon, peppermint, vanilla, and many others are oils in the host plants. We know about oil and water. They don't mix. This means the peppermint taste won't dissolve in water. How do we get the flavor in an extract? We use another solvent. Oils do dissolve in ethanol, so ethanol is used to extract many of our favorite flavors. The ethanol can then be dissolved in water to use the extract in cooking.

Some extracts are made using oil as the solvent. People who like really spicy tastes can get red hot pepper oils. Ground hot peppers are put into light oil, like sesame oil. The oil is a solvent for the really hot substances in the peppers.

The perfume industry relies on extracts. Extracts of roses, orange blossoms, honeysuckle, and lilac are a few of the wonderful scents used for perfume.

Beachcombing Science

An accident in the Pacific Ocean led to an unusual opportunity for **oceanographers**. Oceanographers are scientists who study ocean and wind currents. A storm struck a cargo ship on its way from Hong Kong to Tacoma, Washington, on January 10, 1992. High seas washed a shipping container carrying 29,000 bathtub toys overboard south of the Aleutian Islands. Soon plastic turtles, frogs, beavers, and ducks were floating in the ocean. Ten months after the accident, the toys began to wash up on beaches near Sitka, Alaska.

Scientists at the National Oceanic and Atmospheric Administration (NOAA) took advantage of this opportunity. A group of oceanographers, including Curtis Ebbesmeyer and Jim Ingraham, began to track the toys' journeys around the Pacific Ocean. At first, they followed reports from beachcombers who found many of the toys washed up on beaches. Then they actively went out and searched for the toys themselves. They made charts showing where, when, and how many toys washed up. These observations gave them direct evidence about ocean and wind currents. Scientists hoped to use this information to update existing **models** of ocean currents. With accurate models of currents, scientists would be better prepared to predict the movement of things in the ocean, such as lost sailors or oil spills.

The toys fell off a ship in the North Pacific in 1992 and made their way to southeast Alaska, near Sitka.

The oceanographers learned some surprising things. According to Ingraham, scientists thought it would take from 4 to 6 years for the toys to return to where the shipping container fell into the ocean. Instead, it took just 2.5 years. That might mean that ocean and wind currents are stronger than scientists thought. Scientists also noted that the toys traveled in a counterclockwise path.

Even though the toys washed up on beaches in the northern Pacific, many of them are still out there. Ingraham wouldn't be surprised if some of the toys become trapped in northward-moving ice at the North Pole. If that happened, then those toys might make it all the way to the Atlantic Ocean. That would give scientists an opportunity to gather data about currents in another part of the ocean, all thanks to a container of shipwrecked toys!

The current that carried the bathtub toys around the North Pacific is the Subpolar Gyre (rhymes with *fire*). The bathtub-toy observations improved a computer model of ocean surface currents developed by Jim Ingraham. The Subpolar Gyre model was first developed with data from a Messages in Bottles (MIB) project. The MIB project released 33,869 bottles into the ocean in the 1950s. The beachcombing data collected from the turtles, ducks, beavers, and frogs that washed up near Sitka, Alaska, confirmed the model suggested by the MIB project.

Other data have described a second, larger Pacific gyre, the Subtropical Gyre. The Subtropical Gyre has trapped a Texas-size garbage patch of tiny bits of plastic from decomposing trash.

Map of the North Pacific showing two rotating currents, or gyres

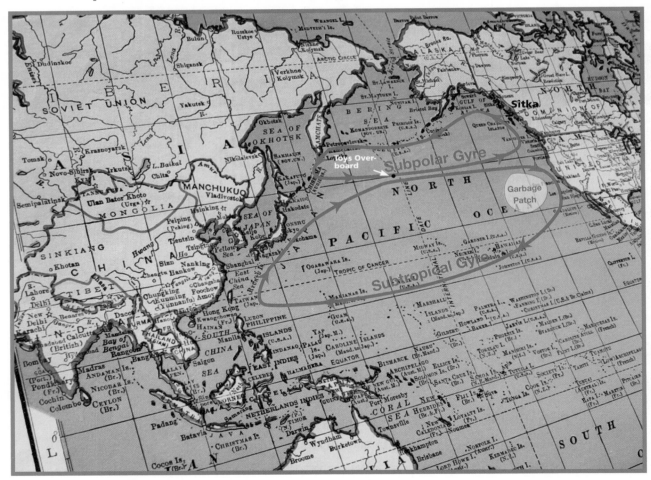

Solid to Liquid

Ice melts. It changes from solid to liquid. An ice cube in a cup on your desk will change into water in about an hour. Chocolate and butter melt, too. But they will not melt on your desk. You have to put them in hot water to make them melt. Wax melts a little bit in hot water. It gets soft. But a pebble won't melt at all. Or will it?

What causes the butter to melt? Heat energy. If you put butter in a cup, nothing happens right away. If you put the cup in hot water, the butter melts. Heat energy **transfers** from the hot water to the butter. Heat energy makes the butter melt.

Heat energy is causing this butter to melt.

23

But ice melts without heat energy. Why is that? Actually, heat energy does make ice melt. When ice is in the freezer, it doesn't melt. It stays solid, or frozen. When you bring ice out into a room that is warmer than the freezer, the ice melts. That's because heat energy from the room transfers to the ice and causes it to melt.

Solid ice melts to form liquid water.

Materials melt at different **temperatures**. Water melts at 0°C. Water **freezes** at 0°C, too. When water is below 0°C, it is solid. When it is above 0°C, it is liquid. Chocolate melts at about 50°C. Candle wax melts into liquid at around 80°C. And yes, the pebble will melt when it is heated to over 1,000°C! Have you ever seen lava flowing from a volcano? That's melted rock.

Metals melt, too. Jewelers melt gold and silver to make rings and other beautiful things. Sculptors melt bronze to make statues. Iron and copper are melted to separate them from the ores taken from mines. Sand is melted to make glass. Many things that we think are always solid will melt if enough heat energy is transferred to them.

Lava flowing down the side of Kilauea Volcano in Hawaii

Gold melts at 1,064°C.

Liquid and Gas Changes

When something is wet, it is covered with water, or it has soaked up a lot of water. When it **rains**, everything outside gets wet. When you go swimming, you and your swimsuit get wet. Clothes are wet when they come out of the washer, and a dog is wet after a bath.

But things don't stay wet forever. Things get dry, often by themselves. An hour or two after the rain stops, stairs, sidewalks, and plants are dry. After a break from swimming to eat lunch, you and your swimsuit are dry. After a few hours on the clothesline, clothes are dry. A dog is dry and fluffy a short time after its bath. Where does the water go?

It evaporates. When water evaporates, it changes from liquid water to **water vapor**, a gas. The gas drifts away in the air.

Wet stairs just after a rainstorm   **Dry stairs the next day**

What causes liquids to evaporate? Heat. When enough heat transfers to a liquid, the liquid changes into a gas. The water vapor leaves the wet object and goes into the air. As the water evaporates, the wet object gets dry.

What happens when you put a wet object in a sealed container? It stays wet. If you put a wet towel in a plastic bag, it's still wet when you take it out of the bag. Why? A little bit of the water in the towel evaporates, but it can't escape into the air. The water vapor has no place to go, so the towel stays wet.

Have you ever seen water vapor in the air? No, water vapor is invisible. When water changes into vapor, it changes into individual water particles. Water particles are too small to be seen with your eyes. The water particles move into the air among the **nitrogen** and **oxygen** particles. Water vapor becomes part of the air. When water becomes part of the air, it is no longer liquid water.

Gas to Liquid

What happens to all that water in the air? As long as the air stays warm, the water stays in the air as water vapor. But when air cools, the water particles start to come together. Tiny droplets of liquid water form.

When gas particles come together to form liquid, it is called **condensation**. Condensation is the change from gas to liquid. When water condenses, it becomes visible again. We see the condensed water as clouds, fog, and dew.

What Else Evaporates?

Water isn't the only liquid that evaporates. Gasoline for cars is a liquid. It is kept in tightly closed gas tanks. If the gasoline was left in open containers, it would evaporate and disappear into the air.

Here's an interesting fact. We breathe oxygen from the air. Oxygen in the air is a gas. But if you put a container of oxygen in a freezer that is –183°C, the oxygen becomes liquid. If there was any liquid oxygen on Earth, it would evaporate because Earth is much warmer than –183°C.

Water vapor condenses indoors, too. On a cold morning, you might see condensation on your kitchen window. Or if you go outside into the cold wearing your glasses, they will get fogged with condensation when you go back inside.

What happens to the bathroom mirror after you take a shower? The air in the bathroom is warm and filled with water vapor. When the air touches the cool mirror, the water vapor condenses on the smooth surface. That's why the mirror gets foggy and wet.

Condensation on a window

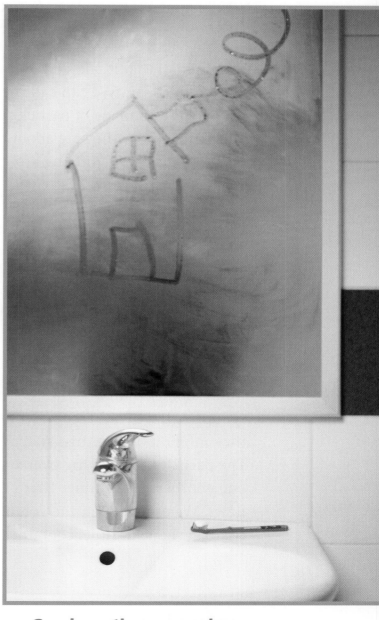

Condensation on a mirror

Solutions Up Close

Salt solutions are transparent. You can't see anything in them. When you look at a salt solution with a hand lens, what do you see? Still nothing. In fact, you can't see anything in a salt solution even with the most powerful light microscope. Does that mean the salt is gone when it dissolves?

No, the salt is still there. To understand what happens to the salt, you have to think very small. You have to think about pieces of salt so small that it takes billions and billions of them to make a tiny grain of salt. We can call the tiniest piece of salt a salt particle.

Water is also made of particles. Water particles are different from salt particles, but they are about the same size. In liquid water, the particles are always moving around and over one another.

Let's imagine that we can see the salt particles. We'll represent one salt particle with this pink circle.

One tiny grain of salt might look like this. The salt is a solid. It has mass, shape, and a definite volume.

Here is a container of water a million times smaller than a 5-milliliter (mL) spoonful. If we could see water particles, they might look like this. Water is a liquid. The particles are moving over and around one another all the time. That's how water flows. Water has a definite volume, but it changes shape to fit its container.

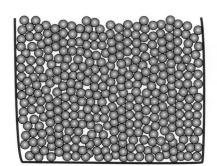

When you put salt in a container, the salt sinks to the bottom.

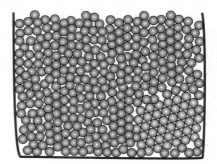

The particles of water bump into the salt. This action knocks salt particles loose. The loose salt particles become surrounded by water particles.

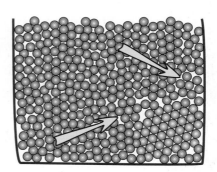

The salt particles are carried into the water. They end up spread evenly among the water particles. The particles of salt among the water particles are the dissolved salt. The particles of salt shown on the bottom of the container represent undissolved solid salt.

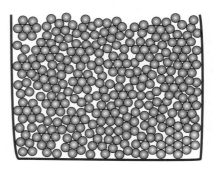

A solution forms when salt particles break free and get carried away by the water particles. The breaking away and getting carried away is the process of dissolving.

Interpreting the Diagrams

Work with a partner. Look at the diagrams on pages 28–29. Describe to your partner what happens when salt dissolves in water.

Concentrated Solutions

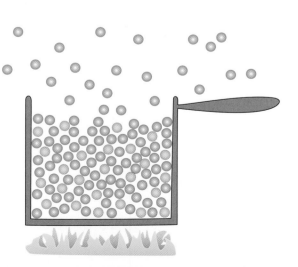

If you stop by the freezer section at the market, you can pick up a can of orange juice. But be careful! If you defrost it and try to drink the orange juice straight from the can, you will be in for a shock. The orange juice is thick and strong. That's because the can contains orange juice concentrate. Most of the water has been removed. The juice is too **concentrated** to drink.

Orange juice straight out of the orange is a solution. Water is the solvent. At the orange juice factory, the orange juice is heated. Water particles leave the solution, but orange juice particles don't. The orange juice particles are still evenly distributed in the water, but there is less water. As a result, the orange juice particles get closer together, because there are fewer water particles between them. Here's how that works.

1 Here is a pot of orange juice. There are 100 water particles (blue) and 25 orange juice particles (orange).

A representation of orange juice in a pot

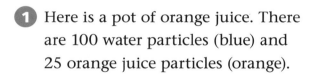

2 The pot of juice is slowly heated. Water particles begin to evaporate.

Water particles evaporate when juice is heated.

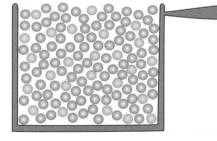

3 When 75 water particles have evaporated, the orange juice looks like this.

The pot of orange juice after most of the water has evaporated

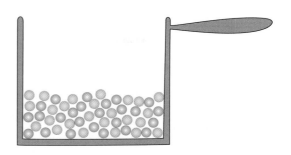

4 Look at the pots before and after evaporation. What is the same? What is different?

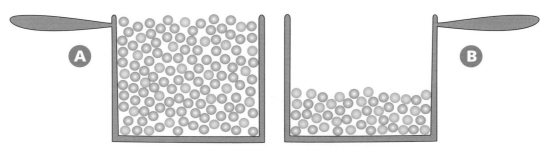

A comparison of a pot of orange juice before (A) and after (B) heating

Both pots contain solutions made with the same materials: water particles and orange juice particles. Both pots also have the same number of orange juice particles.

The important difference is the amount of water. The fresh juice in Pot A has 100 water particles. The evaporated juice in Pot B has only 25 water particles. The orange juice in Pot B is *more concentrated*.

That means that if you scoop up 100 milliliters (mL) of concentrated solution from Pot B, it will contain more orange juice particles than 100 mL of solution from Pot A.

Orange juice from Pot A   **Orange juice from Pot B**

You can also think of **concentration** as the **ratio** of water particles to orange juice particles. There are four times as many water particles as orange juice particles in Pot A. The ratio of water to orange juice is four to one. In math that is written 4:1.

In Pot B there are 25 water particles and 25 orange juice particles. The ratio of water to orange juice is 1:1. There is only one water particle for each orange juice particle in Pot B. So that solution is *more concentrated* than the solution in Pot A. Pot A has four water particles for each orange juice particle.

Comparing Concentrations

If you have two different solutions made with the same materials, such as salt and water, you can often use a balance to figure out which one is more concentrated. Here's how.

- Measure equal volumes of Solution X and Solution Y.
- Weigh them.
- The sample with the greater mass is more concentrated. It's just that simple!

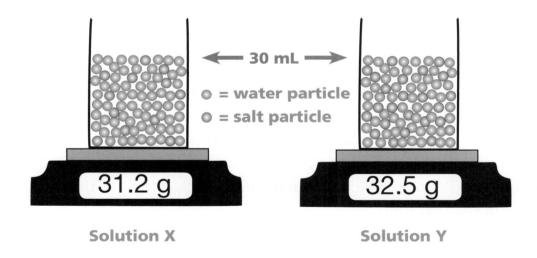

Solution X   Solution Y

How does that work? Particles have mass. Salt particles have mass, and water particles have mass. But here's the important thing: each salt particle has more mass than each water particle. When salt particles go into solution, they take up space. They push some water particles out of the way. When you take a volume of a concentrated salt solution, there are more heavy salt particles in it than there are in an equal volume of a **dilute** salt solution. So when you compare equal volumes of the two salt solutions, one will have more mass because it has more salt particles. And the one with more salt particles is more concentrated.

Thinking about Concentration

1. Which solution on page 30 is more concentrated, Solution X or Solution Y?

2. Look at the four salt solutions below (A, B, C, and D). Put them in order from most concentrated to most dilute.

Each sample on the balance is exactly 150 mL.

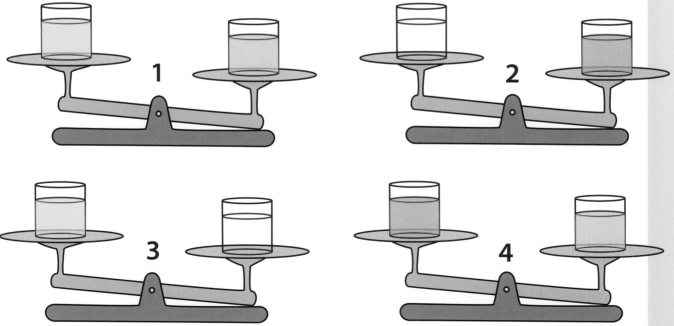

The Air

Air is a mixture of gases. The most common gas in air is nitrogen. Air is about 78 percent nitrogen. The second most common gas is oxygen. Air is about 21 percent oxygen. The other 1 percent is composed of dozens of other gases, with a bunch of tiny solids floating around. Air is a complex mixture.

Another way to look at air is as a solution. Think of air as a bunch of gas particles dissolved in nitrogen. The most concentrated gas dissolved in the nitrogen is oxygen. All other gases are part of the solution, but they are present in low concentrations.

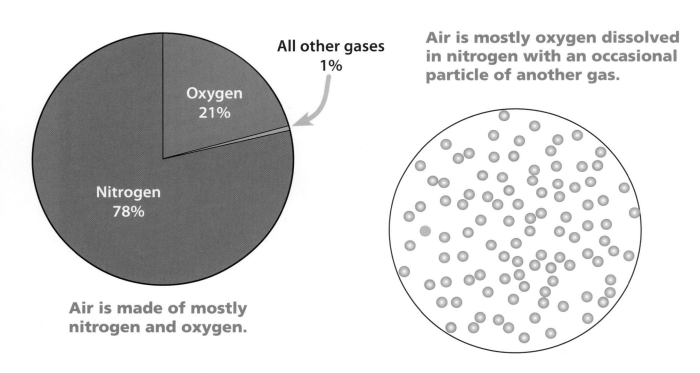

All other gases 1%

Oxygen 21%

Nitrogen 78%

Air is made of mostly nitrogen and oxygen.

Air is mostly oxygen dissolved in nitrogen with an occasional particle of another gas.

Two Other Gases in the Air

You might know the names of a couple of other important gases dissolved in the nitrogen: water vapor and carbon dioxide (CO_2).

When water evaporates, where does it go? It becomes part of the air. Individual water particles change into gas and dissolve in the air. On a warm, humid day, the concentration of water vapor in the air might reach 4 percent. Even so, we never see it. Water in the gas state is invisible.

We don't see water vapor until it cools and condenses. Condensed water vapor is liquid. The tiny liquid droplets form visible clouds. We recognize these processes of water entering the air (evaporation) and leaving the air (condensation) as part of the water cycle.

Water vapor condenses in the air to form clouds.

Fuel is a source of energy. When fuels, like wood, coal, grass, and peanut butter sandwiches, are burned, waste gases are released into the air. One of the most concentrated of them is CO_2. The concentration is low (0.04 percent), but it is significant. Carbon dioxide comes from forest-fire smoke, car exhaust, and the breath you exhale. Carbon dioxide in the air absorbs energy from sunlight. Scientists are concerned about the concentration of CO_2 in the air. Rising CO_2 concentration leads to rising temperatures worldwide.

Air in Other Places

The International Space Station orbits Earth high in the **atmosphere**, about 340 kilometers (km) above Earth's surface. The "air" up there is about 28 percent oxygen and 71 percent helium. The nitrogen is less than 1 percent. The concentration of gases is extremely low. How do astronauts survive in this environment? What do they breathe?

The air inside the space station is just about the same as it is on Earth's surface. The astronauts breathe a mixture of nitrogen and oxygen brought into space in pressurized bottles. Astronauts don't wear space suits inside. But when they go outside, they do wear a protective space suit. The suit is filled with pure oxygen—no nitrogen.

Living and working in small spaces creates a problem. Astronauts exhale CO_2. Carbon dioxide is toxic. A concentration of 1 percent CO_2 makes a person sleepy. A concentration of 7 percent causes dizziness, headache, and blackout. In order to keep the air safe for the astronauts, special filters are used to remove CO_2 from the air supply.

Oceans cover 71 percent of Earth's surface. Scientists explore the deep ocean water in submarines. The space inside is supplied with a mixture of gases similar to air on Earth's surface. But in shallower water, up to 100 meters (m), people dive in and swim around with a supply of air to breathe. Plain pressurized air is fine if you don't go deeper than 30 m. If you go deeper, **pressure compresses** the gas, increasing the concentration of the oxygen and nitrogen. Below 30 m, the pressure makes nitrogen toxic, which causes people to make bad decisions.

To remedy the problem, divers mix oxygen with helium. Helium doesn't affect thinking, so divers can go deeper. A mixture of 80 percent helium and 20 percent oxygen allows divers to go below 30 m safely for short periods of time.

Famous Scientists

Joseph Priestley

Joseph Priestley (1733–1804) was born in England. He grew up expecting to become a minister. But that was only one of his many interests. He was a teacher, a philosopher, and a scientist.

Priestley conducted experiments with electricity. He was the first to describe how electric force worked. This work was the basis for important work of many other scientists.

In the 1770s, Priestley became interested in gases, which he called airs. His experiments led to the discovery of sulfur dioxide, nitric oxide, nitrous oxide, ammonia, and perhaps oxygen. The "perhaps" is because it isn't clear who first isolated oxygen.

Priestley invented soda water. He used pressurized carbon dioxide to saturate water. But he failed to see the commercial value of his invention. J. J. Schweppe took Priestley's idea and made a fortune.

Antoine Lavoisier

Antoine Lavoisier (1743–1794) was born in France. He was well educated and became a lawyer. His second calling was science.

Lavoisier burned things. Most scientists thought things burned because they contained phlogiston, a firelike substance. Lavoisier doubted the existence of phlogiston. Here's how he set out to disprove it.

Most people thought that burning released phlogiston and that's why the ash had less mass. Lavoisier "burned" mercury in a closed container with air. After a couple of hours, the mercury shrank to reddish "ash." The volume of air was smaller, too. Further, the mass of the "ash" was greater than the mass of the starting mercury.

Lavoisier figured out that oxygen in the air reacted with the mercury. This formed mercury oxide. The mercury oxide was heavier than the mercury. Lavoisier went on to describe a new way to think about **chemical reactions**. The phlogiston theory started to lose favor. Because of this work, Lavoisier is sometimes called the father of modern chemistry.

Marie Curie

Maria Sklodowska (1867–1934) was born in Warsaw, Poland. Her father was a science and math teacher. He taught his children basic laboratory science methods. When she was 10 years old, Curie went to boarding school. She graduated at 16 with a gold medal. She was unable to go to college because she was a girl. For a while, she was a governess, teaching young children.

In 1890, Curie moved to Paris. There, she became known as Marie. She studied math, physics, and chemistry on her own. In 1891, she enrolled in the University of Paris. After graduating, she investigated the magnetic properties of steel. She did experiments in the laboratory of Pierre Curie. Pierre convinced Curie to continue studying at the university. Soon after that, Pierre and Curie married.

In 1895 and 1896, physicists discovered powerful radiation called X-rays. The element uranium produces radiation like X-rays. Curie became interested in uranium radiation. She called it **radioactivity**. She investigated many sources of radioactivity. She found several minerals with much stronger radioactivity than uranium. Finally, she isolated the sources of the strong radioactivity. They were two unknown elements. Polonium was named for Curie's home country. The other element was named radium.

Curie's life was very productive. She eventually received two Nobel Prizes. In 1903, she received the Nobel Prize in Physics. That prize honored her pioneering work on radioactivity. In 1911, she received the Nobel Prize in Chemistry. That prize was for discovering polonium and radium. In 1934, Marie Curie died from a blood disease. Her long-term exposure to radiation may have caused her death.

Carbon Dioxide Concentration in the Air

When Charles David Keeling (1928–2005) started working at Caltech University in 1953, he was interested in how carbon dioxide (CO_2) moved around in the environment. How much CO_2 was in Earth's water, rocks, and air?

Keeling realized that understanding these questions would require knowing the concentration of CO_2 in the air. Keeling started measuring CO_2 in Pasadena, California, near the university. His readings varied from day to day because of local CO_2 produced by cars and factories. Keeling moved his sampling equipment to Big Sur on the central California coast, far from urban CO_2 production. There he got much more uniform readings.

Keeling measured CO_2 concentration day and night. Soon he noticed that the CO_2 concentration was lowest in the late afternoon and highest in the early morning. Keeling figured out that plants were taking in CO_2 during the day and giving it off during the night. That explained the daily variation in CO_2 concentration.

Charles David Keeling

Mauna Loa Volcano

In 1956, Keeling moved his monitoring station to the top of Mauna Loa Volcano on Hawaii. He determined the volcano would be least affected by CO_2 from cars and plants. His first sample in March showed a CO_2 concentration of 313 parts per million (ppm). As he monitored CO_2 throughout the year, Keeling found that global CO_2 concentration varied on a seasonal cycle. The amount of CO_2 was highest in May (315 ppm) and lowest in October (311 ppm). The planet was "breathing," as Keeling put it. It was taking in CO_2 during the growing season in the Northern Hemisphere and giving off CO_2 in the fall and winter.

The most important thing Keeling discovered, however, was that the average concentration of global CO_2 increased every year. The Keeling data show a trend of increasing CO_2 concentration in Earth's atmosphere. The pattern in the CO_2 data is related to the burning of **fossil fuels**, like coal, gas, and petroleum. There is a direct relationship between CO_2 gas production by human activities and the concentration of CO_2 in Earth's atmosphere.

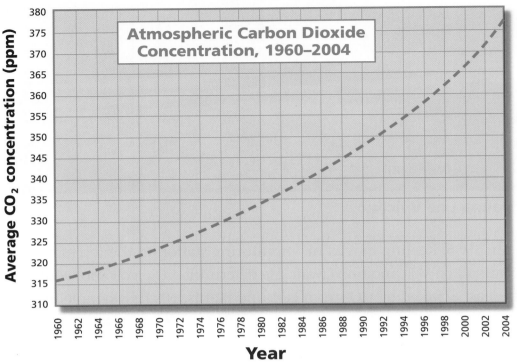

Keeling Curve

Atmospheric Carbon Dioxide Concentration, 1960–2004

Average CO$_2$ concentration (ppm) vs. *Year*

The pattern in the data is known as the Keeling Curve. The curve gets steeper with each passing year. It is possible to use the curve to predict CO$_2$ concentrations into the future. Remember, when Keeling started measuring CO$_2$, the average global concentration was 313 ppm. Fifty years later the concentration was 378 ppm. If we continue to burn fossil fuels at the same rate, by the time we use them all up (in 100–200 years), the CO$_2$ concentration in the atmosphere will be around 1,500 ppm.

Carbon dioxide concentration in the atmosphere is important because CO$_2$ is a **greenhouse gas**. It absorbs energy and contributes to the warming of the atmosphere. This warming contributes to global **climate** change, which will have many effects on life on Earth. The Keeling Curve is a powerful and important scientific contribution to our understanding of the world and how it works.

Thinking about Carbon Dioxide

1. If humans started burning half as many fossil fuels as we did in 2004, what might the graph look like?

2. What might the graph look like if humans stopped burning fossil fuels all together?

The Frog Story

Tyrone B. Hayes

Scientists have noted a significant decline in the worldwide frog and toad populations in the last decade. The causes of the decline are difficult to pin down. There is evidence, however, that toxic chemicals may play a role.

Tyrone B. Hayes (1965–) is a biology professor at the University of California, Berkeley. He has studied frogs for most of his life. The first frogs he saw were in a swamp near his home in South Carolina. Now Hayes studies frogs across the planet, in Africa and North America.

Hayes found something strange going on with some of the frogs he studied. Frogs living in the wild were experiencing sex changes. The "male" frogs were producing eggs. The males were changing into females.

When Hayes and his team analyzed the frogs' environment, they found traces of a common **herbicide** (*herb* = plant; *cide* = kill) in the water. The concentration was only 0.1 parts per billion (ppb). That's one particle in 10 billion. But more tests in the lab showed that the herbicide was causing the changes.

The herbicide does not kill the frogs. But it does affect them. It changes their ability to reproduce. The substance in the frogs' environment, even in very low concentration, makes it impossible for the frogs to produce offspring. The pesticide kills the next generation of frogs, not the current one.

There are about 20,000 different pesticides used in the United States today. Each one is designed to kill unwanted organisms. But the pesticides don't all stay where they are applied. Particles of the substances are carried by wind and water to other locations. In other environments, the pesticides can have unintended results. This problem is growing all over the world, requiring government regulation and careful use of substances that might have an impact on natural environments.

The Bends

Hard-hat diving was invented in 1861. The diver climbed into a watertight suit with a brass helmet. An air hose was attached to the helmet. Air was pumped to the diver walking around on the bottom of the sea 20 meters (m) below the surface.

The **bends** is a condition that happened to deep-sea divers after returning to the surface. Divers felt dizzy, confused, and uncoordinated. They felt pain in their knees, hips, shoulders, and elbows. It became impossible for them to straighten their arms and legs. The pain caused divers to bend their arms and legs for pain relief. That's where the name bends came from.

The cause of the bends wasn't known until 1878. French scientist Paul Bert (1833–1886) figured it out. Nitrogen bubbles in the diver's blood and joints caused the bends. But where did the nitrogen bubbles come from? To answer that question, you need to know more about **saturated** solutions.

A solution is a solute dissolved in a solvent. We know about solids (salt) dissolved in liquids (water). Solutions can also be made when gases dissolve in liquids. That's what happens in the human body. Gases in the air that divers take into their lungs dissolve in the blood. Under normal conditions, the blood is saturated with dissolved nitrogen. No more nitrogen can dissolve.

When a diver goes underwater, the pressure increases. Pressure compresses the air in the diving suit. The air particles are pushed closer together. As a result, more air dissolves in the blood. Air is 78 percent nitrogen, so most of the additional gas that dissolves in the diver's blood is nitrogen. After the diver has been underwater for an hour, his blood is again saturated with nitrogen. But now it is saturated at high pressure, so there is more nitrogen in his blood than there was when he was at the surface.

Hard-hat diving helmet

44

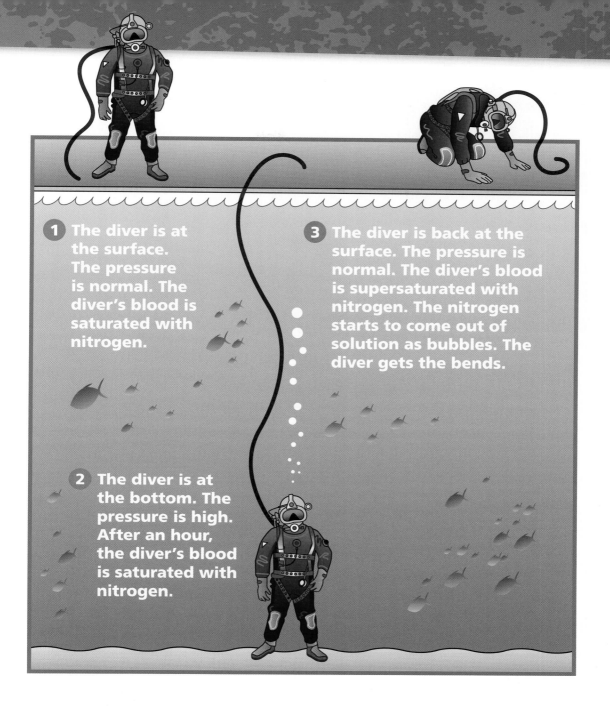

1 The diver is at the surface. The pressure is normal. The diver's blood is saturated with nitrogen.

2 The diver is at the bottom. The pressure is high. After an hour, the diver's blood is saturated with nitrogen.

3 The diver is back at the surface. The pressure is normal. The diver's blood is supersaturated with nitrogen. The nitrogen starts to come out of solution as bubbles. The diver gets the bends.

The trouble starts when the diver rises to the surface. The pressure drops to normal. The blood is holding much more nitrogen than it normally holds at surface pressure. The blood is **supersaturated** with nitrogen. The extra nitrogen comes out of solution (the diver's blood) as nitrogen bubbles. The bubbles get stuck in blood vessels and stop the flow of blood. Bubbles form in the fluids in joints, causing a lot of pain.

The bends is **decompression** sickness. Decompression means changing from higher pressure to lower pressure. That's when the diver feels the effects of too much nitrogen in the blood.

The Eads Bridge

Caisson Disease

Decompression sickness also showed up in a different situation. In 1869, James Buchanan Eads (1820–1887) began building a railroad bridge across the Mississippi River. The bridge needed support in the middle of the river. This required a lot of digging underwater. How could that be done?

Eads used **caissons**. A caisson is a huge box with no bottom. It is placed on the bottom of a river with the open side down. Air is then pumped into the box. The air pushes the water out under the bottom of the box. Workers can dig and build foundations inside the caisson because it is filled with air.

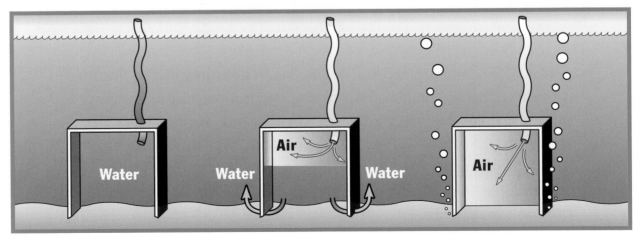

The caisson rests on the bottom of the river.

Pressurized air pushes water out under the bottom of the caisson.

Pressurized air keeps water out of the caisson.

The caisson is fitted with a tube that has tight-fitting doors. Workers can climb down the tube to the open Door 1 and go through it. They close Door 1 behind them. Then they can open Door 2 into the box. Using two doors maintains the pressure. This keeps the water from flowing back under the bottom of the box.

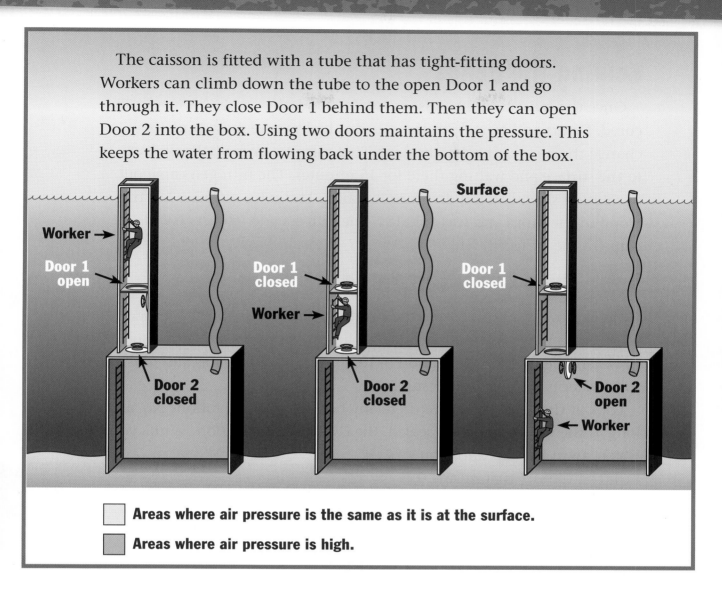

Areas where air pressure is the same as it is at the surface.

Areas where air pressure is high.

The problem is the pressure. The pressure in the box has to be kept high enough to keep the water out. The workers are breathing concentrated nitrogen, so more nitrogen dissolves in their blood. At the end of a workday, their blood is saturated with nitrogen in the pressurized environment. When they return to standard atmospheric pressure at the water's surface, they have the same symptoms as deep-sea divers.

At a depth of 10 m underwater, the pressure is twice as high as standard atmospheric pressure. The workers are in no danger while they are working in the higher pressure in the caisson. The extra nitrogen in their blood does no harm. It is the change of pressure between the caisson and the surface that causes the extra dissolved nitrogen to rush out of the blood as bubbles.

Solving the Bends

Once the cause of the bends was understood, the condition was easily cured. Divers and workers in the caissons had to take more time to change the pressure back to normal. That meant coming halfway back to the surface and waiting there for 15 minutes. The nitrogen came out of solution slowly, so it didn't form bubbles. The extra nitrogen left the blood in the lungs and was exhaled. Then divers and workers could come to the surface safely.

Your Own Supersaturated Solution

Here's how you can observe the bends up close. Get a bottle of soda water. Soda water is a supersaturated solution of carbon dioxide dissolved in water. The high concentration of CO_2 stays in solution because the soda water is kept under pressure.

Look at the soda water. Are there any bubbles in the solution? No, as long as the soda water stays sealed, the CO_2 stays in solution. While you watch, twist the cap until you hear the "pfssst" that means the pressure has been released. Now what do you see? Bubbles!

As soon as the pressure is released, the extra dissolved CO_2 begins to come out of solution. It is the same with the bends. As soon as the diver comes back to the surface, the pressure drops, and nitrogen comes out of solution as bubbles.

A sealed bottle of soda water does not have any bubbles forming. Carbon dioxide bubbles rise from the bottle of soda water when pressure is released.

A Sweet Solution

Do you know what rock candy is? It is crystals of sugar. To make rock candy, you need to know about the science of solutions.

Sugar is a substance that dissolves in water. It takes about 100 grams (g) of sugar to saturate 50 milliliters (mL) of water at **room temperature**. Room temperature is 22° **Celsius** (C). But if you heat the solution, more sugar will dissolve. The hotter you get the solution, the more sugar dissolves in the water.

When the solution reaches its **boiling point**, it won't get any hotter. The boiling point of water is 100°C. When you see undissolved sugar in the pan of boiling sugar solution, you know the solution is saturated. There is about twice as much sugar dissolved in the boiling-hot saturated solution as there is in a room-temperature saturated solution.

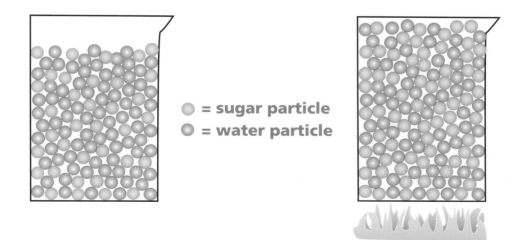

◯ = sugar particle
◯ = water particle

A saturated solution of sugar at room temperature

A saturated solution of sugar at boiling temperature

What will happen to all that extra sugar when the boiling-hot saturated solution cools down? Will it stay in solution? Or will it come out of solution and pile up on the bottom of the container?

The sugar will stay in solution. A solution that has more solute than it should is a supersaturated solution. When the boiling-hot saturated sugar solution cools down, it is supersaturated.

Now the solution is ready to make rock candy. When you roll a wet string in sugar, the sugar sticks to the string. After the sugary string dries, it is covered with tiny sugar crystals.

When you put the string in the supersaturated solution, the extra sugar in the solution comes out of solution in the form of sugar crystals. The crystals stick to other sugar crystals stuck to the string.

The crystals will grow for a couple of days and then stop. Why do they stop growing? Sugar comes out of solution until the solution is no longer supersaturated. Then no more sugar comes out of solution.

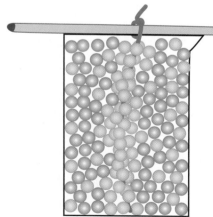

Sugar particles come out of solution on the crystals until the solution is again saturated at room temperature.

Sour Power

Do you like it when a glass of sour lemonade makes your lips pucker? If something that leaves a sour taste in your mouth is okay with you, then you're a fan of **citric acid**!

Citric acid is a white, solid acid. It is highly **soluble** in water. You can dissolve a lot of citric acid in a small amount of water. Like other acids, citric acid has a sour power. If you've ever bitten into a lemon, you know how citric acid tastes. About 6 percent of lemon juice is citric acid. Citric acid is found naturally in other fruits such as oranges, limes, and grapefruits. All of these fruits are known as citrus fruits.

Citric acid is a widely used food additive. It is sour, safe, and inexpensive. Every year tons of citric acid are added to foods for a number of purposes. It gives a sour tang to soft drinks and some candies. In jams and preserves, it helps fruits keep their color and flavor. Look on the backs of the cans and boxes in your cupboard. You will probably find a few packages that include citric acid as an ingredient. Citric acid is also used to make inks, dyes, medicines, and cleansers.

Scientists can extract citric acid from lemons and other citrus fruits. But because citric acid is so widely used today, huge quantities are needed. Factories have been built to produce citric acid by fermenting sugar.

Citric acid is not the only type of acid found in foods. Other weak acids occur in natural substances such as vinegar (acetic acid), tomatoes (acetic acid), and sour milk (lactic acid). There are also acids unrelated to food that are stronger and can be dangerous. They can burn through paper, cloth, and skin, so they must be handled with care. These strong acids are often used by scientists to conduct experiments and make chemicals.

East Bay Academy for Young Scientists

Have you ever wondered what it would be like to be a real scientist? Students in the East Bay Academy for Young Scientists (EBAYS) program don't wonder. They go out in the field and work as scientists. The program serves under-resourced communities in the San Francisco area in California. Some of the students started the program when they were in the sixth grade and stayed through middle school. Students in the program study soil, water, and air-quality problems in their communities. Their environmental work can help protect the families that live in their communities.

In the summer of 2008, students were enjoying the EBAYS summer program. That year it was held at Mills College in Oakland, California. During breaks on warm summer days, students would play in Leona Creek, which runs through the campus. A group of students decided to investigate the water quality of the creek for their summer research project. They first gathered samples of water from the creek. Water-quality kits were used to test the water samples in the classroom. Then they took these samples to the EBAYS laboratory at the Lawrence Hall of Science (LHS) to find how much lead each sample contained. LHS is a science and technology center at the University of California, Berkeley. Students found levels of lead above the legal limits of 15 parts per billion (ppb).

**Water coming out
of a sulfur mine**

After discovering that the lead levels in the creek were so high, the students decided to test the water for other metals. They tested for iron and arsenic. They also wanted to find out how the metals were getting into the creek. They found the water's source at an abandoned sulfur mine. They collected some water samples at the mine and compared them to samples from the creek. They analyzed some of the water samples in the lab. They tested others on-site, using a test kit. Students found high levels of lead, iron, and arsenic at the mine. All the levels were above the legal limits. By comparing the water samples from the mine to those from the creek, the students saw that arsenic levels decreased as the water moved downstream. High levels of iron and lead were still found in these downstream samples.

Now that the students had some results, what was next? As part of the EBAYS project, they had to write a report and develop a poster. But this wasn't enough for the students. They wanted to do something more with the data. According to Elliot, one of the EBAYS students, "When we went to the mine, we were disgusted because it was this really contaminated area. That was when we started to think that we really needed to restore the creek. Water from the creek flows to a lake, and if the lake connected to the creek is polluted, then the water there can also be polluted. And since that water flows to the ocean, that spreads the pollution. Cleaning up one creek may not seem like much, but it is."

The students presented their results to the Oakland Department of Environmental Services. It turns out the mine owner had already been fined for not cleaning up the mine. The city was so impressed with the work the EBAYS students did that they were asked to adopt the creek. They were asked to begin work with other creeks in the area as well. Some of the EBAYS students volunteered for Creek to Bay Day and helped remove trash and nonnative plants.

Elliot (center) and the other students presented their data and results at an American Geophysical Union (AGU) conference in San Francisco.

After the EBAYS summer program ended, the students wrote their findings. They created a poster that presented their results in a way that makes them easy for people to read. The students took their poster to the annual conference of the American Geophysical Union (AGU). At the conference, scientists could review the poster and discuss the findings. Elliot said, "At first, it was a little scary. We didn't see any other middle schoolers, but at the end, we started to get more and more confident. One guy congratulated us and said, 'You guys are really doing advanced stuff.' After that, we started presenting more, and we got a lot more confident." It turns out they were some of the youngest students ever to present at an AGU conference!

The AGU conference was just the beginning for these students. They submitted a research paper related to their work in Oakland to a contest encouraging sustainable development. Their paper won the contest. On May 14, 2010, the students presented their work to the Commission on Sustainable Development at the United Nations headquarters in New York.

Drinking Ocean Water

The world's demand for drinking water is increasing. The human population is over 7 billion. Climate patterns are changing and causing droughts. As a result, people are looking for new sources of drinking water. We already use surface water such as lakes, rivers, and streams. And we pump water from the ground. Where else can we look for drinking water?

The ocean holds 97 percent of Earth's water. Can we use the ocean for drinking water? What do you think?

Ocean water contains dissolved salts. It has a high concentration of sodium chloride. Getting drinking water from ocean water requires separating the water from the salt. This process is called **desalination**.

A view of the
Atlantic Ocean

A view of the
Pacific Ocean

Desalination

How did you separate water and salt? Could that method make drinking water? You evaporated the water, leaving the salt behind. The liquid water became water vapor. It escaped into the air. But now we want to hold onto the water.

An evaporation system with a condenser is possible. A condenser changes water vapor into liquid water. But heating enough water for a community would be very expensive. Evaporation may not be a good design for desalination.

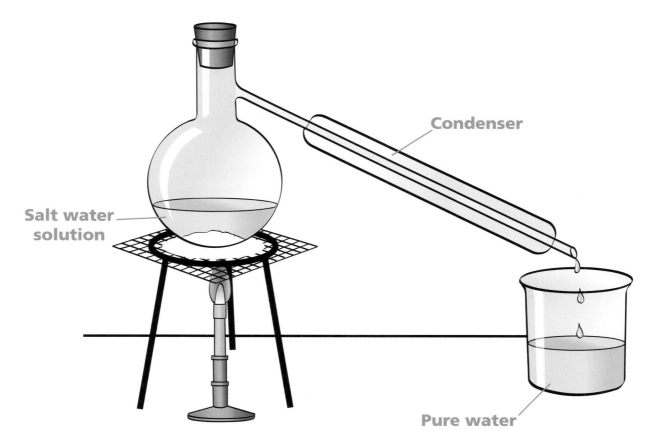

Condenser

Salt water solution

Pure water

Engineers have developed another solution for desalination. The process uses a filter called a **semipermeable membrane**. If something is **permeable**, liquids and gasses can pass through it. For instance, a T-shirt is a permeable membrane. If you stretch a T-shirt across the top of a bucket, you can pour water into the bucket through the T-shirt. Plastic bags are **impermeable**. If you stretch a plastic bag across the top of a bucket, water cannot enter the bucket. A semipermeable membrane allows water to pass through. It blocks dissolved materials.

Look at this setup. A semipermeable membrane is in the bottom of a glass U-tube. A blue salt solution is in one side of the tube. An equal volume of pure water is in the other side. Observe what happens after 30 minutes.

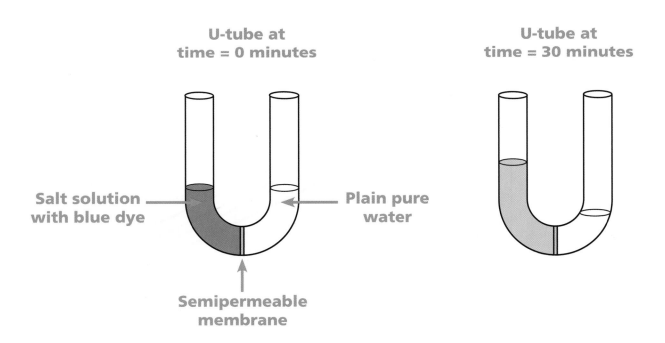

U-tube at time = 0 minutes

U-tube at time = 30 minutes

Salt solution with blue dye

Plain pure water

Semipermeable membrane

What happened to the two solutions after 30 minutes?

The volume of salt solution increased, and the volume of pure water decreased! The membrane is permeable to water molecules. It is impermeable to salt and dye molecules. Water molecules passed through the membrane into the salt solution. The salt solution became less concentrated. This movement of water molecules is **osmosis**. A force drives the water molecules through a semipermeable membrane. This force is **osmotic pressure**.

Here, a pump applies pressure to the salt solution in the U-tube. The pump pressure acts against osmotic pressure. The pump pressure stops water molecules from passing into the salt solution. Say you increased the pump pressure even more. The pressure pushes water molecules out of the salt solution. They move into the pure-water side of the tube. Removing water makes the salt solution more concentrated.

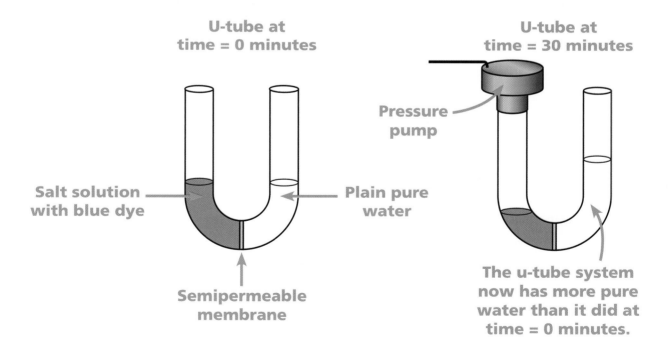

U-tube at
time = 0 minutes

U-tube at
time = 30 minutes

Pressure
pump

Salt solution
with blue dye

Plain pure
water

Semipermeable
membrane

The u-tube system
now has more pure
water than it did at
time = 0 minutes.

Reverse osmosis filters at a water utility plant

The permeability of the membrane does not change under pressure. It still allows only water molecules to pass through. Using high pressure and a semipermeable membrane pushes water out of a salt solution. This process is **reverse osmosis**.

A semipermeable membrane is a special filter. Filters let some things pass through and hold other things. A screen can separate gravel from smaller materials. And a paper filter can separate powder from a salt solution. But a paper filter cannot separate salt from water. You had to use evaporation to separate it.

Criteria and Constraints

Millions of people live near the salty ocean. Reverse osmosis is one way to get water to a thirsty world. Does it meet the **criteria** and **constraints** for a successful solution?

The criteria include producing lots of pure drinking water. The usual constraints are cost and availability of materials. Semipermeable membranes are delicate and expensive. And reverse osmosis requires energy to make pressure. Reducing the energy costs is critical. Semipermeable membranes must be tough and perform well at low pressure.

Another constraint is disposal of waste products. Desalination produces salt as waste. How will we dispose of it?

A water desalination plant in Dubai

Conservation and Recycling

Desalination is one way to get more drinking water. Other ways include conservation and recycling.

Conservation involves sensible practices and engineering solutions. Landscaping with drought-tolerant plants is a sensible practice. We can replace green lawns with native plants that don't need much water. We can use water-efficient appliances. Engineers have designed low-flow washing machines, dishwashers, showerheads, and toilets. Engineers have also designed better ways to irrigate crops.

A lot of water used in our homes and businesses becomes waste water. It ends up in the sewer system. Engineers are developing systems for recycling this waste water. Modern sewage treatment returns clean water to natural environments. Secondary water systems can produce water that is clean enough for watering plants and washing cars. Reverse osmosis can treat waste water and make it safe to drink.

Thinking about Drinking Ocean Water

Look at the environment in each photograph. Why might desalination work well in these environments? Can you think of other environments that might be good for desalination?

Creative Solutions

People face problems every day. Problems may be small or big, from doing homework to curing cancer. Some problems make people work harder than they would like to work. But while some people complain, others act. Inventors are people who solve problems in creative ways. They don't turn away from problems. Inventors look for solutions. They might be scientists in labs. They might be ordinary people at home. Even kids are inventors! Anyone can be an inventor.

The Flying Monkeys

A team of Girl Scouts in Ames, Iowa, called the Flying Monkeys invented a device to help a three-year-old girl named Danielle, who was born without fingers on one hand, write for the very first time.

Their invention, called the BOB-1, is a prosthetic hand device that helps people hold and grip objects, such as a pencil. The device is intended to help people born with limb differences lead normal and healthy lives.

The Flying Monkeys

The Flying Monkeys won the FIRST LEGO League Global Innovation Award and $20,000 in 2011. They also have a short-term patent on their invention.

Arthur Fry

Sometimes inventors have goals in mind. They want to make life easier. They consider a problem, and then they work until it is solved. Arthur Fry (1931–) is such an inventor. Fry sang in his church's choir. He marked pages in his hymnal with scraps of paper. But they fell out as Fry turned from one hymn to another.

Arthur Fry with his invention

Luckily, Fry knew of another inventor's experiment. Spencer Silver had been experimenting with adhesives. He made one that stuck things together and allowed them to be pulled apart without damage. The adhesive could even be reused. No one could think of a use for Silver's invention except Arthur Fry.

Fry tried some of Silver's weak adhesive on his paper scraps. It wasn't perfect. The book pages were sticky after the scrap was removed. Fry experimented for 18 months. He worked until the adhesive was just right. Then he made a machine to apply the adhesive to paper. He called his invention Press and Peel.

Fry showed Press and Peel to his bosses at the 3M Company. They weren't impressed. They couldn't imagine anyone needing sticky note paper. But Fry convinced them to let 3M secretaries try his invention. Soon free samples were sent to other offices. People were enthusiastic! They stuck notes in books and on walls. They thought of many uses for Fry's invention. 3M renamed the product Post-it® notes. By 1980, Post-it notes could be bought all over the United States. Today, Post-its are a best-selling office supply, all because Fry's paper scraps fell out of his hymnal. Arthur Fry worked until he had solved his problem.

Goodyear accidentally discovered how to make rubber strong enough for tires and many other useful things.

Tire swings are one way to recycle Goodyear's invention.

Charles Goodyear

Although most inventions require a lot of hard work, some inventions happen by accident. Charles Goodyear (1800–1860) was interested in rubber. Rubber is made from the sap of rubber trees. It bounces and can erase pencil mistakes. But natural rubber melts in hot weather, and it shatters in cold. Goodyear thought he could make rubber better. He tried mixing it with other materials. None of them made rubber more useful.

Then in 1839, Goodyear dropped rubber and a chemical called sulfur onto his stove by accident. Cleaning up the mess, he found heat had changed the rubber. It was suddenly firm. High temperature didn't melt it, and it didn't shatter when it got cold. Goodyear had made rubber better by accident! He called the heating process vulcanization. Because of Goodyear's accident, now rubber is used to make tires, shoe soles, balls, and many other useful things.

An inventor once said, "When I see something that I don't like, I try to invent a way around it." Inventors not only see what is wrong, but they also see how things can be made better.

George de Mestral

Swiss engineer George de Mestral (1907–1990) loved to hunt. But often he and his dog returned from the woods covered with burrs. They stuck to de Mestral's clothes and to his dog's fur. It took a long time to pull them out. De Mestral didn't understand why the burrs were so hard to remove. He put a burr under his microscope to take a closer look. He saw that it was covered with tiny hooks. They were perfect for grabbing onto fabric and hair. De Mestral wondered if he could use such hooks in a helpful way. Could they hold things together?

De Mestral set out to imitate the burr. He imagined a hook-and-loop system. It would be able to do the work of zippers, snaps, laces, and buttons. The main difficulty was finding the right material. De Mestral wanted to use nylon, a strong material. But nylon was so tough that no one could cut it into hooks. In the end, de Mestral had to invent a special cutting machine for the nylon just so he could use it to produce his invention.

De Mestral called the hooks and loops Velcro® after two French words, *velour* (velvet) and *crochet* (hook). Production of Velcro began in the mid-1950s. Today, Velcro is used on things such as shoes, sports equipment, clothing, toys, backpacks, and watchbands. Velcro has even been used by astronauts to anchor objects in the space shuttle while in space!

De Mestral's hook-and-loop system, which he called Velcro

Velcro is used on shoes and many other things.

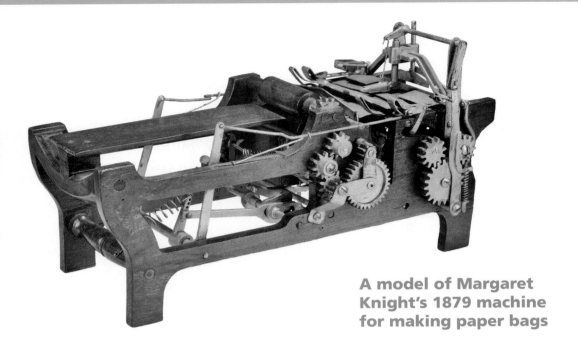

A model of Margaret Knight's 1879 machine for making paper bags

Margaret Knight

Margaret Knight (1838–1914) worked in a cotton mill when she was a child. One day, she witnessed an accident. Cotton strands running through an automated loom became tangled, causing a steeltipped shuttle to fall out of the loom and hit a worker. Knight went home upset but thoughtful. Only 12 years old, she designed a stop-motion device. It made the loom shut down when strands became tangled. Her invention helped keep workers safe.

Knight worked at many jobs as a young woman. At a paper bag company, she became interested in making bags that were more efficient to pack, as well as automating the way they were made. She spent time observing the bags being made by hand. Then she invented a machine to cut, fold, and glue flat-bottomed bags together.

Knight wanted to get a patent for her machine. A patent is a document from the government that credits the inventor for an invention. But when Knight tried to get her patent, she discovered that someone else had stolen her idea! Charles F. Annan had seen Knight's model at a machinist's shop and copied it. Knight fought him in court. She showed her plans, as well as diary entries where she wrote about her work. Knight won the patent. Today's paper bags are still made using her ideas.

Knight never had a formal education. She credited her achievements to a love of tools and machines. In her lifetime, she received 27 patents. She improved automobile motors and machines that made textiles, shoes, and tin cans. Knight was inducted into the National Inventors Hall of Fame in 2006, 92 years after her death.

National Inventors Hall of Fame

The National Inventors Hall of Fame was started in 1973 and is currently located in Alexandria, VA. It's mission is to "honor the women and men responsible for the great technological advances that make human, social, and economic progress possible." As of 2015, there are 516 inventors honored in the Hall of Fame. Each year in February, inventors selected by a panel of experts are inducted into the Hall. Only inventors that have had a US patent that has promoted the progress of science and technology and improved the welfare of society are considered.

Stephanie Kwolek

Stephanie Kwolek (1923–2014) is a **chemist** who worked in a laboratory to create new materials that are useful to society. She started working for the Textile Lab at DuPont® soon after graduating from college in 1946. She thought this job would be temporary so that she could earn enough money to attend medical school. But she really liked the work. She spent her entire career working as a research chemist.

Stephanie Kwolek

Kwolek's job was to develop new synthetic polymers. Polymers are long molecules that can be made into fabric or plastics. In the 1960s, she worked with a team of other chemists to develop high-performance fibers that were strong and stiff. One of the goals of this research was to find a replacement for the steel in steel-belted tires. If the steel could be replaced with a lighter-weight but strong material, then the vehicles would use less gasoline to run. The team also researched fibers that wouldn't melt at very high temperatures.

In her lab, Kwolek mixed substances to make a polymer. Then she melted the polymer into a liquid. The next step in the process was to spin the liquid in a machine called a spinneret. The spinneret turned the liquid into fibers. Other scientists on the team tested the newly created fibers to find their mass, how strong they were, and to determine other properties such as how easily the fibers would stretch or break.

One day, Kwolek created a polymer that would not melt, even at very high temperatures. She decided to see if she could get the polymer into a liquid state by dissolving it in a solvent, rather than melting it with heat. She finally found a solvent that would dissolve the polymer, but the resulting solution was different from any other polymer solution she had observed. Instead of being viscous and clear, like syrup, this new solution was more like water but cloudy. No one expected fibers to form by spinning the liquid in the spinneret. But Kwolek insisted on giving it a try. The result surprised everyone in the lab. The newly created synthetic fibers were much stiffer and stronger than any created before. Kwolek had discovered a new fiber called an aramid fiber. She also discovered a new type of substance called liquid crystalline solution.

The new fiber was named Kevlar®. It is five times stronger than steel (gram for gram), and about half the density of fiberglass. It took almost 10 years from the development of the fiber to the marketing of the first product. Can you name some products made from Kevlar?

One of the most popular uses for Kevlar is bullet-proof vests. These vests, worn by police and other law enforcement officers, save many lives. Kevlar is used to make skis, safety helmets, and bicycle tires. It is used in automobile tires and brake pads, and in cables used for suspension bridges. Kevlar is also used as a protective outer cover for fiberoptic cables. The shells of spacecraft, airplanes, and boats are made out of Kevlar. You can even find Kevlar in some audio speakers and on some smartphones.

Ask a Chemist

Beryl Baker

Beryl Baker's teacher asked her students to do a career report for an assignment. Beryl decided to do her report on a chemist's career. To find out what chemists do, she talked to Angelica Stacy, professor of chemistry at the University of California, Berkeley. Beryl had this interview with Professor Stacy.

BB We are studying mixtures and solutions in our class. My teacher said people who work with mixtures and solutions are called chemists. What does it mean to be a chemist, and what does a chemist do?

AS Those are good questions. Chemists do study mixtures and solutions, but they also study all other states of matter, including gases and solids. We study their properties and try to find out why they do what they do. We then use that information to make new things.

Chemists make many of the things around you: the material of your jacket, the dye in your jeans, medicines, plastics, and lots more.

BB Why do you like chemistry?

AS It's more that I like science, and chemistry is one piece of science. For me, chemistry is a way of thinking about the world and contributing to society at the same time.

Angelica Stacy

BB Was there a person who started you thinking about chemistry?

AS My father. He was an engineer with RCA. He never got a college degree because his family was poor, so he taught himself most of what he needed to know. Because of him, there was always science in our house. He was always making things that interested me and talking about how sound and electricity worked.

BB How long did you go to college to learn about chemistry?

AS Four years of college as an undergraduate to get my bachelor's degree, and then 4 years of graduate work to get the advanced degree so I could become a professor. In my case, it took 8 years of college-level study.

BB Do all chemists work at colleges or universities?

AS No. There is a big chemical industry worldwide. One [industry] that you probably know about is the medicine companies that create and manufacture medicines to fight disease, relieve pain, treat injuries, and so on. Lots of chemists work in this industry. Chemists work in the food industry, enriching and preserving the things we eat. Agriculture depends on chemistry. All those things in the bathroom were developed by chemists: soaps and detergents, cleansers, stain removers, shampoo, hair color, mouthwash, deodorant, toothpaste. Chemists are at work in many industries and government agencies.

BB Does everybody who studies chemistry become a chemist?

AS People may use their understanding of chemistry to launch into other interesting professions. One chemist I know is now a multimedia designer. His chemistry training prepared his mind for the demanding work of creating computer programs that help students learn about science subjects in interesting and fun ways. Others might move into university administration, law enforcement, government work, medicine, or business. And many students who start in chemistry move on to other fields of science and engineering because chemistry is recognized as the basic science. Knowledge of matter and its fundamental behaviors is a good place to start with any career in science.

BB What tools and instruments do you use when you are doing your chemistry work?

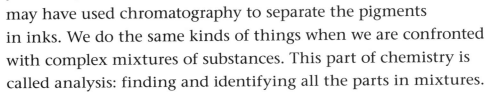

AS We use lots of different instruments to help us find out what things are made out of and how they are put together. As it turns out, some of our most important tools use light to give us information. The way different wavelengths of light are absorbed, reflected, or changed by substances tells us a lot about the structure of those substances.

Separation techniques are important, too. You undoubtedly used evaporation as a way to separate a solvent from a solute in your study of mixtures and solutions. You may have used chromatography to separate the pigments in inks. We do the same kinds of things when we are confronted with complex mixtures of substances. This part of chemistry is called analysis: finding and identifying all the parts in mixtures.

BB Have you invented or discovered anything?

AS My specialty is materials. I was investigating superconductors. Superconductors conduct electricity without resistance. But now I have turned my attention to trying to develop a new kind of refrigerator. Most refrigerators today use a gas called freon. But there is a problem with freon. It damages the ozone layer in the atmosphere, so freon is being phased out. I'm trying to develop a solid refrigerant. When you run electricity through it, it gets hot on one end and cold on the other. Right now it is only 10 percent efficient. Your freon refrigerator is 30 percent efficient. The material must get three times better to be useful on a broad scale. This is what I am trying to discover in my lab. But breakthroughs don't come easily. Discovery is hard work.

BB What are the most interesting things you get to do?

AS Teaching [is one]. My refrigeration research with graduate students is a kind of high-level teaching. I also teach basic chemistry for undergraduates, and I'm developing new ways to teach chemistry at the high school level. Another interesting part of my work is sharing ideas with other chemists all over the world. I have friends and colleagues in many countries as a result of my work in chemistry.

BB Is there anything else you would like to say to students about chemistry?

AS There are lots of opportunities in chemistry and in science generally. Whatever your interests are, knowledge of science can be part of your plans. I'd like to remind girls particularly not to be intimidated by science. In science, you have the opportunity to find things out that might help to solve problems, like my work in refrigeration, or disease control, food production, [or] lots of other things. It's a good feeling to contribute to the knowledge of the world.

When Substances Change

Tina made two solutions. She mixed citric acid and water in one cup. She mixed baking soda and water in another cup.

Citric acid and water

Baking soda and water

Tina poured the citric acid solution and the baking soda solution into an empty cup. At the same time, her brother Leo opened a bottle of soda water and poured some into an empty cup.

Combining citric acid and baking soda solutions

Pouring soda water

The liquids in both cups bubbled and fizzed. In 1 minute, they settled down to a slow, steady stream of bubbles. After 15 minutes, both cups were clear and still.

What happened in the two cups? Tina thought there was a chemical reaction in both cups. When you mix two substances and a change occurs, the change is evidence of a chemical reaction. Tina saw bubbles in both cups. Bubbling is a change. Tina thought there must be reactions going on in both cups.

Leo had a different idea. He knew that the bubbles in Tina's cup were filled with carbon dioxide (CO_2) gas. He observed that there were no CO_2 bubbles in the citric acid solution or the baking soda solution before they were mixed. The CO_2 bubbles formed only after the two solutions were mixed. Carbon dioxide gas was a new substance, evidence of a chemical reaction.

But Leo wasn't sure about the soda water. He didn't mix the soda water with any other substance. He just opened the bottle and poured. And up came the CO_2 bubbles. He didn't think the bubbles in the soda water were the result of a chemical reaction. But where did the CO_2 come from?

Remember, CO_2 dissolves in water. At the soda water bottling plant, water is saturated with CO_2 under high pressure. Leo released the pressure by removing the bottle cap. At the moment the pressure dropped, the solution became supersaturated.

The extra CO_2 then came out of solution in the form of bubbles. Carbon dioxide was not a new substance, so there was no chemical reaction.

Reactions That Don't Fizz

In 1772, Swedish pharmacist Karl Wilhelm Scheele (1742–1786) heated a sample of red-brown mercury oxide powder in a test tube over a flame. He observed a gas coming up and a liquid metal at the bottom of the test tube. The mercury oxide powder was gone. In its place were two new substances, a liquid metal and a gas.

Scheele observed a chemical reaction. A single **reactant**, mercury oxide, had changed into two new **products**, mercury metal and oxygen gas. By conducting this reaction, Scheele isolated and described the element oxygen.

Think about a rusty nail on the sidewalk, a gas burner on a stove, and a magnificent Fourth of July fireworks display. What do they have in common? They are all reactions in progress.

The Rusty Nail

A nail left outdoors in the environment gets rusty. Why is that? What is rust?

The nail contains iron. The iron in the nail reacts with oxygen in the air. The reaction produces a new product that we call rust. The scientific name for rust is iron oxide.

The reaction is very slow. It takes days or weeks for rust to become visible on the nail. It might take a hundred years for the whole nail to change into iron oxide. At the end of that time, the iron nail is gone. In its place is the new substance iron oxide.

The Gas Burner

Natural gas occurs in large quantities underground. It is collected and delivered through pipes to homes and businesses. When the gas is delivered to a stove or furnace, it is burned to produce heat. The heat cooks food and warms the air.

Gas changes into heat. How does that work? Natural gas is made of carbon and hydrogen. When the gas (one reactant) is mixed with oxygen from the air (the second reactant), a reaction is ready to happen. But nothing happens until the reaction is started with a spark or flame. Once the reaction starts, it will continue by itself until one of the reactants is used up. If the natural gas is used up, the reaction stops. If the oxygen is used up, the reaction stops.

While the natural gas flame is burning, the reaction is happening. Three things are given off by the reaction, two products and heat. The products are CO_2 and water. Here's one way to illustrate the reaction.

The major ingredient in natural gas is a substance called **methane**. The methane particle is made of carbon and hydrogen and looks like this.

The oxygen particle in the air looks like this.

In the burning flame, each particle of methane reacts with two particles of oxygen. The methane particles and the oxygen particles break apart and form new particles of CO_2 and water. This is how the reactants change to form the new products.

Methane	Oxygen	Carbon dioxide	Water	Water

Reactants = Products

79

You can see that matter is conserved during the reaction. The number of carbon particles, hydrogen particles, and oxygen particles is the same on both sides of the arrow. In other words, the matter in the reactants is exactly the same as the matter in the products.

The natural gas reaction is a fast reaction. The change from reactants to products occurs in a flash. The products are both gases, CO_2 and water vapor, so the reaction is "clean." The only concern is the waste product CO_2, which enters the air.

Fireworks

Another fast reaction is a stunning fireworks display. This kind of reaction is called an **explosion**. To qualify as an explosion, the reaction must happen very fast and must produce light, heat, and sound energy, plus a lot of gas. Because the gases expand so rapidly, explosions come with a loud kaboom. The people who design fireworks know what substances to put into each charge to produce different colors. The green color is the product of one substance, the red color is from another substance, and so on. The result is a thrilling experience for your eyes and ears.

Air Bags

The automotive air bag was invented in 1952 as a safety device for people. Twenty years later, air bags started to appear in American cars as an extra. Today, all cars sold in the United States have air bags in front, one for the driver and one for the passenger. Many cars have additional air bags in the ceiling and doors.

An air bag is a fabric bag that inflates like a big balloon the moment a car crashes into something. The bag has to inflate fully in a few thousandths of a second! How is that possible?

It's a chemical reaction. When a car smacks into a solid object, sensors in a triggering device start the action. A pulse of electricity flows to the igniter, and a wire gets hot. The hot wire starts a very fast reaction, which produces a large volume of gas, usually nitrogen. The expanding gas bursts open the steering wheel or dashboard, and the bag pops out. It has to be fully inflated before the driver's or passenger's head and chest reach the steering wheel or dashboard. That's fast inflation!

The air bag is full of carefully designed holes. When the person's body contacts the bag, the force of the impact squeezes air out of the holes. The air bag doesn't stop the forward motion of the person. It slows the speed of the forward motion. This is important because the longer it takes for the person's body to come to a stop, the less he or she will be hurt by the collision.

The inflation reaction is pretty close to being an explosion. The definition of an explosion is a fast reaction that produces gas, heat, light, and sound energy. The air bag reaction is fast, produces a lot of gas, gets warm, and makes a bang, but has no flash of light. It is close to an explosion, but not quite. Still, the action is forceful. People have been injured by air bags. The benefits, however, far outweigh the hazards. Thousands of lives have been saved by air bags since they were first installed in cars more than 40 years ago.

An air bag inflates completely in 20–30 milliseconds.

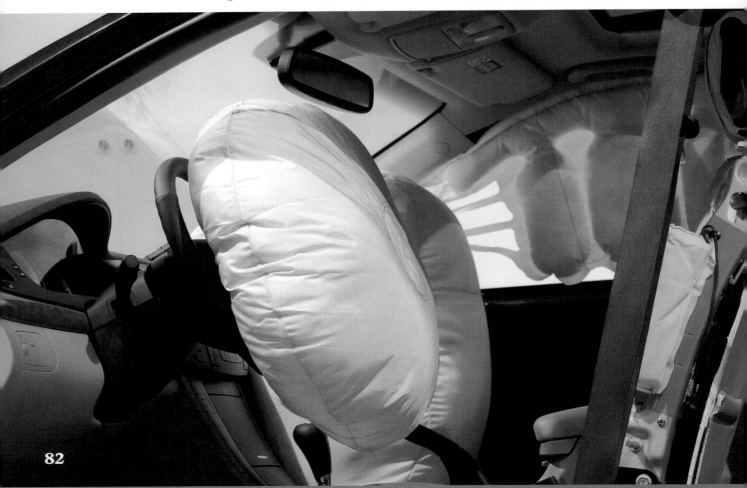

Celsius and Fahrenheit

Celsius and Fahrenheit are two **scales** used to measure temperature. Both scales are based on the **freezing point** and boiling point of pure water at sea level. The Celsius scale has 100° between the two points. The Fahrenheit scale has 180° between the freezing point and boiling point.

Today most countries use the Celsius scale to measure temperatures. The United States, however, still uses the Fahrenheit scale.

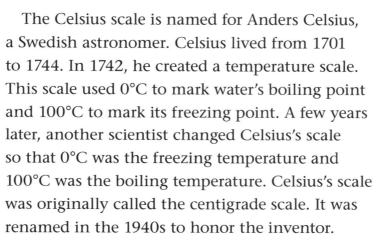

Celsius

Body temp 37°

Room temp 22°

Freezing point of water 0°

Anders Celsius

The Celsius scale is named for Anders Celsius, a Swedish astronomer. Celsius lived from 1701 to 1744. In 1742, he created a temperature scale. This scale used 0°C to mark water's boiling point and 100°C to mark its freezing point. A few years later, another scientist changed Celsius's scale so that 0°C was the freezing temperature and 100°C was the boiling temperature. Celsius's scale was originally called the centigrade scale. It was renamed in the 1940s to honor the inventor.

Daniel G. Fahrenheit

The Fahrenheit scale is named for German scientist Daniel G. Fahrenheit. Fahrenheit lived from 1686 to 1736. In 1714, he invented the first mercury thermometer. He invented a temperature scale to go along with it. Fahrenheit's thermometer marked normal human body temperature as 98.6°F.

Fahrenheit thought he had found the lowest possible temperature by mixing ice and salt. He set the temperature of this mixture at 0°F. Then he set the freezing point of water at 32°F. He also set the boiling point of water at 212°F.

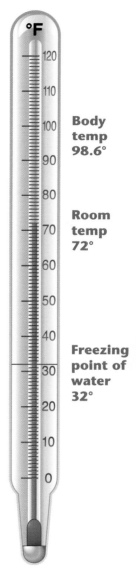

Fahrenheit

Body temp 98.6°

Room temp 72°

Freezing point of water 32°

Earth Science

FOSS Science Resources

Earth and Sun

Table of Contents

Table of Contents (continued)

Investigation 5: Water Planet

Changing Shadows

Objects you can't see through, such as people, birds, buildings, balls, and flagpoles, have **shadows** on sunny **days**. That's because opaque objects block sunlight. A shadow is the dark area behind an **opaque** object. Shadows give information about the position of the **Sun**. If you see your shadow in front of you, then the Sun is behind you.

Did you know that a shadow tells you what time of day it is? Let's see how that works. First, if you are in North America, you need to be facing south. When you are facing south, north is behind you.

It is 12:00 noon. Let's look at the flagpole and observe its shadow. What direction is the shadow pointing?

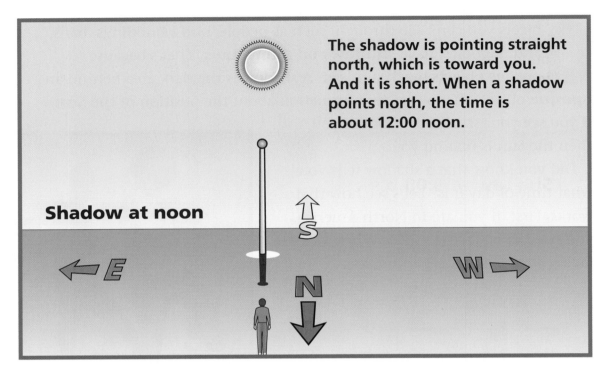

The shadow is pointing straight north, which is toward you. And it is short. When a shadow points north, the time is about 12:00 noon.

Shadow at noon

What does the flagpole's shadow look like at 9:00 in the morning? Did you see your shadow this morning? Do you remember what direction it was pointing? Do you remember how long it was?

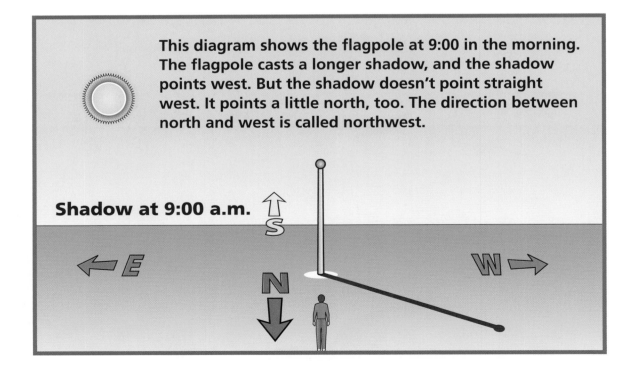

This diagram shows the flagpole at 9:00 in the morning. The flagpole casts a longer shadow, and the shadow points west. But the shadow doesn't point straight west. It points a little north, too. The direction between north and west is called northwest.

Shadow at 9:00 a.m.

What happens to the shadow in the afternoon?

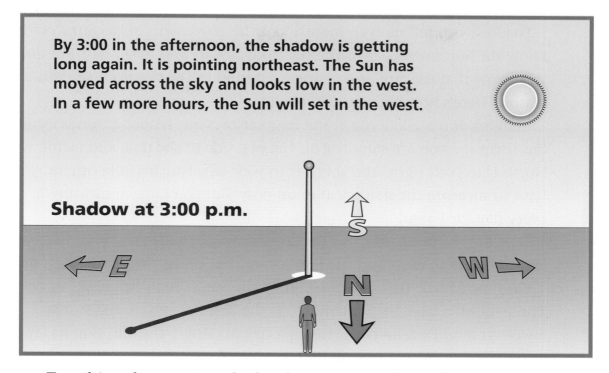

By 3:00 in the afternoon, the shadow is getting long again. It is pointing northeast. The Sun has moved across the sky and looks low in the west. In a few more hours, the Sun will set in the west.

Shadow at 3:00 p.m.

Two things happen to a shadow between **sunrise** and **sunset**: its length changes and its direction changes. Early in the morning, a shadow is long, and it points west. We observe that the Sun moves across the sky from east to west, and the shadow changes.

At noon, the Sun reaches its highest point in the sky. Now the shadow is as short as it will get. It points straight north. We observe that the Sun keeps moving across the sky. Just before sunset, a shadow is very long, and it points east.

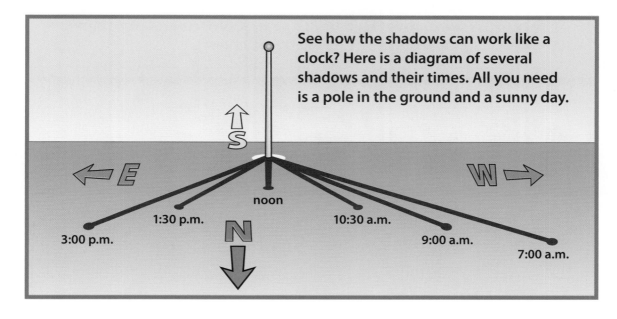

See how the shadows can work like a clock? Here is a diagram of several shadows and their times. All you need is a pole in the ground and a sunny day.

noon

1:30 p.m.   10:30 a.m.

3:00 p.m.   9:00 a.m.

7:00 a.m.

The Sun and Seasons

Shadows can tell us even more about the movement of the Sun. We know the Sun moves across the sky from east to west every day. But did you know that the Sun also changes position in the sky from **season** to season? Here's how you can observe it.

Imagine you are looking at the flagpole on your school grounds again. But this time you are standing on the east side of the pole and facing west. North is to your right, and south is to your left. For this experiment, you have to measure the shadow at noon only. But you have to measure it every day for 1 year!

Here are the noon shadows for just five times during the year. Look at the length of the shadow and the position of the Sun in the sky on each date.

On June 21, the first day of summer, the Sun is high in the sky at noon. Three months later, on September 21, the first day of fall, the Sun is lower. And on December 21, the first day of winter, the Sun is at its lowest noon position. After December 21, the Sun begins to climb higher in the sky again. On March 21, the first day of spring, it is as high as it was in September. One year after starting the experiment, on June 21, the Sun is again at its highest noon position.

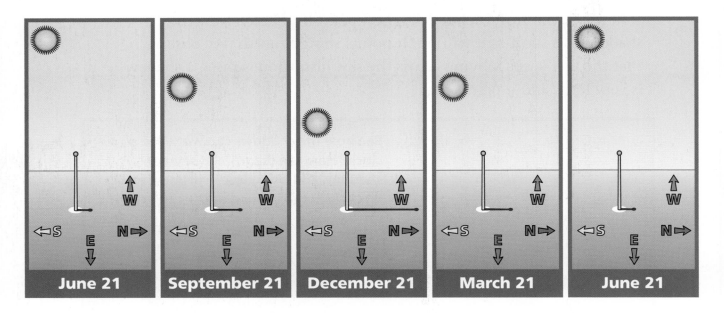

June 21 | September 21 | December 21 | March 21 | June 21

The Sun's change of position in the sky minute by minute during a day is predictable. The Sun's position in the sky season to season during a year is also predictable.

Thinking about Shadows

1. How does the Sun's position in the sky change over 1 day?

2. In what ways do shadows change during the day?

3. What causes shadows to change during the day?

4. Think about a flagpole. How does its shadow change over 1 year?

5. Look at the photo at the top of the page. Can you see the shadow of the person? Can you see the shadows of the four flagpoles? Why or why not?

The Sun rising over a cornfield in Minnesota

Sunrise and Sunset

The Sun has just come up in this picture. It is sunrise. What direction are you looking?

The Sun always rises in the east. If you are in Portland, Maine, the Sun rises in the east. If you are in Portland, Oregon, the Sun rises in the east. If you are in Raleigh, North Carolina, the Sun rises in the east.

If you are in Brownsville, Texas, or Broken Bow, Oklahoma, the Sun rises in the east. Wherever you are on **Earth**, the Sun rises in the east.

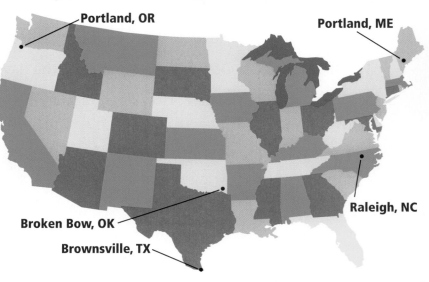

Portland, OR

Portland, ME

Raleigh, NC

Broken Bow, OK

Brownsville, TX

In this picture, the Sun is just about to go down. It is sunset. What direction are you looking now?

That's right, you're looking west. The Sun always sets in the west. If you are in Portland, Maine, the Sun sets in the west. If you are in Portland, Oregon, the Sun sets in the west. If you are in Raleigh, North Carolina, the Sun sets in the west. If you are in Brownsville, Texas, or Broken Bow, Oklahoma, the Sun sets in the west. Wherever you are on Earth, the Sun sets in the west.

Every day the Sun rises in the east and sets in the west. To get from east to west, the Sun appears to slowly travel across the sky. In the early morning, when the Sun first comes up, it is touching the horizon in the east. At noon, the Sun is at its highest position in the sky. At sunset, the Sun is touching the horizon in the west. The Sun's position in the sky changes all day long.

The Sun setting over the city of Boston, Massachusetts

There is one thing you can depend on for sure. The Sun will come up tomorrow morning. And you can be sure it will come up in the east. When the Sun is in the sky, you can feel its warmth. At the end of the day, it will set in the west. You can count on it.

As the day goes along, it looks as though the Sun travels across the sky from east to west. During the morning, it rises higher and higher in the sky. At noon, it is at its highest position in the sky. From noon to sunset, the Sun continues to travel west. And it gets lower and lower in the sky. At sunset, the Sun disappears below the horizon in the west. Another day has passed. And tomorrow will be the same.

Earth's Rotation

The Sun looks as though it moves across the sky. But it really doesn't. It is Earth that is moving. Here's how it works.

Earth is spinning like a top. It takes 1 day (24 hours) for Earth to **rotate** once. Because Earth is rotating, half of the time we are on the sunny side of Earth. We call the sunny side day. The other half of the time we are on the dark side of Earth. We call the dark side **night**.

Imagine it's just before sunrise. You can't see the Sun because you are still on the dark side of Earth. But in 5 minutes, Earth will rotate just enough for you to see the Sun come over the horizon. That moment is sunrise.

Earth turns toward the east, the direction of the orange arrow. That means the first sunlight of the day will be in the east. And, of course, Earth keeps turning. You keep moving with it. In 4 or 5 hours, you have turned so far that the Sun is high over your head. And 5 hours after that, the Sun is low in the western sky. This is because Earth is moving in an eastward direction. It looks as though the Sun is moving across the sky in a westward direction. Finally, it is sunset. The Sun slips below the horizon in the west. It is dark again.

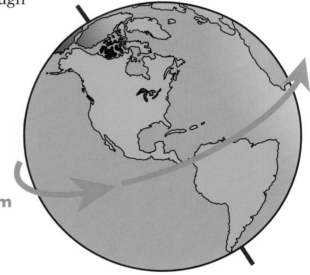

Earth turns toward the east. So the Sun seems to move from east to west across the sky.

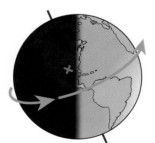

The x shows your position just before sunrise.

The x shows your position just after sunrise.

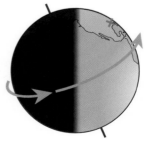

The x shows your position near noon.

97

Shadows

A shadow is the dark area behind an opaque object. It is created where an object blocks sunlight. A steel pole, like a flagpole, casts a shadow. The direction of the pole's shadow changes as the Sun's position changes. At noon, the Sun is highest in the sky. Noon is also when the flagpole's shadow is the shortest of the day.

We can watch the noon shadow to see how the Sun's position changes from season to season. The length of that shadow changes a little bit every day. Why does the length of the shadow change? It changes because the position of the Sun at noon changes a little bit every day.

The Sun's position changes all day from sunrise to sunset.

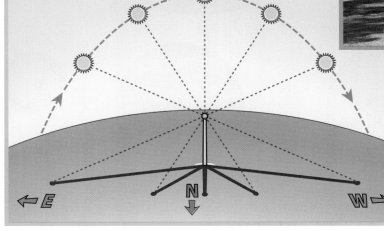

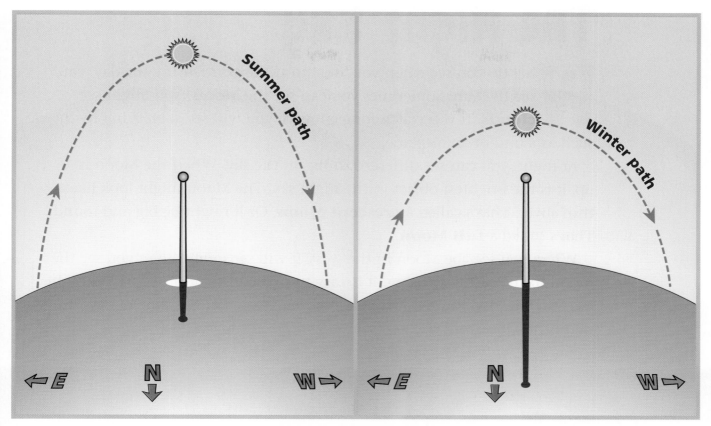

The Sun's path through the sky is higher in summer.

The pattern of change is predictable. In North America, the position of the noon Sun gets higher in the sky from December 21 to June 21. On June 21, the Sun is highest in the sky. That's also the day when the flagpole's shadow is the shortest of the year.

The position of the noon Sun gets lower in the sky each day between June 21 and December 21. On December 21, the noon Sun is lowest in the sky. That's also the day that the flagpole's shadow is the longest of the year.

The Sun's position in the sky changes in two ways. Every day the Sun rises in the east, appears to travel across the sky, and sets in the west. The other way the Sun's position changes is in its daily path. In summer, the Sun's path is high in the sky. In winter, the Sun's path is lower in the sky.

The Night Sky

What do you see when you look up at the sky? During the day, you see the Sun. Sometimes you can see the **Moon**. You might see **clouds**. If you watch long enough, you will see something fly by, such as a bird or an airplane.

At night, you can see different things in the sky. When the Moon is up, it is the brightest object in the night sky. The Moon might look like a thin sliver. That's called a **crescent Moon**. Or it might be big and round. That's called a **full Moon**.

When you see the Moon in the west, it will set soon. When you see the Moon in the east, it is rising. It is easy to **predict** the time of day or night the Sun will rise and set. It is much harder to predict the time of day or night the Moon will rise and set.

A full Moon over New York City

A crescent Moon

The Moon during the day

On a clear night, you can see about 2,000 stars in the sky.

Stars

When it is clear, you can see **stars** in the night sky. Night is the only time you can see stars. Well, almost the only time. There is one star we can see in the daytime. It's the Sun. The Sun shines so brightly that it is impossible to see the other stars. But after the Sun sets, we can see that the sky is full of stars. It looks like there are millions of stars in the sky on a clear night. But actually you can see only about 2,000 stars with your **unaided eyes**.

Venus and Jupiter in the eastern sky just before sunrise

Planets

Some stars are brighter than others. They are the first ones you can see just after the Sun sets. Did you ever make a wish on the first star that appears in the evening sky? "Star light, star bright, first star I see tonight. I wish I may, I wish I might, have the wish I make tonight." That star might not be a star at all. The brightest stars are actually **planets**. That's one way you can tell a planet from a star, by how brightly it appears to shine.

Earth **orbits** the Sun with seven other planets and several **dwarf planets**. You can see five planets in the night sky. Venus is one of the planets you might see. Ancient sky watchers called Venus the evening star. It is seen near the western horizon after sunset. Venus was also called the morning star. It is also seen near the eastern horizon just before sunrise. What caused the confusion?

Two planets orbit closer to the Sun than Earth does. Mercury is closest to the Sun. Then comes Venus. Venus takes only 225 days to go around the Sun. Sometimes Venus is positioned where we can see it from Earth just before sunrise as the morning star. A few months later, Venus has traveled to the other side of the Sun. Now it is positioned for us to see it after sunset as the evening star. That's why ancient sky watchers thought Venus was two different stars.

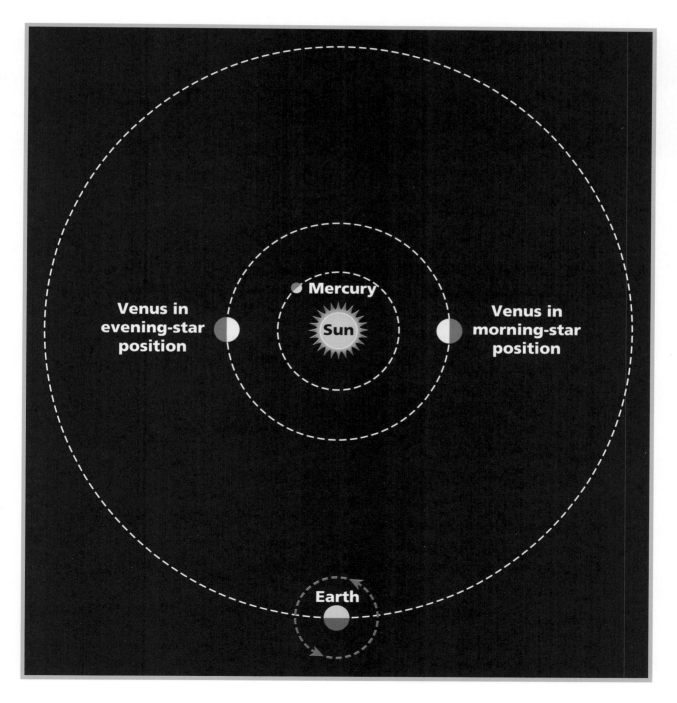

Venus is often visible from Earth.

Four other planets can be seen with unaided eyes. Mercury is visible sometimes. Because it is so close to the Sun, it is often lost in the bright glare of the Sun. Mars is the fourth planet from the Sun. It shines with a slightly red light. Jupiter and Saturn are the farthest of the visible planets. Still, they are pretty bright because they are so big.

It is a special night when you can see all five planets at the same time in the night sky. It doesn't happen very often. It happened in 2004. It won't happen again until 2036!

Thinking about the Night Sky

1. What are some of the objects you can see in the night sky that you can't see in the day sky?

2. Which object is the brightest object in the night sky?

3. Which star is the closest to Earth?

4. Look at the picture of the crescent Moon. What is the other bright object you can see in the night sky?

Looking through Telescopes

What do you see when you look at the sky on a clear night? You probably see many twinkling stars. Maybe you see the Moon or a planet. People saw the same objects in the sky thousands of years ago.

The way we look at objects in the sky changed in 1608. In that year, the **telescope** was invented. A telescope is a tool that **magnifies** distant objects so that they appear larger and closer.

Galileo Galilei (1564–1642) was a scientist who lived in Italy. In 1609, he improved the telescope and used it to observe the night sky. He could see many more stars through the telescope than with his unaided eyes. He could see mountains and **craters** on the Moon. And he could see that planets were spheres, not just points of light. Then Galileo turned his telescope toward Jupiter. He became the first person to observe moons orbiting another planet.

Galileo Galilei

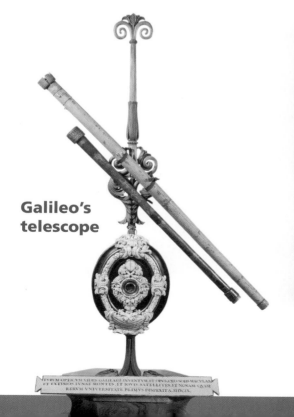

Galileo's telescope

You can see more stars through a telescope than with your unaided eyes.

105

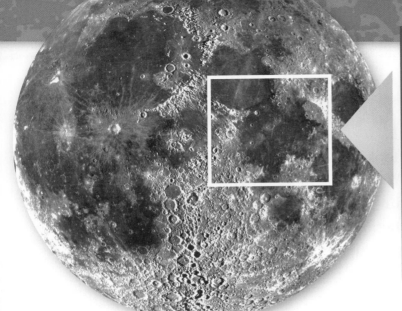

The Apollo 11 landing site on the Moon

As telescopes got more powerful, **astronomers** could see more details on planets. They could also see more stars in the night sky. By the mid-1900s, the surface of the Moon could be studied in detail with telescopes on Earth. Scientists used pictures taken through telescopes to plan the first Moon landing in 1969.

Modern Telescopes

Most telescopes are built on mountain peaks. The telescopes are above most of the dust and pollution in the **air**. And they are far away from city lights. The telescopes are protected inside dome-shaped buildings called **observatories**.

Keck Observatory is on top of Mauna Kea, a 4,205-meter peak on the island of Hawaii.

The space shuttle placed a very important telescope in Earth's orbit in 1990. It is called the Hubble Space Telescope. The Hubble Space Telescope takes pictures of planets and other objects in the **solar system**. It also takes pictures of objects beyond the solar system. Because the telescope orbits above Earth's **atmosphere**, it gets a clear view of outer space.

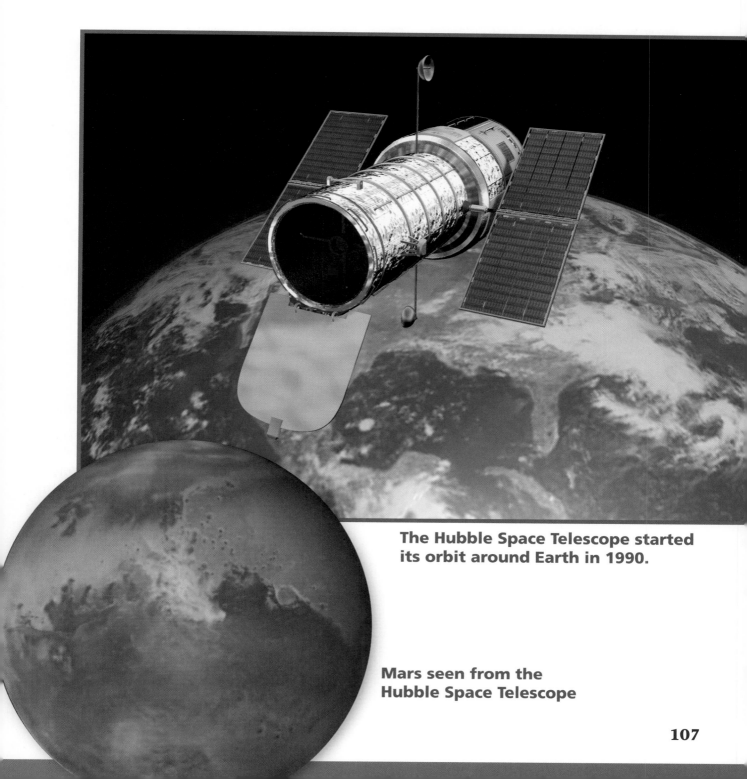

The Hubble Space Telescope started its orbit around Earth in 1990.

Mars seen from the Hubble Space Telescope

When you look up at the sky on a clear, moonless night, you can see about 2,000 stars. But that view changes a lot when you look through the Hubble Space Telescope. You can see millions of stars that are too dim to see with your unaided eyes. Telescopes make distant objects look bigger and closer. With telescopes, astronomers can explore space without leaving Earth.

Part of the Milky Way seen with unaided eyes on a clear night

Part of the Milky Way seen through the Hubble Space Telescope

On April 24, 2015, Hubble was 25 years old. For 25 years, it had provided information about the structure and organization of the universe. Hubble looked into the most distant parts of our **galaxy** to observe the birth of stars.

The Westerlund 2 cluster, a collection of about 3,000 newly-formed stars

Hubble has also allowed astronomers to determine the size and age of the universe. By looking between the stars in the night sky, Hubble observed objects in deep, deep space. Hubble observed that in every direction in the sky, the deep field of view is filled with millions of other galaxies. Each galaxy is made up of billions of stars. Measurements made by Hubble show that the galaxies are all moving away from one another. This is evidence that the universe is expanding at a rapid rate. These observations allowed astronomers to figure out that the universe is between 13 and 14 billion years old.

Each point of light in this image is a galaxy composed of billions of stars.

Thinking about Telescopes

1. Who was Galileo, and what was he the first to do?

2. Why is a telescope a useful tool to an astronomer?

3. Why are modern telescopes built on mountaintops or put into space?

Comparing the Size of Earth and the Moon

Apollo 11 Space Mission

On July 16, 1969, the world's most powerful booster rocket thundered off launch pad 39A at Cape Canaveral, Florida. Perched on top of the mighty Saturn 5 rocket was a tiny command module and a smaller, spindle-legged, lunar module. The mission was Apollo 11. On board were three American astronauts. Neil Armstrong was the mission commander. Michael Collins was the command module pilot. Edwin "Buzz" Aldrin Jr. was the lunar module pilot.

The goal of the Apollo 11 mission was to land two men on the Moon and return them safely to Earth. The mission was complex. It involved the development of many new technologies, including some of the most advanced engineering ever attempted by humans. The 36-story-tall Saturn 5 three-stage rocket was the largest, most powerful booster rocket ever designed.

The first stage of the rocket lifted the 3,000-ton spacecraft off Earth's surface. After 8 minutes, the first stage was used up and fell away. At that point, the second stage fired up to propel the spacecraft into orbit 189 kilometers (km) above Earth's surface. After orbiting Earth one and a half times, the third stage of the booster rocket fired up and sent the spacecraft on its way toward the Moon.

Neil Armstrong, Michael Collins, and Buzz Aldrin

The lunar module after it is separated from the command module. The two parts are shown in orbit around the Moon.

The lunar module as it approaches the command module for docking and the return trip to Earth. Earth is seen in earthrise.

As soon as the spacecraft was up to speed, it separated from the third rocket stage and coasted its way to the Moon. Four days later, the spacecraft arrived and moved into orbit around the Moon.

The spacecraft had two separate parts. The first part was the lunar module, the craft that would land on the Moon and later take off from the Moon. The second part was the command module, the craft that would orbit the Moon while waiting for the lunar module to return. The two parts would undock, or separate, during an orbit around the Moon.

When all was ready, Armstrong and Aldrin moved into the lunar module. Mission Control in Houston, Texas, gave the command to the lunar module to start its descent toward the Moon's surface. The two modules separated. *Eagle*, the lunar module, started its long process of slowing down and descending to the Moon's surface. *Columbia*, the command module, stayed in its lunar orbit to await the return of *Eagle* after it completed its mission to the surface.

The preprogrammed descent brought *Eagle* close to the Moon's surface. As *Eagle* approached the landing site, Armstrong and Aldrin could see that they were headed for a pile of boulders. At the last minute, Armstrong took the controls to pilot *Eagle* to a safer landing spot.

Footprints left by the astronauts on the Moon are permanent.

Armstrong took this picture of Aldrin. What can you see in the visor of Aldrin's helmet?

After a few tense seconds, Armstrong guided *Eagle* to a soft, safe landing on the southwestern edge of the Sea of Tranquility. Soon after, Armstrong and Aldrin reported to Mission Control in Texas: "Houston, Tranquility Base here. The *Eagle* has landed!" Dozens of technicians at Mission Control cheered for this amazing event. Humans had arrived safely on the surface of the Moon.

After checking all systems in the lunar module to make sure it was secure and undamaged, Armstrong and Aldrin dressed for a trip outside. The Moon's surface, with no atmosphere, is a deadly place for a person without proper protection. The **temperature** is more than 115 degrees Celsius (°C) in the sunshine and –173°C in the shade. The pressure is 0, and there is no air.

Dressing involved putting on a pressurized space suit that was temperature controlled. The suit provided air and communication. The helmet had a gold-covered lens that could be lowered to protect the astronauts' eyes from dangerous ultraviolet rays from the Sun.

At 10:39 p.m. eastern daylight time, Armstrong squeezed out of the exit hatch onto the ladder leading down to the Moon's surface. As he hopped from the lowest rung onto the Moon's surface, he said, "That's one small step for a man, one giant leap for mankind."

The lunar soil onto which Armstrong stepped was like powder. The bulky, stiff suit worked perfectly. Armstrong was comfortable and able to move around easily. Aldrin joined him on the Moon's surface, and together they began their tasks. They set up several experiments on the surface. They put up an American flag, took photos of the terrain, and collected samples of lunar rocks and soil.

After 2 hours and 21 minutes of exploring the Moon's surface, the astronauts gathered their equipment and scientific samples, including 108 kilograms (kg) of Moon rocks, and returned to the lunar module. They repressurized the cabin and settled in for some much needed rest before leaving the Moon's surface.

Aldrin climbs down to step on the Moon's surface.

Armstrong and Aldrin left the American flag on the Moon.

After 7 hours of rest, Mission Control sent the astronauts a wake-up call. Two hours later, they fired the ascent rocket that propelled the lunar module upward. *Eagle* reunited with *Columbia*, which had been orbiting while *Eagle* was on the Moon's surface.

Once the two spacecrafts were reunited, the landing crew transferred to *Columbia*. No longer needed, *Eagle* was left behind in lunar orbit and probably crashed into the Moon in the next few months. Then *Columbia* used its rockets to start its voyage back to Earth. After the long ride home, *Columbia* moved into Earth's orbit. When the time and location were right, rockets fired to push *Columbia* out of orbit and into Earth's atmosphere.

Soon after, huge parachutes opened to slow *Columbia*'s reentry. The historic mission came to a successful end on July 24, when *Columbia* splashed down safely in the Pacific Ocean. They landed only 24 km from the recovery ship waiting for their return.

Six more Apollo missions followed this adventure. The last mission, Apollo 17, was in December 1972. A total of 12 people have walked on the Moon. The Moon is the only **extraterrestrial** object that humans have visited.

Columbia safely landed in the Pacific Ocean.

How Did Earth's Moon Form?

Counting out from the Sun, Earth is the first planet with a **satellite**, or moon. Mercury and Venus, closer to the Sun, don't have moons. Mars, the fourth planet from the Sun, has two moons. Earth probably didn't have a moon at first. Earth got its Moon early in Earth's history as a result of a gigantic collision. The event might have happened about 4.5 billion years ago. This is how it might have happened.

Earth formed from **gas** and dust in the solar system. **Gravity** pulled the gas and dust together to form the planet. As soon as it formed, Earth traveled around the Sun in an almost-circular orbit.

The early solar system was messy. It had lots of large rocks and debris flying around in it. Some of the rocks, called planetesimals, were huge. Scientists now think that one of these planetesimals, the size of Mars, started heading for Earth.

Imagine you had been on Earth to witness the event. The planetesimal first appeared as a dot in the sky. Over a period of days and weeks, it appeared bigger and bigger. Then it completely blocked the view from Earth in that direction. Finally, it struck, traveling at perhaps 40,000 kilometers (km) per hour. The collision lasted several minutes.

The crash created a chain of events. First, the impact seemed to destroy the incoming object. The planetesimal turned to gas, dust, and a few large chunks of rock. Some surviving chunks traveled deep into the interior of Earth. A large portion of Earth was destroyed as well. The energy that resulted from the crash produced a huge explosion. Earth itself might have been in danger of being blasted apart.

Second, the explosion threw a tremendous amount of **matter** into motion. Some of this debris flew far out into space. Other matter flew up into the air and then returned to Earth. This debris came in many sizes. Some of it was huge rocks that immediately returned to Earth. A short time later, smaller granules of different sizes fell to Earth. Months or even years later, some of the debris was still floating up in the air.

A large portion of the debris didn't fly off into space, and it didn't return to Earth. It began orbiting Earth. This orbiting debris formed a disk, like the rings of Saturn. The ring was probably about two Earth **diameters** from the surface of Earth. Right away, the pieces of debris started to attract one another. Gradually, they formed into larger and larger chunks. After several weeks, the chunks of debris formed Earth's Moon.

Earth now had a satellite where previously there was none. It must have been quite a sight up there only about 30,000 km above Earth. Today the Moon is much farther above Earth, about 385,000 km.

A representation of how the Moon might have formed

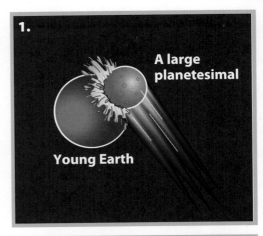

1. A large planetesimal
Young Earth

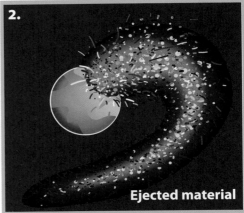

2. Ejected material

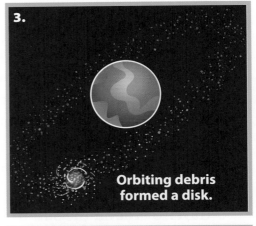

3. Orbiting debris formed a disk.

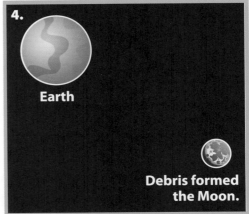

4. Earth
Debris formed the Moon.

118

Changing Moon

Earth has one large satellite. It is called the Moon. The Moon completes one orbit around Earth every 28 days. One complete orbit is also called a **cycle**.

The Moon is the second-brightest object in the sky. It shines so brightly that you can see it even during the day. But did you know that the Moon doesn't make its own light? The light you see coming from the Moon is **reflected** sunlight. Sunlight reflected from the Moon is what we call moonlight.

The Moon is a sphere. When light shines on a sphere, the sphere is half lit and half dark. Wherever you position the sphere, if the light source is shining on it, one half will always be lit and the other half dark.

The same is true for the Moon. It is always half lit and half dark. The half that is lit is the side toward the Sun. The half that is dark is the side away from the Sun.

These spheres are all half lit and half dark.

119

The Moon's Position

From Earth, the Moon never looks the same 2 days in a row. Its appearance changes all the time. Sometimes it looks like a thin sliver, and sometimes it looks completely round. Why does the Moon's appearance change?

The Sun is in the center of the solar system. The planets orbit the Sun. The Moon orbits Earth.

It takes 4 weeks for the Moon to orbit Earth. Where is the Moon during those 4 weeks? Let's take a look from out in space.

We'll start the observations when the Moon is at position 1 between Earth and the Sun.

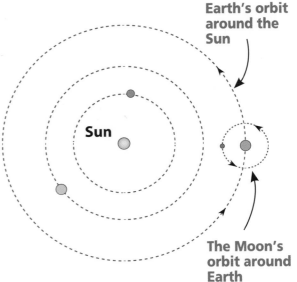

Earth's orbit around the Sun

The Moon's orbit around Earth

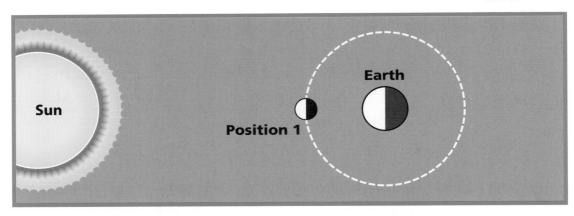

The Moon orbits Earth in a counterclockwise direction. After 1 week, the Moon has moved to position 2.

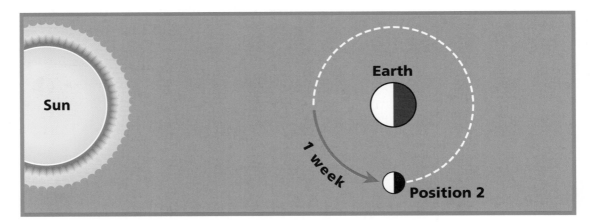

After 2 weeks, the Moon has moved to position 3, on the other side of Earth. The Moon has traveled halfway around Earth.

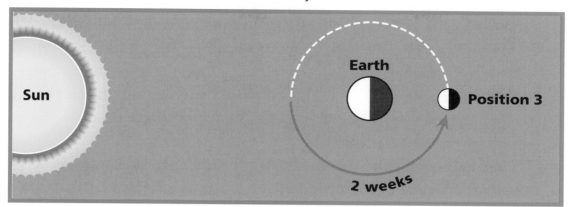

After 3 weeks, the Moon has moved to position 4. It is now three-quarters of the way around Earth.

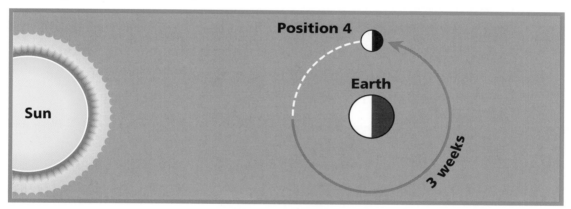

In another week (a total of 4 weeks), the Moon has returned to position 1. It has completed one **lunar cycle**.

Look at the Moon in each of the illustrations. You will see that the lit side is always toward the Sun. In each position during the lunar cycle, the Moon's bright side is always toward the Sun.

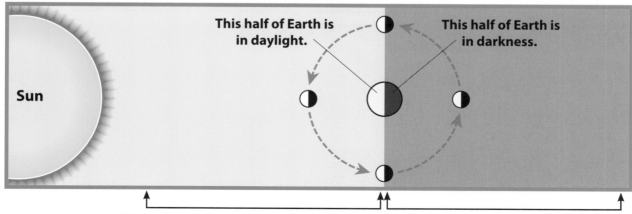

The Moon's Appearance

The shape of the Moon doesn't change. It is always a sphere. The amount of the Moon that is brightly lit doesn't change. Half of the Moon is always lit by the Sun. What changes is how much of the lit half is visible from Earth. You might see just a tiny bit of the lit half. Or you might see the entire lit half. The lit portion you see from Earth changes in a predictable way. The different shapes you see have been named, and each one is called a **phase**.

Let's look at the phase of the Moon in position 1. The Moon is between the Sun and Earth. When you look up at the Moon from Earth, what do you see? Nothing. All of the lit half of the Moon is on the other side. This is the **new Moon**. The new Moon has no light visible from Earth. The new Moon is shown as a black circle.

Let's move forward 2 weeks. The Moon has continued in its orbit and is in position 3. What do you see when you look up at the Moon? The whole lit side of the Moon is visible from Earth. This is the full Moon. The full Moon is shown in the illustration as a white circle.

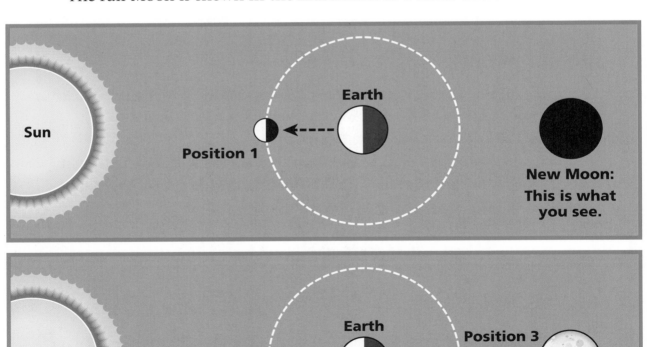

Now let's look at positions 2 and 4. At both positions, you see half of the lit part of the Moon and half of the dark part of the Moon. At position 2, when you look up at the Moon, the lit part is on the right side. At position 4, the lit part of the Moon is on the left side. Position 2 is the **first-quarter Moon**. Position 4 is the **third-quarter Moon**.

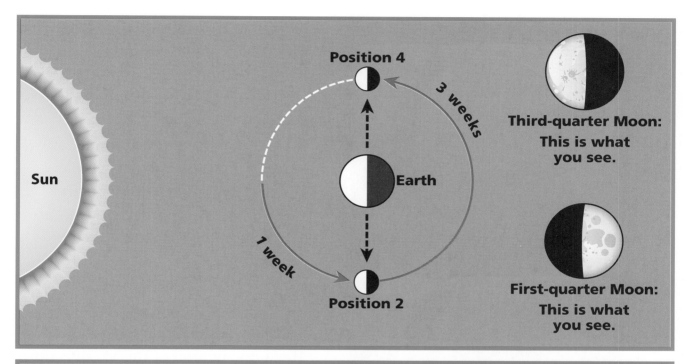

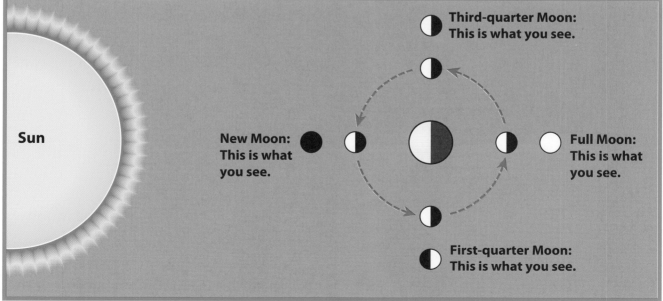

This is the Moon's orbit during one lunar cycle.

Lunar Cycle

Day 0: New Moon

Day 3: Waxing crescent Moon

Day 5: Waxing crescent Moon

Day 6: Waxing crescent Moon

The new Moon is invisible for two reasons. First, no light is coming to your eyes from the Moon. The lit side is facing away from Earth. Second, to look for the new Moon, you would have to look toward the Sun. The glare is too bright to see the Moon. (And remember, you should never look directly at the Sun.)

Three days later, the Moon has moved in its orbit, and it is visible. The first sighting of the Moon after a new Moon is a tiny sliver of visible light. The curved shape is called the crescent Moon.

On day 5, the Moon looks larger. About one-quarter of the Moon is now bright. Each day the visible bright part of the Moon is a little larger. We say the Moon is **waxing** when it appears to be growing.

By day 6, almost half of the Moon appears brightly lit. This is the last day of the waxing crescent Moon. Tomorrow the Moon will appear as the first-quarter Moon.

The first-quarter Moon is the phase seen on day 7. The Moon has completed the first quarter of its lunar cycle. Observers on Earth see half the sunlit side of the Moon and half the dark side of the Moon. The brightly lit side is on the right side.

Day 7: First-quarter Moon

On day 9, you can see more than half the sunlit side of the Moon. The Moon appears to be oval shaped. A Moon phase that is larger than a quarter but not yet full is called a **gibbous Moon**. Because the Moon is still getting bigger, it is a waxing gibbous Moon.

Day 9: Waxing gibbous Moon

On day 11, the Moon is almost round. It is still a waxing gibbous Moon. Observers on Earth can see most of the sunlit half of the Moon. They can see only a small sliver of the dark side of the Moon. Can you see the dark crescent?

Day 11: Waxing gibbous Moon

On day 14, you can see the whole sunlit side of the Moon. This is the full-Moon phase. A full Moon always rises at the same time the Sun sets.

Day 14: Full Moon

Day 18: Waning gibbous Moon

Each day after the full Moon, the bright part of the Moon gets smaller. Getting smaller is called **waning**. On day 18, the Moon looks oval again. Because it is still between full-Moon phase and quarter phase, it is still a gibbous Moon, a waning gibbous Moon.

Day 21: Third-quarter Moon

On day 21, the Moon has completed three-quarters of its orbit around Earth. The Moon appears as the third quarter, again half bright and half dark. But notice that the bright side of the third-quarter phase is on the left. Compare the appearance of the third-quarter Moon and the first-quarter Moon.

Day 24: Waning crescent Moon

As the Moon starts the last 7 days of its orbit, it returns to crescent phase. But because it is getting smaller each day, it is the waning crescent phase. By day 24, an observer on Earth sees just a small part of the sunlit side of the Moon. A lot of the dark side is visible again.

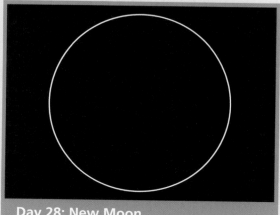

Day 28: New Moon

On about day 28, the Moon has completed one lunar cycle. It is back at its starting point. It is at the new-Moon phase again. The night sky is moonless. The day sky has no Moon. For a couple of days, observers on Earth can't see the Moon.

Then, in the evening sky, just after sunset, the Moon reappears. It is a thin, silver-colored crescent. And if you are in the right place at the right time, you could see something special. It is a bright crescent on the edge of a dim full Moon. It is called the old Moon in the new Moon's arms.

How can you see a bright crescent Moon and a pale full Moon at the same time? When the Moon appears as a thin crescent, it is almost between Earth and the Sun. A lot of light reflects from Earth onto the Moon. The whole Moon is dimly lit by earthshine.

The old Moon in the new Moon's arms

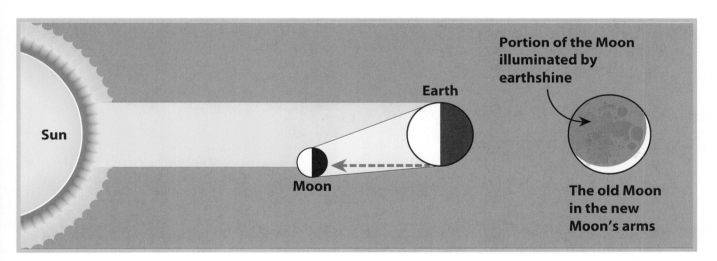

Thinking about the Phases of the Moon

1. How long does it take the Moon to complete one lunar cycle?

2. What is a new Moon, and what causes it?

3. What is the difference between a waxing Moon and a waning Moon?

4. What is the difference between a crescent Moon and a gibbous Moon?

5. Describe the Moon's appearance 1 week, 2 weeks, 3 weeks, and 4 weeks after the new Moon.

Lunar Cycle Diagram

The position of the Moon in its lunar cycle determines the Moon's phase.

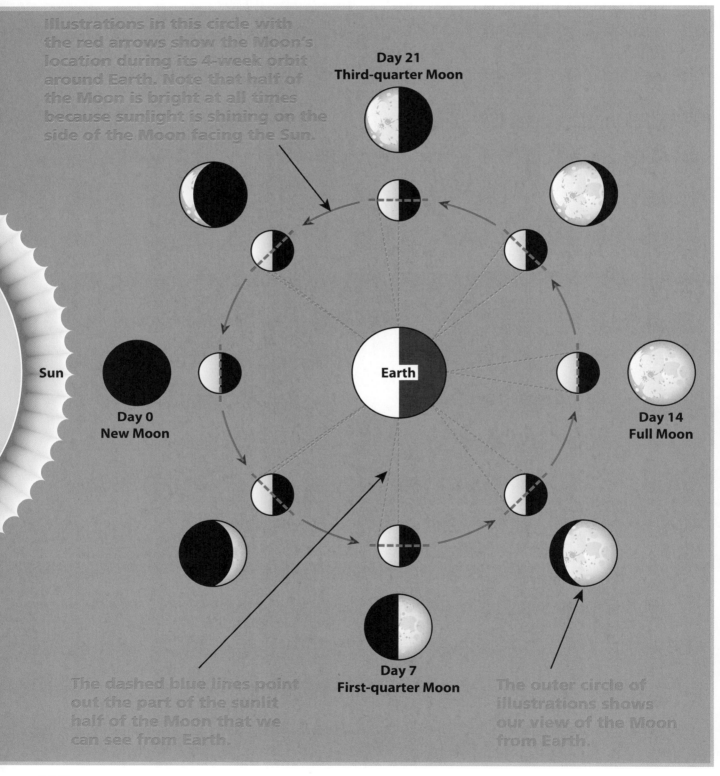

Illustrations in this circle with the red arrows show the Moon's location during its 4-week orbit around Earth. Note that half of the Moon is bright at all times because sunlight is shining on the side of the Moon facing the Sun.

Day 21
Third-quarter Moon

Sun

Day 0
New Moon

Earth

Day 14
Full Moon

Day 7
First-quarter Moon

The dashed blue lines point out the part of the sunlit half of the Moon that we can see from Earth.

The outer circle of illustrations shows our view of the Moon from Earth.

A total
solar
eclipse

A total
lunar
eclipse

Eclipses

Occasionally, people on Earth are able to observe a lovely orange-colored eclipse of the Moon (a **lunar eclipse**). Less frequently, they can observe a black-centered eclipse of the Sun (a **solar eclipse**). What causes these interesting events? When can you see a lunar eclipse? When can you see a solar eclipse?

What Is a Solar Eclipse?

A solar eclipse occurs when the Moon passes exactly between Earth and the Sun. The Moon completely hides the disk of the Sun when this happens. This diagram shows the alignment of Earth, the Moon, and the Sun during a solar eclipse.

A total solar eclipse

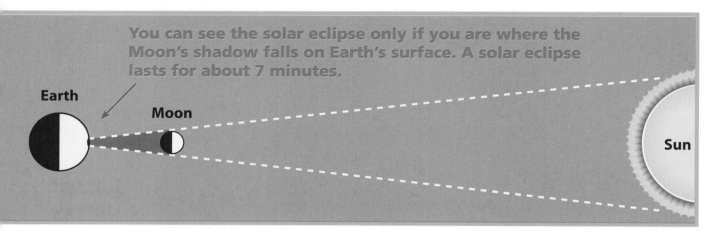

You can see the solar eclipse only if you are where the Moon's shadow falls on Earth's surface. A solar eclipse lasts for about 7 minutes.

Earth

Moon

Sun

You can see a solar eclipse only on a very small area of Earth's surface. A total eclipse of the Sun is visible for a bit more than 7 minutes, as long as it takes for the disk of the Moon to pass across the disk of the Sun.

The Moon travels around Earth once every month. Why doesn't a solar eclipse occur every month? The Moon's orbit around Earth is not in the same plane as the orbit of Earth going around the Sun. The Moon's orbit is tilted a little bit. Most months, Earth, the Moon, and the Sun are not in a straight line.

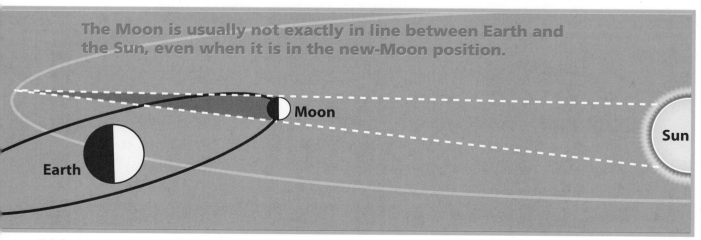

The Moon is usually not exactly in line between Earth and the Sun, even when it is in the new-Moon position.

Moon

Sun

Earth

What Is a Lunar Eclipse?

A lunar eclipse occurs when Earth passes exactly between the Moon and the Sun. Earth's shadow completely covers the disk of the Moon when this happens. This diagram shows the alignment of Earth, the Moon, and the Sun during a lunar eclipse.

A lunar eclipse

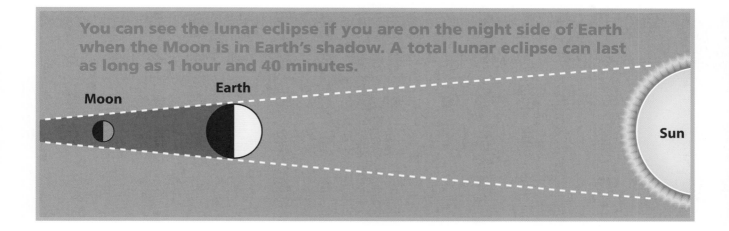

You can see the lunar eclipse if you are on the night side of Earth when the Moon is in Earth's shadow. A total lunar eclipse can last as long as 1 hour and 40 minutes.

Moon   Earth   Sun

You can see a lunar eclipse from anywhere on Earth where it is night. A total lunar eclipse lasts almost 2 hours and its beautiful red color is safe to view without eye protection.

Why don't we see a lunar eclipse every month? Again, it's because of the tilt of the Moon's orbit around Earth. The Moon's orbit around Earth is not in the same plane as the orbit of Earth going around the Sun. In most months, Earth's shadow does not fall on the Moon.

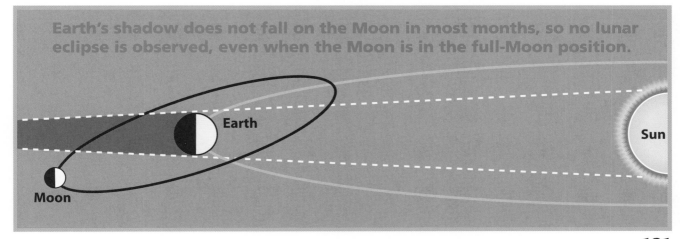

Earth's shadow does not fall on the Moon in most months, so no lunar eclipse is observed, even when the Moon is in the full-Moon position.

Earth   Sun

Moon

Look at the sequence of photos showing a total lunar eclipse. The Moon moves across Earth's shadow. The diagram below the photos explains what's happening. Note the reddish-brown color of the last photo.

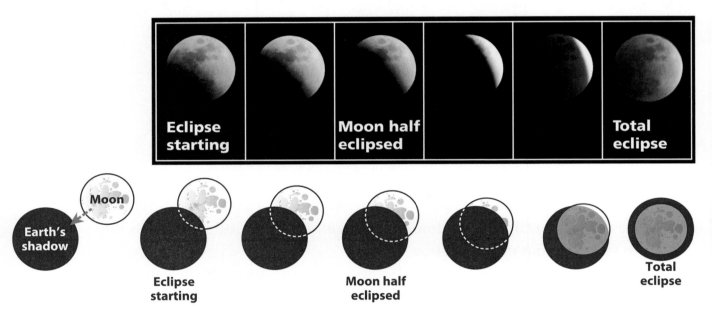

Why is the totally eclipsed Moon reddish-brown? Why is it visible at all? When light passes through Earth's atmosphere, it is bent and scattered by the air. As a result, some reddish light falls on the Moon's surface. This makes the Moon appear reddish-brown. If this bending and scattering did not occur, a totally eclipsed Moon would be invisible because no light would hit the Moon. If no light hit the Moon, no light would be reflected back into our eyes on Earth.

Thinking about Eclipses

1. During what phase of the Moon can you observe a lunar eclipse?

2. During what phase of the Moon can you observe a solar eclipse?

Sizes and distances of solar-system objects are not drawn to scale.

Exploring the Solar System

Imagine you are coming to the solar system as a stranger on a tour. There is a tour guide to provide information. You have a window to look out. The tour is about to start. What will you see?

The first view of the solar system is from space. From here, you can see the whole solar system. The most surprising thing is that the solar system is mostly empty. The matter is concentrated in tiny dots. And the dots are far apart. Most of the dots are planets.

There is a star in the center of the solar system. Four small planets orbit pretty close to the star. These are the rocky **terrestrial planets**.

Next, there is a region of small bits of matter orbiting the star. This is the **asteroid** belt.

Out farther, four large planets orbit the star. These are the **gas giant planets** made of gas.

Beyond the gas giant planets is a huge region of icy chunks of matter called the **Kuiper Belt**. Some of the chunks are big enough to be planets. A dwarf planet, Pluto, is one of the Kuiper Belt objects. Others, called comets, have orbits that send them flying through the rest of the solar system.

The Sun

The Sun is a fairly average star. It is much like millions of other stars in the **Milky Way**. The Sun formed about 5 billion years ago. A cloud of gas began to spin. As it spun, it formed a sphere. The sphere got smaller and smaller. As it got smaller, it got hotter. Eventually, the sphere got so hot that it started to radiate light and heat. A star was born.

The Sun is made mostly of hydrogen (72 percent) and helium (26 percent). It is huge. The diameter is about 1,384,000 kilometers (km). The diameter is the distance from one side of the Sun to the other through the center. That's about 109 times the diameter of Earth.

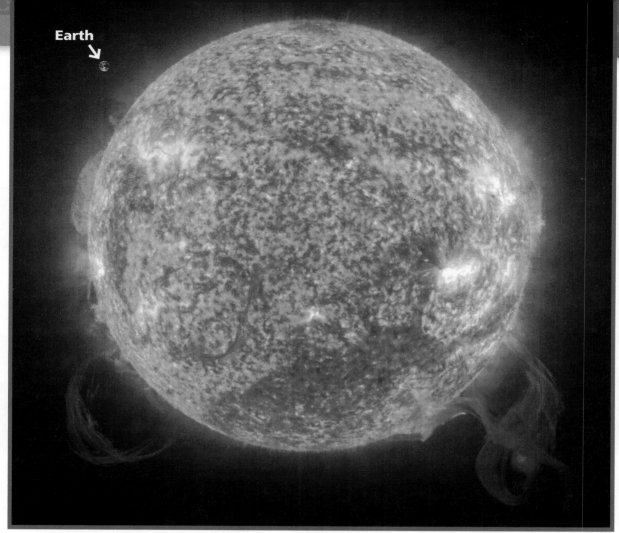
Earth

The Sun's diameter is about 109 times the diameter of Earth.

The Sun is incredibly hot. Scientists have figured out that the temperature at the center of the Sun is 15,000,000 degrees Celsius (°C). The temperature of the Sun's surface is lower, about 5,500°C. Hydrogen is constantly changing into helium in **thermonuclear reactions**. These reactions create heat and light. About 3.6 tons of the Sun's **mass** is being changed into heat and light every second. This energy radiates out from the Sun in all directions. A small amount of it falls on Earth.

Another name for the Sun is Sol. That's why the whole system of planets is called the solar system. The solar system is named for the ruling star. The Sun rules because of its size. It has 99.8 percent of the total mass of the solar system. All the other solar-system objects travel around the Sun in predictable, almost-circular orbits. The most obvious objects orbiting the Sun are the planets.

Terrestrial Planets

The terrestrial planets are the four planets closest to the Sun. They are small and rocky.

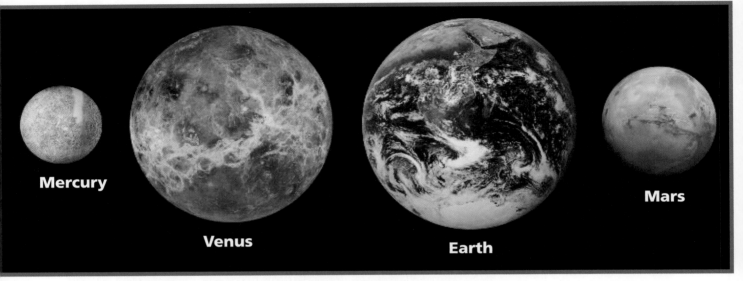

Relative sizes of the terrestrial planets

Mercury

Mercury is the planet closest to the Sun. Mercury is smaller than Earth and has no satellite (moon). By human standards, it is an uninviting place. Mercury is very hot on the side facing the Sun and very cold on the dark side. It has no atmosphere or water.

Mercury is covered with craters. The craters are the result of thousands of collisions with objects flying through space. The surface of Mercury looks a lot like Earth's Moon.

Mercury is the planet closest to the Sun.

Venus

Venus is the second planet from the Sun. Venus is about the same size as Earth and has no satellites. The surface of Venus is very hot all the time. It is hot enough to melt lead, making it one of the hottest places in the solar system.

There is no **liquid** water on Venus. But Venus does have an atmosphere of carbon dioxide. The dense, cloudy atmosphere makes it impossible to see the planet's surface. Modern radar, however, allows scientists to take pictures through the clouds. We now know that the surface of Venus is dry, cracked, and covered with volcanoes.

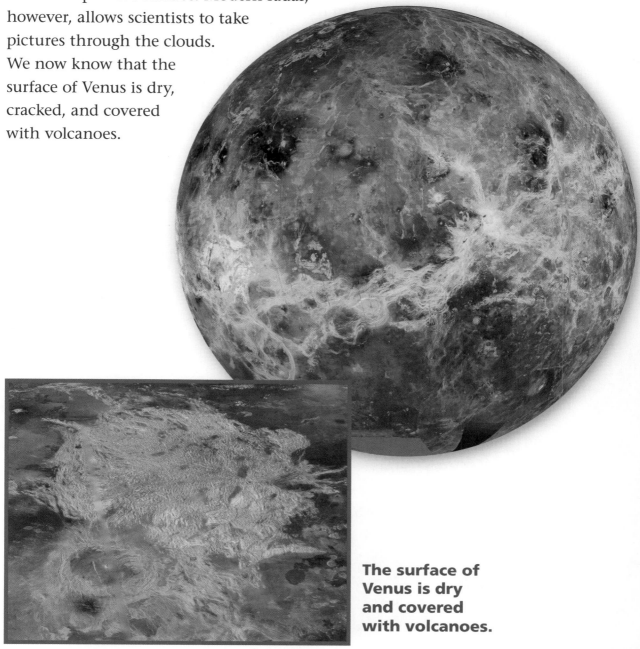

The surface of Venus is dry and covered with volcanoes.

Earth

Earth is the third planet from the Sun. Earth has a moderate, or mild, temperature all the time. It has an atmosphere of nitrogen and oxygen, and it has liquid water. As far as we know, Earth is the only place in the universe that has life. Earth also has one large satellite called the Moon. The Moon orbits Earth once a month. The Moon is responsible for the tides in Earth's ocean. The Moon is the only extraterrestrial place humans have visited.

Earth is 150 million km from the Sun. This is a huge distance. It's hard to imagine that distance, but think about this. Sit in one end zone of a football field and curl up into a ball. You are the Sun. A friend goes to the other end zone and holds up the eraser from a pencil. That's Earth. Get the idea? Earth is tiny, and it is a long distance from the Sun. Still, the light and heat that reach Earth provide the right amount of energy for life as we know it.

The Moon orbits Earth once a month.

Water frost on the surface of Mars

A robotic lander exploring Mars

Mars

Mars is the fourth planet from the Sun. It has two small satellites, Phobos and Deimos. Mars is a little like Earth, except it is smaller, colder, and drier. There are some places on Mars that are like Death Valley in California. Other places on Mars are more like Antarctica, and others are like the volcanoes of Hawaii.

Mars is sometimes called the red planet because of its red soil. The soil contains iron oxide, or rust. The iron oxide in the soil tells scientists that Mars probably had liquid water at one time. But liquid water has not been on Mars for 3.5 billion years. It has frozen water in polar ice caps that grow and shrink with its seasons.

Mars is likely the next place humans will visit. But exploring Mars will not be easy. Humans can't breathe the thin atmosphere of carbon dioxide. And explorers will need to wear life-support space suits for protection against the cold.

Several robotic landers, including *Viking*, *Spirit*, *Opportunity*, *Sojourner*, and *Curiosity* have observed Mars and sent back information about the surface and presence of water. Evidence suggests that there is a lot of frozen water just under the surface.

Asteroids

Beyond the orbit of Mars are millions of chunks of rock and iron called asteroids. They all orbit the Sun in a region called the asteroid belt. The asteroid belt surrounds the terrestrial planets. The planets farther out are quite different from the terrestrial planets.

Some asteroids even have moons. When the spacecraft *Galileo* flew past asteroid Ida in 1993, scientists were surprised to discover it had a moon. They named it Dactyl. The largest object in the asteroid belt is Ceres, a dwarf planet. It is about 960 km around.

Asteroid Ida with moon Dactyl

Gas Giant Planets

The four planets farthest from the Sun are the gas giant planets. They do not have rocky surfaces like the terrestrial planets. So there is no place to land or walk around on them. They are much bigger than the terrestrial planets. What we have learned about the gas giant planets has come from probes launched on rockets to fly by and orbit around the giants. Even though they are made of gases, each gas giant planet is different.

Neptune

Uranus

Saturn

Jupiter

Relative sizes of the gas giant planets

Jupiter and its four largest moons

Jupiter

Jupiter is the fifth planet from the Sun. It is the largest planet in the solar system. It is 11 times larger in diameter than Earth. Scientists have found 67 moons orbiting Jupiter. The four largest moons are Ganymede, Callisto, Io, and Europa.

Jupiter's atmosphere is cold and poisonous to life. It is mostly hydrogen and helium. Jupiter's stripes and swirls are cold, windy clouds of ammonia and water. Its Great Red Spot is a giant storm as wide as three Earths. This storm has been raging for hundreds of years. On Jupiter, the atmospheric pressure is so strong that it squishes gas into liquid. Jupiter's atmosphere could crush a metal spaceship like a paper cup.

An artist's drawing of Jupiter, its moon Io, and the *Galileo* spacecraft

Saturn

Saturn is the sixth planet from the Sun. It is the second largest planet and is very cold. At least 60 satellites orbit Saturn. Most of the planet is made of hydrogen, helium, and methane. It doesn't have a solid surface.

It has clouds and storms like Jupiter, but they are harder to see because they move so fast. Winds in Saturn's upper atmosphere reach 1,825 km per hour.

The most dramatic feature of Saturn is its ring system. The largest ring reaches out 200,000 km from Saturn's surface. The rings are made of billions of small chunks of ice and rock. All the gas giant planets have rings, but they are not as spectacular as Saturn's.

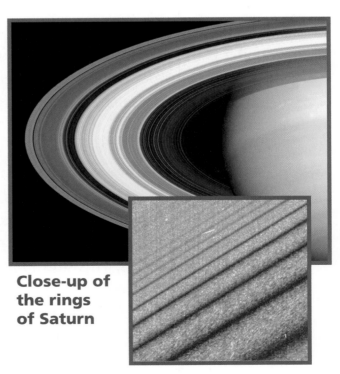

Close-up of the rings of Saturn

Uranus

Uranus is the seventh planet from the Sun. Uranus has 27 moons and 11 rings. Uranus is very cold and windy, and would be poisonous to humans. It is smaller and colder than Saturn.

Uranus has clouds that are extremely cold at the top. Below the cloud tops, there is a layer of extremely hot water, ammonia, and methane. Near its core, Uranus heats up to 4,982°C. Uranus looks blue because of the methane gas in its atmosphere.

Neptune (far right) and its largest moon, Triton

Neptune

Neptune is the eighth planet from the Sun. Neptune has 13 moons and 4 thin rings. It is the smallest of the gas giant planets, but is still much larger than the terrestrial planets.

Neptune is made mostly of hydrogen and helium with some methane. It may be the windiest planet in the solar system. Winds rip through the clouds at more than 2,000 km per hour. Scientists think there might be an ocean of super-hot water under Neptune's cold clouds. It does not boil away because of the atmospheric pressure.

Pluto and Charon, one of its moons

Kuiper Belt

Out beyond the gas giant planets is a disk-shaped zone of icy objects called the Kuiper Belt. Some of the objects are fairly large.

Pluto

Pluto is a large Kuiper Belt object. Some scientists considered Pluto a planet because it is massive enough to form a sphere. Others did not consider Pluto a planet. To them, Pluto is one of the large pieces of debris in the Kuiper Belt. Scientists have agreed to call Pluto a dwarf planet.

Pluto has a thin atmosphere. When Pluto is farthest from the Sun, the atmosphere gets so cold that it freezes and falls to the surface. Even though Pluto is smaller than Earth's Moon, it has its own moons. Charon is the largest (about half the size of Pluto). Nix and Hydra are much smaller, and in 2011-12, two even smaller moons named Kerberos and Styx were discovered. And there may be more!

Eris

In July 2005, astronomers at the California Institute of Technology announced the discovery of a new planet-like object. It is called Eris. Like Pluto, Eris is a Kuiper Belt object and a dwarf planet. But Eris is more than twice as far away from the Sun as Pluto is. This picture is an artist's idea of what the Sun would look like from a position close to Eris.

The Sun would look like a bright star from Eris.

Comets

Comets are big chunks of ice, rock, and gas. Sometimes comets are compared to dirty snowballs. Scientists think comets might have valuable information about the origins of the solar system.

Comets orbit the Sun in long, oval paths. Most of them travel way beyond the orbit of Pluto. A comet's trip around the Sun can take hundreds or even millions of years, depending on its orbit. A comet's tail shows up as it nears the Sun and begins to warm. The gases and dust that form the comet's tail always point away from the Sun.

A comet's tail always points away from the Sun.

Comet orbits can cross planet orbits. In July 1994, a large comet, named Comet Shoemaker-Levy 9, was on a collision course with Jupiter. As it got close to Jupiter, the comet broke into 21 pieces. The pieces slammed into Jupiter for a week. Each impact created a crater larger than Earth.

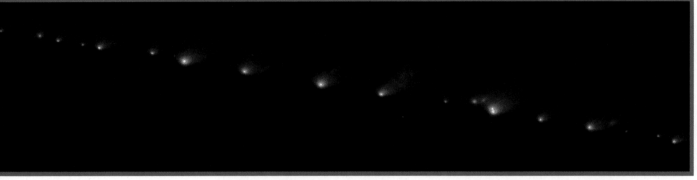

Comet Shoemaker-Levy 9 broke into 21 pieces as it got close to Jupiter.

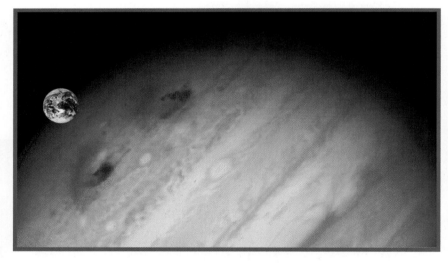

Two of the comet's craters on Jupiter. The picture of Earth gives an idea of how big the craters are.

Thinking about the Solar System

1. What is the Sun, and what is it made of?

2. What is the solar system?

3. Which planets are terrestrial planets? Which planets are gas giant planets?

4. What is the Kuiper Belt, and what is found there?

5. Which planet has the most moons orbiting it?

6. How are asteroids and comets alike and different?

Planets of the Solar System

Mercury

Venus

Earth

Pluto (dwarf planet)

Mars

Relative sizes of planets

Sun

Jupiter

Saturn

Neptune

Uranus

Why Doesn't Earth Fly Off into Space?

Earth travels around the Sun in a predictable, almost-circular path once every year. That's a distance of about 942 million kilometers (km) each year. That's an incredible 2.6 million km each day! Earth travels at a speed over 100,000 km per hour. That's fast.

One important thing to know about objects in motion is that they travel only in straight lines. Objects don't change direction or follow curved paths unless a **force** pushes or pulls them in a new direction. If nothing pushed or pulled on Earth, it would fly off into space in a straight line.

But Earth doesn't fly off into space in a straight line. Earth travels in an almost-circular path around the Sun. In order to travel a circular path, Earth has to change direction all the time. Something has to push or pull Earth to change its direction. What is pushing or pulling Earth? The answer is gravity.

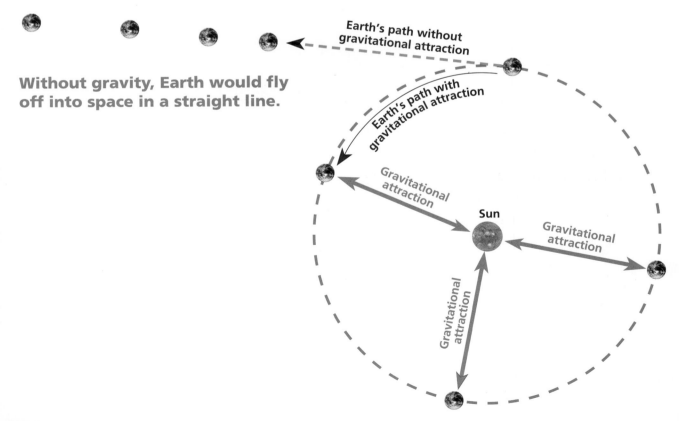

Earth's path without gravitational attraction

Earth's path with gravitational attraction

Without gravity, Earth would fly off into space in a straight line.

Gravitational attraction

Sun

Gravitational attraction

Gravitational attraction

Gravity

Think about a ball resting motionless on a table. A gentle push on the ball will put it into motion. The ball will roll across the table. What will happen when the ball comes to the edge of the table? The ball will roll off the edge and fall to the ground. The ball's motion changes when it rolls off the edge of the table. It moves in a different direction and starts to move faster.

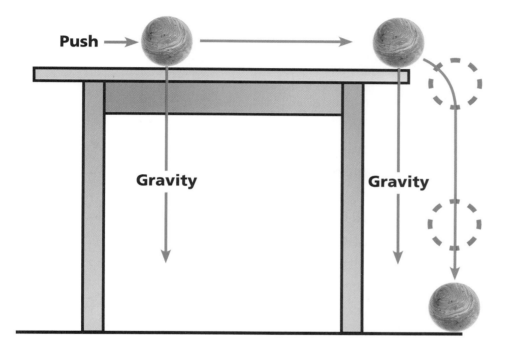

Push

Gravity   **Gravity**

Gravity makes a ball fall to the ground.

What causes this change of motion? That's right, force. What force makes the ball move toward the ground? The force that makes the ball fall to the ground is gravity. Gravity is a pulling force between two objects, and it draws them toward each other. The bigger the objects, the stronger the gravitational force between them. Earth is a huge object, so it pulls strongly on all other objects. It is the force of gravity that pulls objects to Earth's center.

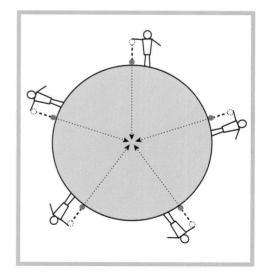

Wherever an object, such as a dropped ball, falls on Earth, it falls toward the center of Earth.

If you return the ball to the flat tabletop, it will again rest there motionless. Why doesn't the ball fall to the ground? The ball doesn't move because the forces acting on it are balanced. There are two forces. First, the table is pushing upward on the ball. Second, gravity is pulling the ball downward toward Earth's center. When two equal forces act on an object in opposite directions, the forces are balanced. When the forces acting on an object are balanced, the object's motion does not change.

But what happens if you tip the table? The ball starts to roll down the table. For the ball to start moving, a force must act on the ball. Tipping the table unbalances the forces. The forces are no longer opposite and equal. Gravity pulls the ball downhill toward Earth's center. The round ball rolls across the table, over the edge, and down to the ground. When you're on a slide, can you feel the moment when the forces become unbalanced and gravity pulls you down?

The force of gravity pulls the ball to the ground.

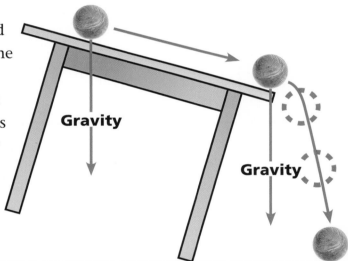

150

Gravity is the force of attraction between objects, or masses. The Sun is an object. Earth is an object. The force of attraction between the Sun and Earth pulls hard enough to change Earth's direction of travel.

Remember the string-and-ball demonstration? The hand pulled on the string. The string pulled on the ball. The ball traveled in a circular orbit. Gravity is like the string. The force of **gravitational attraction** between the Sun and Earth pulls on Earth, changing its direction of travel. The pull of gravity doesn't change Earth's speed, just its direction. That's why Earth travels in an almost-circular orbit around the Sun.

The Sun's gravity keeps all the planets in their orbits. Otherwise, each planet would fly off in a straight line right out of the solar system.

Earth travels around the Sun.

Thinking about Orbits

1. What happens to balls dropped on opposite sides of Earth?

2. Why do planets stay in orbit around the Sun?

3. How is a ball on a string like a planet in its orbit?

4. What keeps the Moon in its orbit around Earth?

Stargazing

Stars are twinkling points of light in the night sky. When you get into bed at night, the sky is filled with stars. But in the morning, they are gone. Where did they go?

The stars didn't go anywhere. They are exactly where they were when you went to sleep. But you can't see the stars in the day sky. This is because the light from our star, the Sun, is so bright.

Where Are the Stars?

Stars are huge balls of hot gas. Most stars are located in groups of stars called galaxies. The Sun is in the galaxy called the Milky Way. There are several hundred billion other stars in the Milky Way with us. If we could see the entire Milky Way from above, it might look something like the picture below. The Sun is out on one of the arms where the arrow is pointing.

The Sun is one of the billions of stars in the Milky Way.

As you can see, we are surrounded by stars. Think about the 2,000 or so stars you can see and the billions of stars you can't see in the Milky Way. All these stars, including the Sun, are moving slowly around in a huge circle. Because all the stars move together, the positions of the stars never change. You can see the same stars in the same places in the sky year after year.

Did you ever see the **Big Dipper**? It is seven bright stars in the shape of a dipper. The Big Dipper is part of a **constellation** called Ursa Major, or the Great Bear.

Most of the stars you see in the night sky are part of a constellation. A constellation is a group of stars in a pattern. Thousands of years ago, stargazers imagined they could see animals and people in the star groups. They gave names to these constellations. Some of the names are Orion the hunter, Scorpius the scorpion, Aquila the eagle, Leo the lion, and Gemini the twins. Those same constellations are still seen in the sky today. They are unchanged.

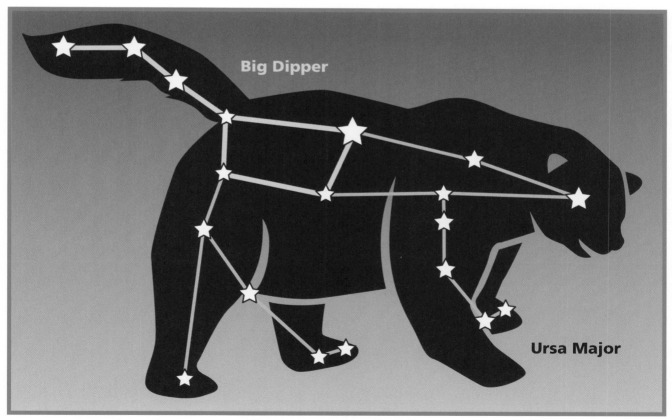

The constellation Ursa Major (the Great Bear)

Constellations in Motion

Even though the stars don't change position, they appear to move across the night sky. Stars move across the sky for the same reason that the Sun and the Moon move across the sky. The stars are not moving. Earth is moving. As Earth rotates on its **axis**, constellations rise in the east. They travel across the night sky and set in the west.

If you look at the stars every day for 1 year, you will see something interesting. The stars you see in winter are different from the stars you see in summer. If the stars don't move around, how is that possible? To answer this, we have to look at how Earth orbits the Sun.

Here is a simple drawing of the Milky Way. The Sun and Earth appear much larger than they really are. That's so we can study what happens as the seasons go by.

The side of Earth facing the Sun is always in daylight. The side facing away from the Sun is always in darkness. You can only see stars when you are on the dark half of Earth.

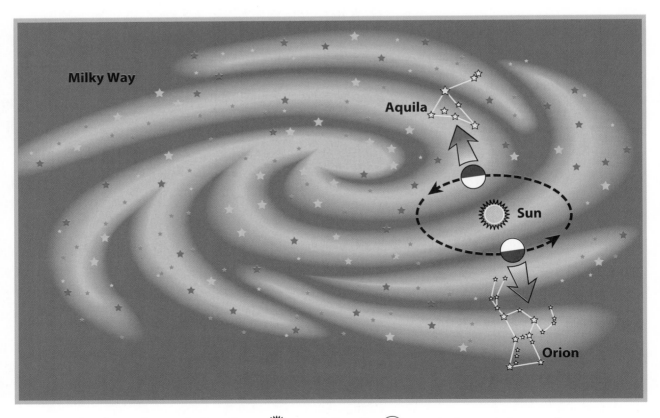

Milky Way

Aquila

Sun

Orion

A simple drawing of the Sun ☀ **and Earth** ◑**, not drawn to scale.**

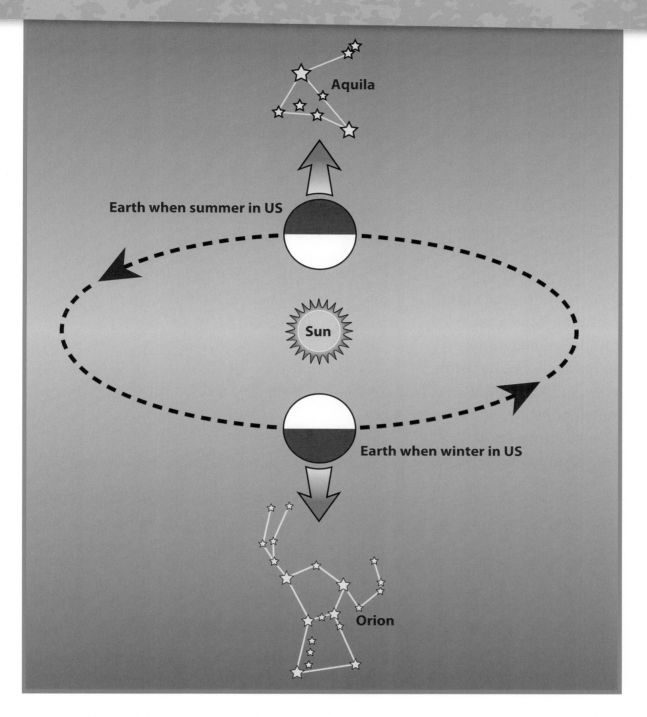

When it is summer in the United States, Earth is between the Sun and the center of the Milky Way. The constellation Aquila is in that direction. The dark side of Earth is toward the center of the galaxy in summer. On a summer night, you see Aquila high overhead.

Six months later, Earth is on the other side of the Sun. It is winter in the United States. Now the dark side of Earth faces away from the center of the galaxy. The constellation Orion is in that direction. On a winter night, you see Orion high overhead.

This is Orion. Can you see his belt and sword? The brightest stars in the Orion constellation appear in this picture. You can see Orion in the sky on a clear winter night.

When you see Orion, you are seeing the same pattern of stars that a hundred generations of stargazers looked at before you. And a hundred generations into the future, stargazers will still see Orion marching across the winter sky.

The constellation Orion is visible in the winter sky.

Thinking about the Stars

1. Why do stars appear to move across the night sky?

2. What is a constellation?

3. Why are the constellations in the summer sky different from those in the winter sky?

4. Imagine that you could see stars during the day. What constellation would you see at noon in winter? Why do you think so?

Star Scientists

Sometimes a childhood fascination with stars lasts a lifetime. Scientists who try to find out the secrets of stars are called astronomers. Meet five scientists who have taken star study in different directions. They truly are star scientists.

Stephen Hawking

When you drop a ball on Earth, the force of gravity pulls it down. Gravity keeps your feet on the ground, too. When a star reaches the end of its life, it collapses. Gravity pulls together all the matter in the star. In collapsed stars, gravity can even pull in light.

When a really big star collapses, it can become a **black hole**. In a black hole, gravity is so strong that nothing, not even light, can escape. Everything for millions of kilometers (km) around is pulled into the black hole, where it disappears.

Today, the best-known scientist who studied black holes is Stephen Hawking (1942–2018). Using mathematics, Hawking helped prove that black holes exist.

Since 1994, the Hubble Space Telescope has been used to search

Stephen Hawking

for evidence of black holes. Hubble images show stars and gases swirling toward a central point. Hawking says this could be the effect of a black hole. A black hole's strong gravity would pull in everything around it, including stars. Future images from the Hubble Space Telescope and its successor, the James Webb Space Telescope, might help scientists improve their understanding of black holes.

Edna DeVore

Many people wonder if there is life anyplace else in the universe. But Edna DeVore (1947–) does more than wonder. DeVore is the Deputy Chief Executive Officer (CEO) of the SETI Institute. SETI is short for Search for Extraterrestrial Intelligence.

Edna DeVore

The scientists at SETI think that there might be other intelligent beings in the universe. If they are out there, they live on a planet orbiting a star. And intelligent life could develop technologies that send signals into space. Radio, TV, navigation systems, and telephones on Earth send messages in all directions into space. Is someone else out there doing the same thing?

The SETI Institute watches the sky for any signs of life in the universe. It uses big sets of antennae to listen for any sounds of life, like radio signals.

DeVore is a scientist and educator at SETI. She grew up on a ranch in Sattley, California. DeVore remembers watching the stars and the Milky Way in the clear night sky as a child. She didn't think about becoming a star scientist, but in college, DeVore became more and more interested in the stars. After getting her degree in **astronomy**, she became a teacher and a **planetarium** director. But the question she always asked herself was "Are we alone in the universe?"

DeVore is in charge of education and public outreach for the SETI Institute and NASA's Kepler Mission. And what's the latest report from the universe? The scientists at SETI haven't heard or seen anything yet. But they keep watching and listening.

SETI uses radio telescopes like this one.

Neil deGrasse Tyson

You put water and fish in an aquarium. You put soil and plants in a terrarium. But what do you put in a planetarium? Planets! A planetarium is filled with information about planets, stars, galaxies, and everything else seen in the night sky.

A planetarium is a theater with a dome-shaped ceiling. In the middle of the room is a projector. The projector shines points of light all over the dome. The points of light are in the same positions as the stars in the sky. The projected stars make it seem as though you are outside watching the stars.

Neil deGrasse Tyson

One of the fun things about a planetarium is that you can control the night sky. Do you want to see the stars as they were the day you were born? Or how the sky looked at different times in Earth's history? The projector operator can put you under the stars at any time and any place.

When he was a child, Neil deGrasse Tyson (1958–) never dreamed that he would one day be in charge of a planetarium. Tyson took a class at the Hayden Planetarium in New York City when he was in middle school. He was awarded a certificate at the end of the class. It meant a lot to him.

Tyson's love of the stars grew as he got older. After getting a PhD in astrophysics, Tyson spent time doing research and promoting education. He researched how stars form and explained space science to the public. He works hard to make science interesting for everyone. In 1996, Tyson became the youngest person ever to direct the Hayden Planetarium. It is the same place he visited as a child.

The Hayden Planetarium

Mae Jemison

Mae Jemison (1956–) was born in Decatur, Alabama. She moved to Chicago, Illinois, as a child. There an uncle introduced her to astronomy. In high school, Jemison began reading books on astronomy and space travel. She was only 16 years old when she entered college. She earned degrees in chemical engineering and African and Afro-American studies from Stanford University. She went on to earn her medical degree from Cornell University.

Mae Jemison, astronaut

After becoming a doctor, Jemison spent time in western Africa as a Peace Corps physician. But she continued to think about astronomy and space travel. She wanted to be part of the space program.

Jemison joined the astronaut program in 1987. On September 12, 1992, Jemison became the first African American woman in space. She was a science mission specialist on the space shuttle *Endeavour*. Jemison conducted experiments to find out more about the effects of being in space. She studied motion sickness, calcium loss in bones, and weightlessness.

The crew of *Endeavour*

**The space shuttle _Endeavour_ docked at
the International Space Station**

Space shuttle mission STS-47 was the 50th space shuttle flight, but
only the second flight for _Endeavour_. The space shuttle was in space
for 8 days. During those 8 days, Jemison orbited Earth 127 times at an
altitude of 307 km. The space shuttle traveled 5,234,950 km.

In 2011, after 30 years of flying and many firsts, the space shuttle
program ended. Did the space shuttles actually fly in space? No, they
orbited Earth in the upper atmosphere. What kept the shuttles in orbit?
The answer is gravity. Shuttles traveled very fast. Earth's gravity pulled
on the shuttles, constantly changing their direction of travel. Engineers
from NASA figured out exactly how high above Earth's surface and how
fast the shuttles needed to travel. Since they knew the force of gravity,
the space shuttles were able to stay in orbit until the astronauts changed
the speed. Then gravity pulled them back to Earth.

Ramon E. Lopez

As strange as it may sound, there is **weather** in space. But it's not weather like we have on Earth. There are no clouds, **hurricanes**, or snowstorms in space. Space weather is the result of activities on the Sun. The Sun is always radiating energy into the solar system. The regular flow of light and gases is called **solar wind**. But what happens when the Sun goes through a period of violent solar flares? That's what Ramon E. Lopez (1959–) studies.

Ramon E. Lopez

Solar flares are huge solar explosions. They send intense blasts of electrified gas into Earth's atmosphere. The blasts can produce electric effects in the atmosphere and on Earth's surface. The electricity can disable satellites orbiting Earth and interfere with radio transmissions and cell phones. Space weather can cause blackouts over large areas.

Lopez and his team understand how space weather can damage communication and navigation systems. And they understand how important these systems are to modern society. Can Lopez and his team learn how to predict space weather? Will it be possible to warn the world when a dangerous solar storm is coming? Lopez and the team he works with are developing a computer program to predict space weather about 30 minutes before it hits Earth. And that may be just long enough to protect communication and navigation systems from damage.

The Sun with a large solar flare

Our Galaxy

Stars are huge balls of hot gas. They produce bright light that travels out into space. When we go outdoors on a clear night, we see the stars as tiny points of light. There are billions of them sending light our way. But because most of them are so far away, the light is too dim for us to see. We can enjoy the 2,000 or so stars that we can see with our unaided eyes.

Astronomers study stars and other objects in the sky. One of the most important tools they use is the telescope. Telescopes **magnify** objects in the sky. When an astronomer looks at an object through a telescope, the object looks bigger and closer. With a telescope, you can see many more stars. Objects in the night sky can be studied in greater detail with a telescope.

The great Italian scientist Galileo Galilei used a telescope to observe the Moon and planets. He saw things no one had seen before. He observed mountains and craters on the Moon and discovered moons orbiting the planet Jupiter. Galileo's telescope brought the science of astronomy to a new level.

Galileo's record of the movement of Jupiter's moons

Galileo's painting of the phases of the Moon

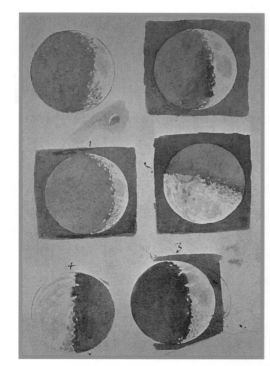

Moving Objects in the Sky

The Sun, the Moon, and the stars all move in the sky. But they all move in a different way. The Sun rises in the east in the morning and sets in the west at night. We see the Sun only during the day, never at night. Every day the Sun has the same pattern.

The Moon rises in the east and sets in the west, just like the Sun. But it doesn't always rise and set at the same time. Sometimes it rises in the morning, and sometimes it rises in the afternoon. There is a chance you might see the Moon in the daytime, but it might appear at night, depending on the lunar cycle.

The Moon and the Sun rise in the east and set in the west because Earth rotates on its axis. To people on Earth, the Sun and the Moon appear to move across the sky. The Moon rises and sets at different times because the Moon is orbiting Earth. The Moon is changing its position all the time.

Stars are different. We see them only at night. They are up in the sky all the time. But we can't see them during the day because the Sun is too bright. As soon as the Sun sets, the sky gets dark. Then we can see the stars. Stars rise and set, too. If you watch one star, you can see it rise above the eastern horizon. It then appears to move across the night sky, and set in the west. Why? Because Earth is rotating.

Earth's Orbit

One more thing is different about stars. Earth is completely surrounded by stars in all directions. But you can't see all of them at once. This is because half of them are on the day side of Earth. Also, the stars you can see in winter are different from the ones you can see in summer.

Here's why. Earth orbits the Sun. One complete orbit takes a year. At all times, half of Earth is in daylight and half is in darkness. It is always the side of Earth toward the Sun that is in daylight. The day side of Earth is always "looking" toward the Sun.

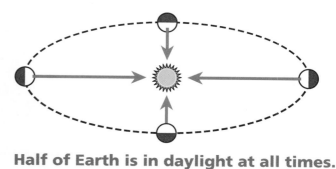

Half of Earth is in daylight at all times.

The side of Earth away from the Sun is always in darkness. The dark side of Earth is always "looking" away from the Sun. We can only see stars at night when it is dark. So stargazers always look in the direction away from the Sun.

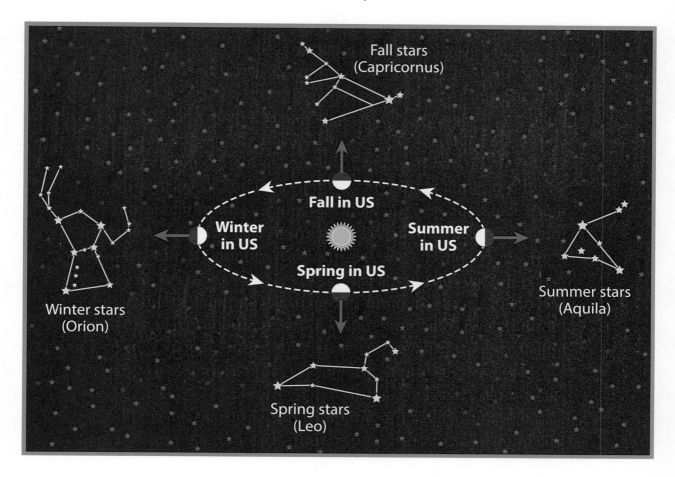

Fall stars
(Capricornus)

Fall in US

Winter
in US

Summer
in US

Spring in US

Winter stars
(Orion)

Summer stars
(Aquila)

Spring stars
(Leo)

As Earth orbits the Sun, the dark side of Earth is aimed at different parts of the star-filled sky. Because stars don't move, the stars and constellations you see change from season to season.

In the United States, look for Aquila the eagle in summer. Look for Capricornus the goat in the fall, Orion the hunter in winter, and Leo the lion in spring.

Leo the lion

Clouds float in air.

What Is Air?

You can't see it or taste it. You can't even smell it. But you might feel it as a gentle breeze brushing across your skin. Air is difficult to understand because it is not easy to observe with your senses. Is air one thing or a mixture of things? And where is air? Is it everywhere or just in some places?

As we go about our everyday lives, we usually travel with our feet on solid Earth and our heads in the atmosphere. The atmosphere is all around us, pressing firmly on every part of our bodies—top, front, back, and sides. Even if we attempt to get out of the atmosphere by going inside a car or hiding in a basement, the atmosphere is there, filling every space we enter.

An atmosphere is the layer of gases surrounding a planet or star. All planets and stars have an atmosphere around them. The Sun's atmosphere is mostly hydrogen. Mars has a thin atmosphere of carbon dioxide (CO_2) with a bit of nitrogen and a trace of **water vapor**. Mercury has almost no atmosphere at all. Each planet is surrounded by its own mixture of gases.

167

A view from space, looking down through Earth's atmosphere

Earth's atmosphere is made up of a mixture of gases we call air. Air is mostly nitrogen (78 percent) and oxygen (21 percent), with some argon (0.93 percent), carbon dioxide (0.039 percent), **ozone**, water vapor, and other gases (less than 0.04 percent together).

Nitrogen is the most abundant gas in our atmosphere. It is a stable gas, which means it doesn't react easily with other substances. When we breathe air, the nitrogen goes into our lungs and then back out unchanged. We don't need nitrogen gas to survive.

Oxygen is the second most abundant gas. It makes up about 21 percent of air's volume, and it accounts for 23 percent of air's mass. Oxygen is a colorless, odorless, and tasteless gas. Oxygen combines with hydrogen to form water. Without oxygen, life as we know it would not exist on Earth.

Oxygen and nitrogen are called permanent gases. The amount of oxygen and nitrogen in the atmosphere stays constant. The other gases in the table are also permanent gases, but are found in much smaller quantities in the atmosphere.

Permanent Gases of the Atmosphere	
Gas	Percentage by volume
Nitrogen	78.08%
Oxygen	20.95%
Argon	0.93%
Neon	0.002%
Helium	0.0005%
Krypton	0.0001%
Hydrogen	0.00005%
Xenon	0.000009%

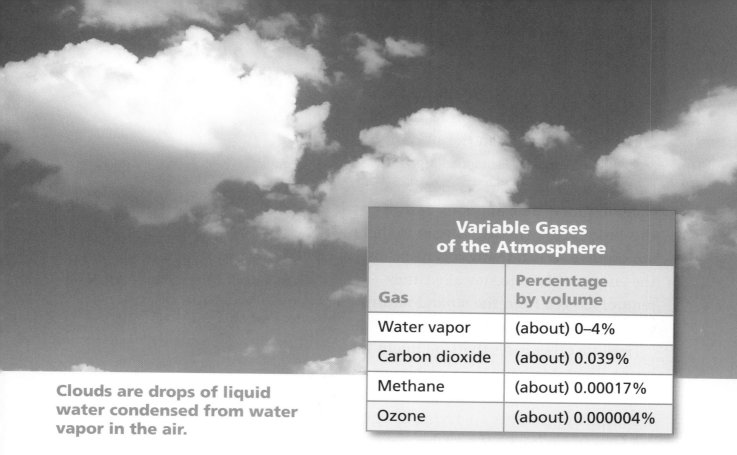

Variable Gases of the Atmosphere	
Gas	Percentage by volume
Water vapor	(about) 0–4%
Carbon dioxide	(about) 0.039%
Methane	(about) 0.00017%
Ozone	(about) 0.000004%

Clouds are drops of liquid water condensed from water vapor in the air.

Air also contains variable gases. The amount of each variable gas changes in response to activities in the environment.

Water vapor is the most abundant variable gas. It makes up about 0.25 percent of the atmosphere's mass. The amount of water vapor in the atmosphere changes constantly. Water moves between Earth's surface and the atmosphere through **evaporation**, **condensation**, and **precipitation**. You can get an idea of the changes in atmospheric water vapor by observing clouds and noting the stickiness you feel on your skin on humid days.

Carbon dioxide is another important variable gas. It makes up only about 0.039 percent of the atmosphere. You can't see or feel changes in the amount of carbon dioxide in the atmosphere.

Precipitation, such as rain and snow, comes from water vapor in the air.

169

Carbon dioxide plays an important role in the lives of plants and algae. Carbon dioxide is removed from the air during **photosynthesis**. Plants and algae use light from the Sun, carbon dioxide, and water to produce sugar (food). During this process, they release oxygen to the atmosphere. When living organisms use the energy of food to stay alive, they remove oxygen from the air and return carbon dioxide to the air.

Here are other gases that you might have heard about. Methane is a variable gas that is increasing in concentration in the atmosphere. Scientists are trying to figure out why this is happening. They suspect several things. Cattle produce methane in their digestive processes. Methane also comes from coal mines, oil wells, and gas pipelines. It is a by-product of rice cultivation and melting permafrost in arctic regions. Methane **absorbs** energy and transfers heat to the atmosphere.

Ozone is a variable gas. It is a form of oxygen that forms a thin layer high in the atmosphere. The ozone layer protects life on Earth by absorbing dangerous ultraviolet (UV) light from the Sun. But ozone in high concentrations can cause lung damage. In the lower atmosphere, ozone is an air pollutant.

Plants make sugar out of sunlight, carbon dioxide, and water.

Some methane gas comes from the digestive processes of cows.

Thinking about Air

What is air?

Earth's Atmosphere

Earth's atmosphere is made up of a mixture of permanent and variable gases. These gases are all mixed together. Any sample of air is a mixture of all of them. The gases mix because the air particles are always moving near Earth's surface. Above about 90 kilometers (km), the gases mix less, and there are more light gases, such as hydrogen and helium.

There are extreme temperatures in the universe. The temperature can be as cold as −270 degrees Celsius (°C). Near hot stars, such as the Sun, it can be very hot, up to thousands of degrees. But there are a few places in the universe that have a temperature between those extremes of hot and cold. Earth is one of those places where the temperature is just right.

On a typical day, the temperature range on Earth is only about 100°C. It might be 45°C in the hottest place on Earth and −55°C at one of the poles. The measured extremes are 57°C in Death Valley, California, recorded on July 10, 1913, and −89°C in Vostok, Antarctica, on July 21, 1983. That's a range of temperature on Earth of 147°C.

Space-shuttle astronauts took this photo while orbiting Earth. You can see a side view of Earth's atmosphere. The black bumps pushing into the troposphere are tall cumulus clouds.

The crew of Apollo 17 took this photo of Earth in December 1972, while on their way to the Moon. The small green box at the top of Earth's image shows about how much area is in the atmosphere photo.

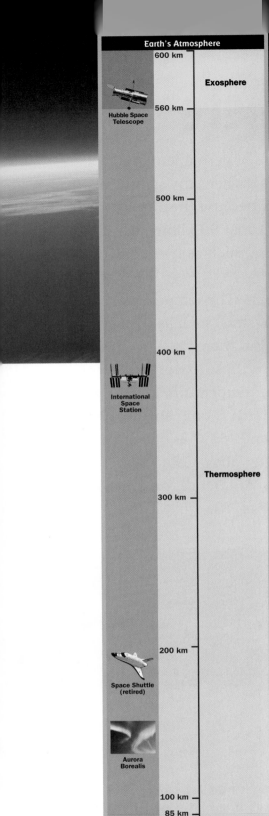

Earth's Atmosphere

600 km	
	Exosphere
560 km	
Hubble Space Telescope	
500 km	
400 km	
International Space Station	
	Thermosphere
300 km	
200 km	
Space Shuttle (retired)	
Aurora Borealis	
100 km	
85 km	
Meteor	Mesosphere
50 km	
Ozone Layer	Stratosphere
15 km	
Weather	Troposphere
0 km	

Earth's atmosphere looks like a thin, blue veil.

It's not only because we are at the right distance from the Sun that Earth's temperatures are moderate. Earth's atmosphere keeps the temperature within a narrow range so that it is just right for life on Earth.

From space, Earth's atmosphere looks like a thin, blue veil. Some people like to think of the atmosphere as an ocean of air covering Earth. The depth of this "ocean" is about 600 km. The atmosphere is most dense right at the bottom, where it rests on Earth's surface. It gets thinner and thinner (less dense) as you move away from Earth's surface. There is no real boundary between the atmosphere and space. The air just gets thinner and thinner until it disappears.

Imagine a column of air that starts on Earth's surface and extends up 600 km to the top of the atmosphere. Scientists have discovered several layers in this column of air. Each layer has a different temperature. Here's how it stacks up.

The four seasons occur in the troposphere.

The layer we live in is the **troposphere**. It starts at Earth's surface and extends upward for 9–20 km. Its thickness depends on the season and where you are on Earth. Over the warm equator, the troposphere is a little thicker than it is over the polar regions, where the air is colder. It also thickens during the summer and thins during the winter. The average thickness of the troposphere is 15 km.

This ground-floor layer has most of the organisms, dust, water vapor, and clouds found in the entire atmosphere. It has most of the air as well. And, most important, weather occurs in the troposphere. The troposphere is where differences in air temperature, **humidity**, **air pressure**, and **wind** occur.

These properties of temperature, humidity, air pressure, and wind are important **weather variables**. **Meteorologists** launch weather balloons twice each day to monitor weather variables. The balloons float up through the troposphere to about 18 km.

The troposphere is the thinnest layer. It has only about 2 percent of the depth of the atmosphere. It is the most dense layer, however, containing four-fifths (80 percent) of the total mass of the atmosphere.

Earth's surface (both land and water) absorbs heat from the Sun and warms the air above it. Because air in the troposphere is heated mostly by Earth's surface, the air is warmest close to the ground. The air temperature drops as you go higher. At its highest point, the temperature of the troposphere is about –60°C. The average temperature of the troposphere is about 25°C.

Mount Everest, located in Nepal and Tibet, is the highest landform on Earth, rising 8.848 km into the troposphere. The air temperature at the top of the mountain is far below freezing most of the time. There is also less air to breathe at the top of Mount Everest. Climbers usually bring oxygen to help them survive the thin air.

Mount Everest

Jets usually fly in the region between the lower stratosphere and the upper troposphere.

The **stratosphere** is the layer above the troposphere. It is 15–50 km above Earth's surface and has almost no moisture or dust. It does, however, have a layer of ozone that absorbs ultraviolet (UV) **radiation** from the Sun. The temperature stays below freezing until you reach the top part of the stratosphere, where ozone absorbs energy and warms the air to about 0°C.

The jet stream, a fast-flowing stream of wind, travels generally west to east in the region between the lower stratosphere and the upper troposphere. Many military and commercial jets take advantage of the jet stream when flying from west to east. The jet stream winds move cold air over North America. This brings cold temperatures and storms.

The **mesosphere** is above the stratosphere, 50–85 km above Earth's surface. The temperature is colder than in the stratosphere. Its coldest temperature is around –90°C in the upper mesosphere. This is the layer where meteors burn up while entering Earth's atmosphere. We call these burning meteors shooting stars.

Beyond the mesosphere, 85–560 km (or higher) above Earth, is the **thermosphere**. The thermosphere is the most difficult layer of the atmosphere to measure. The air is extremely thin. The thermosphere is where the atmosphere is first heated by the Sun. A small amount of energy coming from the Sun can result in a large temperature change. When the Sun is very active with sunspots or flares, the temperature of the thermosphere can be 1,500°C or higher!

Temperature defines these four layers. The boundaries between the layers are not fixed lines and they can change with the seasons.

Meteors burn up in the mesosphere.

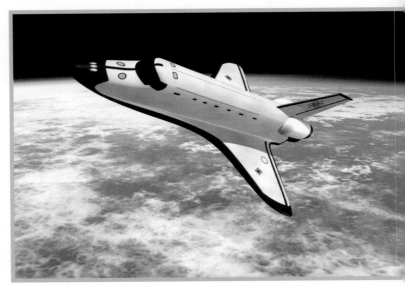
The space shuttle orbited Earth in the thermosphere.

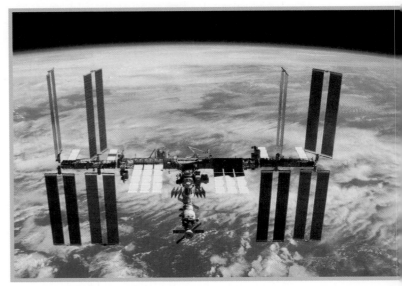
The International Space Station is in the thermosphere above Earth.

Earth's atmosphere fades into space.

Beyond the thermosphere, Earth's atmosphere fades into space. The **exosphere** is where gas particles escape into space. In this region, the temperature drops to the extreme –270°C of outer space.

That 600 km column of air pushes down on the surface of Earth with a lot of force. We call the force air pressure. We are not aware of it because we are adapted to live under all that pressure. But there is a mass of about 1 kilogram (kg) pushing down on every square centimeter (cm) of surface on Earth. Your head has a surface area of about 150 square cm. This means you have about 150 kg of air pushing down on your head. That's like having a kitchen stove or a motorcycle pushing down on your head all the time!

Here's another way to look at it. If all the air were replaced with solid gold, the entire planet would be covered by a layer of gold about half a meter deep. The mass of the entire atmosphere is about the same as half a meter of gold. But the atmosphere is much more valuable.

Thinking about the Atmosphere

1. How is Earth's atmosphere like the ocean? How is it unlike the ocean?

2. What is the average temperature of the troposphere? Why is that important?

Weather Instruments

Meteorologists are scientists who study weather. Weather is the condition of the air in an area. The conditions can change, so they are called weather variables. The most important weather variables to meteorologists are temperature, air pressure, humidity, and wind. Meteorologists use weather instruments to measure each variable.

A weather tower with a weather station on top

Temperature

Temperature is a measure of how hot the air is. Temperature is measured with a **thermometer**. There are many kinds of thermometers. The most common kind is a liquid thermometer. A liquid thermometer is a thin glass tube connected to a small bulb of liquid. As the liquid warms and cools, it expands and contracts. The height of the column of liquid in the tube changes in response to the temperature. By labeling the liquid tube to show temperatures, the meteorologist can read the temperature directly from the thermometer.

Metals also expand and contract in response to temperature change. Some thermometers use strips made of two different metals to detect temperature changes. These are called bimetallic thermometers. The two metals have different rates of expansion. One side of the strip expands more than the other as it heats up, and the strip bends. A pointer on the end of the bending strip points to the temperature.

A liquid thermometer

A bimetallic thermometer

cold   hot

Air Pressure

Air pressure is the force of air pushing on things around it. Air pressure changes with the density of the air. When air heats up, it becomes less dense; when it cools, it becomes more dense. The instrument that measures air pressure is called a **barometer**. Air pushes on a closed container, one side of which is attached to a dial in the barometer. The harder the air pushes, the higher the dial goes. The dial measures in units called millibars. Changes in air pressure mean that weather conditions will change. Falling air pressure means **rain** is coming. Rising air pressure means fair and dry weather is coming.

A barometer

Humidity

Water vapor is water (H_2O) in its gas state. As vapor, water can enter the air. The water vapor will eventually condense and form drops of water, which can fall as rain. Meteorologists measure humidity, the amount of water in the air, with instruments called **hygrometers**. Humidity is measured as a percentage.

A hygrometer

Wind Speed

Moving air is called wind. Meteorologists are interested in how fast the wind is moving. To measure wind speed, meteorologists use **anemometers** and **wind meters**. An anemometer uses a rotating shaft with wind-catching cups attached at the top. The harder the wind blows, the faster the shaft rotates, and the faster the cups move through the air. The moving cups measure the wind speed.

A wind meter is an instrument with a small ball in a tube. When wind blows across the top of the tube, the flow of air up the tube lifts the ball. The harder the wind blows, the higher the ball rises. Both instruments are adjusted to report wind in miles per hour (mph) or kilometers (km) per hour.

An anemometer

A wind meter

Wind Direction

Meteorologists are also interested in the direction the wind is blowing. To determine wind direction, meteorologists use a **wind vane**. A wind vane is a shaft with an arrow point on one end and a broad paddle shape at the other end. When wind hits the paddle, it rotates the shaft so that the arrow points into the wind. Using a compass, the meteorologist determines the direction the shaft is pointing. Wind direction is the direction from which the wind is blowing. It is reported in compass directions, such as north or south.

A wind vane

A compass

Modern Weather Instruments

Meteorologists now use a combination of traditional weather instruments and computer-based digital weather instruments. Meteorologists get information from advanced electronic instruments that are placed in good locations for monitoring weather. Those instruments use radio transmitters (like those in cell phones) to send information to weather centers where meteorologists work.

This weather device for home use has electronic instruments inside for detecting and reporting temperature and humidity. Some models measure air pressure and are connected to anemometers to measure wind speed.

Uneven Heating

Stars create a lot of energy. Energy radiates from them in all directions. Most of this energy streams out into space and never hits anything. A small amount, however, hits objects in the universe. When you look into the sky on a dark, clear night, you see thousands of stars. You see them because a tiny amount of energy from the stars goes into your eyes.

During the day, you are aware of the energy coming from a much closer star, the Sun. When sunlight comes to Earth, you can see the light and feel the heat when your skin absorbs the light. Heat and light from the Sun are called **solar energy**.

When light from the Sun hits matter, such as Earth's surface, two important things can happen. The light can be reflected or absorbed by the matter. If the light is reflected, it simply bounces off the matter and continues on its way in a new direction. But if the light is absorbed, the matter gains energy. Usually the gained energy is heat. When matter absorbs energy, its temperature goes up.

Heating It Up

The amount of solar energy coming from the Sun is about the same all the time. But the temperature of Earth's surface is not even. Some locations get warmer than other locations. Why is that?

There are several variables that affect how hot a material will get when solar energy shines on it. The table below lists several variables and how each affects the temperature change of a material.

Variable	Effect
Length of exposure	Longer exposure leads to higher temperature.
Intensity of solar energy	Greater intensity leads to higher temperature.
Angle of exposure	More direct angle leads to higher temperature.
Color of material	Darker color leads to higher temperature.
Properties of material	Water shows the least temperature change.

Length of exposure is how long the Sun shines on an object.

Intensity of solar energy is how bright and concentrated the energy is. For example, if the light travels through clouds, it will be less intense. Clouds reflect and absorb some of the energy before it gets to Earth's surface. The brighter the sunlight falling on an object, the warmer the object will get.

Angle of exposure changes throughout the day. Morning sunshine comes at a low angle and is less intense and weak. Midday sunshine radiates down from a high angle and is intense and strong.

Different colors absorb solar energy differently. Black absorbs the most solar energy. White absorbs the least solar energy.

The chemical properties of materials affect how hot they get when they absorb solar energy. Water heats up slowly and soil heats up rapidly when they absorb the same amount of energy. Water cools slowly and soil cools rapidly when they are moved to the shade.

Solar Energy in Action

Imagine a summer trip to the beach. On a cloudless day, the Sun shines down with equal intensity on the sandy beach and the ocean. It's a hot day.

When the car stops in the parking lot in the early afternoon, the pavement in the parking lot is hot. The black asphalt has absorbed a lot of solar energy, and its temperature is 50 degrees Celsius (°C). You walk across the parking lot (ouch, hot!) and onto the white sand. Whew! The white sand isn't as hot. It is a bearable 32°C. You keep moving toward the water. You finally get relief from the intense heat. The temperature of the ocean water is 22°C.

The asphalt, sand, and ocean water were all exposed to the same intensity of solar energy for the same length of time. But they are all different temperatures.

Black asphalt absorbs a lot of energy and gets very hot. White sand reflects a lot of solar energy. Light-colored sand doesn't get as hot as asphalt. Water absorbs a lot of energy, but it stays cool.

The temperature of Earth's surface is not the same everywhere. Land gets hotter than water in the sunlight. Land gets colder than water when the Sun goes down. Land heats up and cools off rapidly. Water heats up and cools off slowly. The result is uneven heating of Earth's surface.

Uneven Heating Worldwide

You can experience uneven heating of Earth's surface with your bare feet when walking on asphalt. The difference in temperature between the asphalt and water is obvious. On a larger scale, the whole planet is heated unevenly. The tropical areas (the tropics, near the equator) are warmer. The polar areas are cooler. That's because the angle of exposure of the solar energy is more direct in the tropics.

You can feel uneven heating of Earth when you are barefoot on asphalt.

The illustration shows how sunlight comes straight down on the tropics. But the sunlight comes at a sideways angle toward the poles. You can see how the same amount of light is spread over a much larger area in the north than in the tropics. This results in more heating in the tropics and less heating in the northern areas.

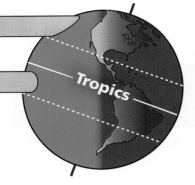

Tropics

Two identical beams of sunlight. The upper beam spreads over a larger area toward the poles.

Thinking about Uneven Heating

1. What causes Earth's surface to heat up?

2. What are some of the variables that cause uneven heating of Earth's surface?

3. What happens to the temperature of equal volumes of soil and water when they are placed in the sunlight for 30 minutes?

Heating the Air: Radiation and Conduction

You might have had an experience like this one. The campfire has burned down to a bed of hot coals. Now it is time to toast some marshmallows. You put a marshmallow on a long stick and stand at a safe distance from the coals to toast your treat. You can feel the heat coming from the coals. After a minute, the marshmallow is brown and gooey. You pop it into your mouth. Yikes, that's hot! You didn't wait long enough for it to cool.

That story includes a couple of heat experiences. Have you ever stopped to think about what heat really is? What is the heat that you felt coming off the coals and the heat in the marshmallow that burned your tongue?

Heat = Movement

Objects in motion have energy. The faster they move, the more energy they have. Energy of motion is called **kinetic energy**.

Matter, like soccer balls, juice bottles, water, and air, is made of particles that are too small to see. The particles are in motion. They are in motion even in steel nails and glass bottles. In solids, the particles vibrate back and forth. In liquids and gases, the particles move all over the place. The faster the particles vibrate or move, the more energy they have.

Particle motion is kinetic energy, which can produce heat. The amount of kinetic energy in the particles of a material determines how much heat it produces. The particles in hot materials are moving fast. The particles in cold materials are moving more slowly.

The particles in solids are held close to each other. They move by vibrating.

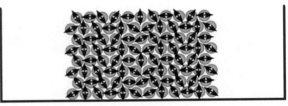

When solids get hot, the particles vibrate more. Hotter solids have more kinetic energy than colder solids.

The particles in liquids move by bumping and sliding around each other.

When liquids get hot, the particles bump and push each other more. Hotter liquids have more kinetic energy than colder liquids.

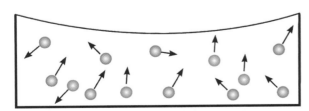

The particles in gases fly individually through the air in all directions.

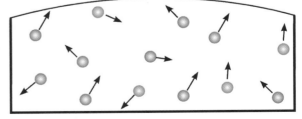

When gases get hot, the particles fly faster and are farther apart. Hotter gases have more kinetic energy than colder gases.

Energy Transfer

Heat can transfer (move) from one place to another. We can observe the **energy transfer** when energy is present as heat. Scientists sometimes describe heat transfer as heat flow, as though it were a liquid. Heat is not a liquid, but flow is a good way to imagine its movement.

Heat flows from a hotter location (high energy) to a cooler one (less energy). For example, if you add cold milk to your hot chocolate, heat flows from the hot chocolate to the cold milk. The hot chocolate cools because heat flows away. The cold milk warms because heat flows in. Soon the chocolate and the milk arrive at the same warm temperature, and you gulp them down.

Energy Transfer by Radiation

Burning gas, like the burner on a stove, can get very hot. When this happens, the burner is radiating heat and light. If you are close to a lightbulb, you can see light and feel heat, even though you are not touching the lightbulb. Energy that travels through air is **radiant energy**.

Radiant energy travels in rays. Heat and light rays radiate from sources like hot campfire coals, lightbulbs, and the Sun.

Radiation from the Sun passes through Earth's atmosphere. We call this solar energy. When solar energy hits a particle of matter, such as a gas particle in the air, a water particle in the ocean, or a particle of soil, the energy can be absorbed. Absorbed radiation increases the kinetic energy (movement) of the particles in the air, water, or soil. Increased kinetic energy produces a higher temperature, so the material gets hotter.

Radiation is one way energy moves from one place to another. Materials don't have to touch for energy to transfer from one place to the other.

Energy Transfer by Conduction

Imagine that hot toasted marshmallow or maybe a slice of pizza straight from the oven going into your mouth. This is another kind of energy transfer. When energy transfers from one place to another by contact, it is called **conduction**.

The fast-moving particles of the hot pizza bang into the slower particles of your mouth. The particles in your tongue gain kinetic energy. At the same time, particles of the hot pizza lose kinetic energy, so the pizza cools off. Some of the pizza's kinetic energy is conducted to heat receptors on your tongue, which sends a message to your brain that says, "Hot, hot, hot!"

When you heat water in a pot, the water gets hot because it touches the hot metal of the pot. Kinetic energy transfers from the hot metal particles to the cold water particles by contact, which is conduction.

A "hot" particle with a lot of kinetic energy collides with a "cold" particle with little kinetic energy. Energy transfers at the point of contact. The cold particle gains energy, and the hot particle loses energy.

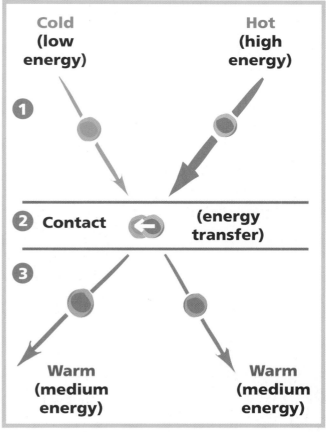

Cold (low energy)   Hot (high energy)

1

2 Contact (energy transfer)

3

Warm (medium energy)   Warm (medium energy)

Energy Transfer to the Air

We have learned about energy transfer by radiation and conduction. Now let's explore energy from the Sun and what happens when it interacts with the air. Many kinds of rays radiate from the Sun. The most important rays are visible light and infrared light, which is invisible. So how do the Sun's rays heat up the air?

Air is 99 percent nitrogen and oxygen particles. Neither kind of particle absorbs visible light or infrared radiation. Only water vapor and carbon dioxide absorb significant amounts of radiant energy, and this is mostly infrared rays, not visible light.

If only a tiny part of the air absorbs the incoming radiant energy, how does the rest of the air get hot? We need to consider parts of two other systems, the **hydrosphere** (water) and **geosphere** (land).

Earth's surface absorbs visible light. The land and water warm up. The air particles that touch the warm land and water particles gain energy by conduction. But there is more.

The warm land and water also radiate energy. This is a very important idea. Earth gives off infrared radiation that can be absorbed by water particles and carbon dioxide particles in the air. The energy transferred to the small number of water particles and carbon dioxide particles is transferred throughout the air by conduction. This happens when energized water particles and carbon dioxide particles bang into oxygen and nitrogen particles.

The air is not only heated from above. It is also heated from below.

Hydrosphere
Water particles warmed by radiation coming up from Earth

Atmosphere
Air particles warmed by conduction

Geosphere
Earth warmed by solar energy radiates infrared radiation.

Wind and Convection

Kite flying can be a lot of fun if the conditions are right. If the conditions are wrong, kite flying can be boring. What makes conditions right for kite flying? Wind.

Wind is air in motion. Air is matter. Air has mass and takes up space. When a mass of air is in motion, it can move things around. Wind can blow leaves down the street, lift your hat off your head, and carry a kite high in the air.

Sometimes air is still. Other times the wind is blowing. What causes the wind to blow? What puts the air into motion? The answer is energy. It takes energy to move air. The energy to create wind comes from the Sun.

Wind lifts a kite high in the air.

Air is particles of nitrogen, oxygen, and a few other gases. The particles are flying around and banging into each other, the land, and the ocean. Let's imagine we are at the beach. It's early morning. The air over the land and the air over the ocean are both the same cool temperature.

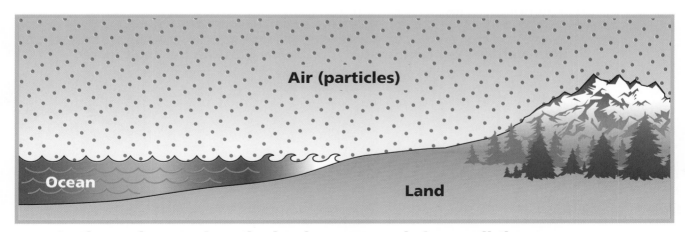

In the early morning, the land, ocean, and air are all the same cool temperature.

As the Sun shines down on the land (part of the geosphere) and ocean (part of the hydrosphere), solar energy is absorbed. The land heats up quickly. The ocean heats up very slowly. By noon the land is hot, but the ocean is still cool. Earth's surface is heated unevenly. The afternoon wind starts. Here's why.

When air particles bang into the hot surface of the land, energy transfers to the air particles. Because of this energy transfer, the air particles fly around faster. The air gets hot. The hot-air particles bang into each other harder. That pushes the particles farther apart.

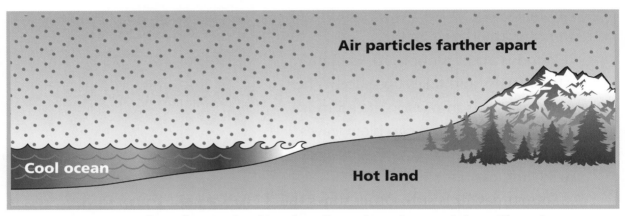

Energy transfers from the hot land to the air particles. The air particles move farther apart.

Over the ocean, air particles are banging into the cool surface of the water. The air stays cool. The air particles continue to move at a slower speed. The cool-air particles don't hit each other as hard, so they stay closer together.

A cubic meter of hot air has fewer particles than a cubic meter of cool air. The hot air is less dense than an equal volume of cool air.

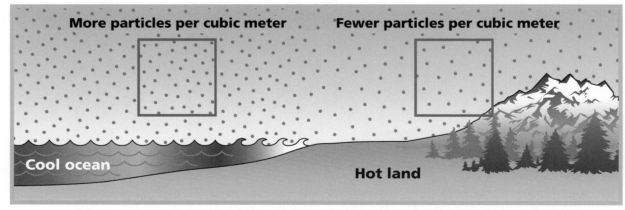

A cubic meter of hot air has fewer particles than a cubic meter of cold air. Hot air is less dense than cool air.

The Wind Starts

You know that cork floats on water. Cork floats on water because it is less dense than water. If you take a cork to the bottom of the ocean and let it go, it will float to the surface.

That's exactly what happens with warm and cold air. The warm air over the land floats upward because it is less dense than the cool air over the ocean. The more-dense, cool air flows into the area where the less-dense, warm air is and pushes it upward. The movement of more-dense air from the ocean to the warm land is wind. Wind is the movement of more-dense air to an area where the air is less dense.

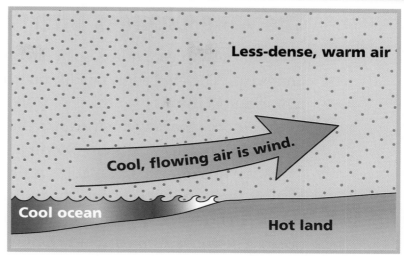

Dense, cool air flows from the ocean to the land. Less-dense, warm air rises.

There is more to the story of wind. Two things happen at the same time to create wind. The warm air cools as it rises, becoming more dense than the surrounding air. At the same time, the dense air from the ocean warms up as it flows over the hot land.

As a result, air starts to move in a big circle. Air that is warmed by the hot land moves upward. The warm air cools as it moves up, gets more dense, and starts to fall. The rising and falling air sets up a big circular air current. The circular current is called a **convection current**.

As long as Earth's surface continues to be heated unevenly, the convection current will continue to flow. The part of the convection current that flows across Earth's surface is what we experience as wind. But what happens at night?

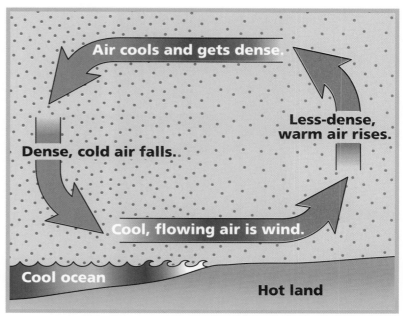

A convection current is the result of the uneven heating of Earth's surface.

The Wind Changes Direction

When the Sun goes down, solar energy no longer falls on the land and ocean. The land cools rapidly, but the ocean stays at about the same temperature. The air over the cool land is no longer heated. The density of the air over the land and ocean is the same. The convection current stops flowing. The wind stops blowing.

What will happen if the night is really cold? The land will get cold. The air over the land will get cold. The cold air will become more dense than the air over the ocean. The more-dense air will flow from the land to the ocean. The convection current will flow in the opposite direction, and the wind will blow from the land to the ocean.

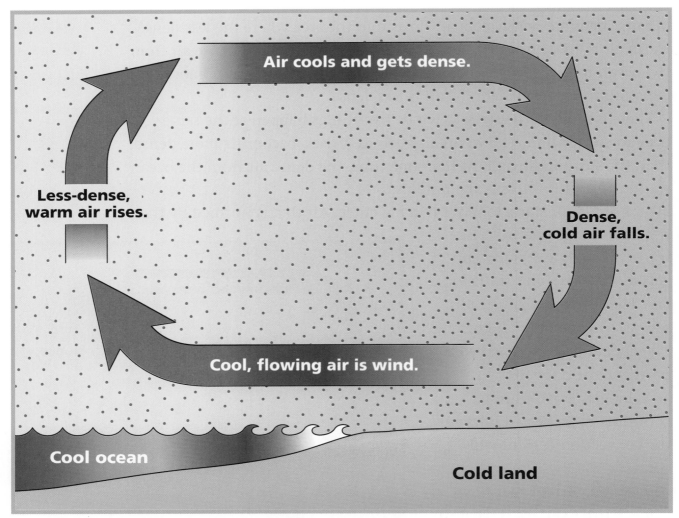

Air cools and gets dense.

Less-dense, warm air rises.

Dense, cold air falls.

Cool, flowing air is wind.

Cool ocean

Cold land

This convection current creates wind that blows from the land to the ocean.

194

Convection Summary

Uneven heating of Earth's surface by the Sun causes uneven heating of the air over Earth's surface. Uneven heating of air causes wind. Warm air is less dense than cold air. Cold, dense air flows to an area where the air is warmer and less dense. The less-dense air is pushed upward. As the warm air moves upward, it cools. Cool air is more dense, so it falls back to Earth. This circular pattern of air flow is a convection current. Convection currents are important ways that air masses move from place to place in the atmosphere. Convection currents transport energy from place to place.

Convection currents produce wind. The greater the difference in temperature between the warm and cold air masses, the harder and faster the wind will blow. Uneven heating of Earth's surface is the cause of many weather changes on Earth, including hurricanes, **tornadoes**, and **thunderstorms**.

Convection currents produce wind.

Uneven heating of Earth can cause hurricanes.

Thinking about Wind

1. How are convection currents produced in the air?

2. Explain what causes wind.

3. What happens to air particles when air is heated?

4. What is the source of energy that causes the wind to blow?

Wind Power

Heat isn't the only energy resource that starts with the Sun. Wind, which is caused by the Sun's uneven heating of Earth, can also be used to generate power.

Wind is created when cool air rushes in to take the place of warmer, less-dense air. People have used wind power for thousands of years. In the past, sailing ships were the quickest and easiest way to travel. These ships had large sails to catch the wind and move them across the water.

Wind energy has powered sailing ships for thousands of years.

One ancient use of wind power is windmills. Arabic people introduced windmills to Europe in about the 12th century. Ancient windmills were used to grind grain into flour. These windmills caught the wind in sails made of wood and cloth. The sails turned an axle, which transferred its motion to a turning pole. The pole turned the millstones that ground the grain. Windmills were also used to pump water.

Inventors and engineers have made many improvements to windmill technologies. Modern "windmills" are called **wind turbines**. Wind turbines can operate in gentle winds. They can turn in wind speeds in the 8–16 kilometers (km) per hour range. Wind speeds in the 8–16 km per hour range are light winds that you can just feel on your face and are about right for flying a kite.

Windmills have provided power for pumping water and grinding grain in Europe since the 12th century.

Part of the wind farm at Palm Springs, California.

Sometimes dozens or even hundreds of wind turbines are set up on a wind farm. One well-known wind farm is at Altamont Pass in California. As warm valley air rises in the central part of the state, cool air from the ocean flows over the coastal mountains. Narrow gaps between mountains, called passes, channel the air and increase its speed.

There are over 13,000 wind turbines in California at Altamont Pass, Tehachapi Pass, and Palm Springs. In 1995, these areas produced 30 percent of the world's wind-generated electricity. Roscoe Wind Farm in Texas is the largest land-based wind farm in the world. It has 627 wind turbines over 100,000 acres of west Texas. This wind farm can provide electricity to 230,000 homes. In 2010, wind power provided about 2 percent of the electricity generated in the United States.

Wind power has some disadvantages. The power produced depends on how strongly the wind is blowing. Therefore, wind farms can produce too much energy at some times and too little energy at others. Excess energy needs to be stored. It can be used to heat water or oil, or stored in batteries.

Some people don't like wind farms because they think the turbines are ugly. The turbines also create a whipping sound as they turn. The sound annoys some people and scares away animals. Birds can be killed by flying into spinning turbines.

Even though wind power has limitations, it is still an important source of energy. Each year the United States generates wind turbine electricity equal to burning 320 million barrels of oil in oil-fired power plants. Using wind power in place of burning **fossil fuels** prevents 96 million tons of carbon dioxide from being released into the air each year. Eventually fossil fuels will run out and burning carbon-based fuels will no longer be an option. Wind power will be an important part of our energy future.

Solar Technology

People use solar energy in a number of ways. People use it to heat water, to cook food, to warm and cool buildings, and to generate electricity.

Solar Water Heaters

Solar water heaters have been around for thousands of years. The ancient Romans created public baths supplied with water that flowed through heating channels. These channels were like canals, open to the Sun. The water channels were lined with black slate to absorb as much of the Sun's energy as possible. Centuries later, people painted metal tanks black and tilted them toward the Sun to warm the water inside.

In 1891, the first American commercial solar water heater, the Climax, was built. It was a black iron tank inside a wooden box. The box was lined with black felt and covered with glass. It sat on a roof exposed to the Sun.

The Climax worked fine on a sunny day. But what about cloudy days or nighttime? In 1909, the Day and Night water heating system was invented. This system included a solar heater and a separate insulated storage tank. After the Sun heated the water, it was piped into the storage tank where it remained warm.

Today, there are many types of solar water heaters, some of them shown on these pages.

A thermosyphon system solar water heater

198

A flat-plate collector solar water heater

One type of solar water heater available today uses a flat-plate solar collector in an insulated box. On top of the collector are small tubes filled with water to absorb the Sun's rays. The system is placed on the roof of a house. The Sun-heated water is piped down into an insulated storage tank in the house.

The many types of modern solar water heaters share some common features. They must be positioned to capture the Sun's energy so they are often on top of roofs. They are made of materials that absorb the heat energy and transfer the energy to water. The systems are insulated so the heat energy doesn't escape from the water. The water moves through pipes to a storage tank and is accessible by turning a faucet.

A glass tube collector solar water heater

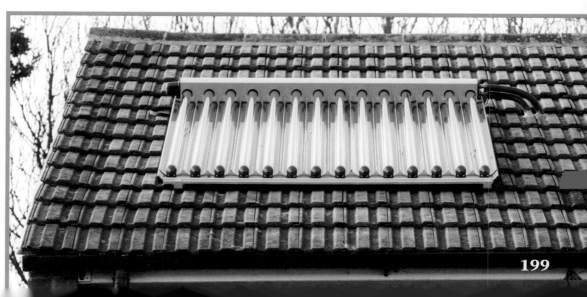

Solar Cookers

Most of your meals are probably cooked in an oven or on a stove powered by electricity or natural gas. Electric microwave ovens are also popular for cooking food. But what about cooking where there is no access to gas or electricity? In developing countries, more than 2 billion people burn wood for cooking. But burning wood is bad for the environment and creates health risks for people. Large numbers of trees have to be cut down. Wood burning creates smoke that pollutes the air and causes breathing problems.

People can use solar cookers as a safe, inexpensive, pollution-free way to cook. A number of organizations have developed solar ovens in countries all over the world.

A solar cooker in the Zanskar Mountains of northern India

One of the most successful solar cooking projects is in Kenya. Professor Daniel Kammen, of the University of California, Berkeley, has introduced solar cookers to villages in Kenya. His simple solar ovens are boxes lined with reflective foil and covered with glass. First, he demonstrates how easy they are to use. Kammen and his coworkers mix up a stew or cake. They put it in the oven. Then Kammen explains how the oven works. He also explains how to build one. Finally he opens the oven and lets everyone eat some of the cooked food.

It takes about 3 hours to cook a pot of stew in a solar oven and about half an hour to boil a pot of water. Cooking food over a traditional fire takes less time.

A solar oven in Kenya

However, solar ovens eliminate the time-consuming chore of gathering firewood. Solar cooking also eliminates many respiratory illnesses, which are a common cause of death in Kenya.

If the community is interested in the solar oven, Kammen and his coworkers come back with plywood, foil, glass, and nails. They teach the villagers how to build their own ovens. So far, Kammen and his team have introduced hundreds of solar ovens in eastern Kenya.

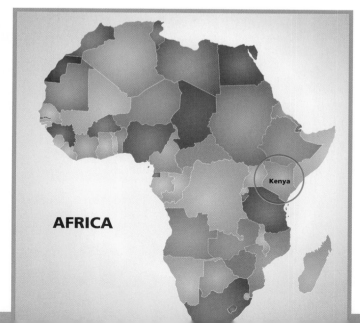

201

Solar Electricity

The Sun's energy can be converted into electricity. This process uses solar cells or steam-powered turbines. Solar cells are devices used to transform solar energy directly into electricity.

Solar cells are made of silicon, which is found in sand. The silicon is purified, crystallized, and cut into wafers or squares. Two wafers or squares are sandwiched together to form a solar cell. The cells are arranged on a flat panel made of glass, metal, or wood and sealed behind glass or plastic. One solar cell with a diameter of 10 centimeters (cm) can produce 1 watt of electric power. The electricity is then used immediately or stored in batteries.

Many solar cells are connected to make large panels called solar arrays. Solar arrays can generate enough electricity to store. The biggest challenge facing the use of solar cells is to bring down their cost. If this happens, many energy experts believe that solar cells could provide most of our energy needs by the end of this century.

Solar furnaces use huge mirrors to concentrate a lot of light in one place. Large solar furnaces can use this energy to produce steam, which can be used to turn large generators to produce large quantities of electricity. The solar furnace in Odeillo, France, has an 8-story-tall mirror and can produce temperatures up to 3,000 degrees Celsius (°C). That's hot enough to melt a steel plate in just 3.5 seconds!

The solar furnace in Odeillo, France

Maria Telkes

Dr. Maria Telkes (1900–1995) was the world's most famous female inventor in the field of solar energy. Some people even called her the Sun Queen!

Maria Telkes was born in Hungary. She lived most of her life in the United States. She first became interested in solar energy when she was with the Massachusetts Institute of Technology (MIT) in the 1940s. During her 50-year career, she worked for many top universities.

Dr. Maria Telkes

Solar cooking was of special interest to Telkes. She realized that we need to **conserve** fuel. The heat of the Sun provided a clean source of energy. During the 1950s, she invented a model of a solar oven that is still used today. Later the Ford Foundation gave Telkes a $45,000 grant to work on her solar oven. This allowed Telkes to improve her design.

Telkes also helped to create a solar house. In 1981, she worked to design and build the Carlisle House in Carlisle, Massachusetts. MIT and the US Department of Energy also worked on the project. This house features a solar heating and cooling system. It uses no fossil fuels, such as natural gas, oil, and coal. The house generates so much power that it is able to share its extra energy with the local utility company.

The solar-powered Carlisle House was built by Telkes in 1981.

Solar Buildings

Imagine a house or office building where the electric, heating, and cooling systems don't rely on oil, natural gas, or coal. Instead, all these systems use energy from the Sun for power. Homes like this do exist. They are called solar houses.

Solar houses have many different systems that use energy from the Sun. Some of these systems are passive. They don't use any mechanical devices such as pumps or generators. An example of passive space heating would use large windows that face the Sun. The windows let sunlight shine in to warm the house. When the weather is warm, window coverings come down over the windows and keep the house cool. Solar houses are designed to work with the Sun to maintain a comfortable temperature at all times of the year.

Other solar systems are active. They use mechanical devices, such as fans and pumps, to move captured solar energy throughout the house. For example, many solar houses use flat-plate collectors to heat water and air. A flat-plate collector sits in a box that is insulated on the bottom and sides. The top is covered by one or more layers of clear glass or plastic. The system is placed on the roof of a house. The visible light goes through the glass, where it is absorbed by the plate and converted into heat. The glass traps the heat inside the box. The hot air is pumped to rooms in the house where it heats the space.

Solar energy is good for the environment! That's why some houses and apartment buildings use solar panels.

Solar energy can also be used to cool buildings during the summer. Most solar air-conditioning systems use solar collectors and materials called desiccants. Desiccants can absorb large amounts of water. Fans force air from outdoors through the desiccants, which remove moisture from the air. Next the dry air flows through a heat exchanger that removes some of the heat. Then the air passes over a surface soaked with water. As the water comes in contact with the dry air, it evaporates and removes more heat from the air. Finally the cooled air is pumped throughout the building.

Other types of active systems involve solar cells. Solar arrays (also called solar panels) can generate electricity for all kinds of household uses. Solar panels can be placed on the roof of a house or on the sides of apartment buildings. It is important that the solar cells capture as much sunlight during the day as possible.

Solar houses have many advantages. They are environmentally friendly. Solar energy is a **renewable resource**. It does not use up Earth's resources the way burning fossil fuels or wood does. In addition, solar collectors are pollution-free. They don't create fumes or other dangerous chemicals that can poison the environment or make people sick.

Thinking about Solar Technology

1. What are some features of solar water heaters used today?

2. What are the advantages of solar cookers?

3. What did Maria Telkes contribute to solar technology, and when did she do this?

Condensation

When water evaporates, where does it go? It goes into the air. Water is always evaporating. Clothes are drying on clotheslines. Wet streets are drying after a rain. Water is evaporating from lakes and the ocean all the time. Every day more than 1,000 cubic kilometers (km) of water evaporates worldwide. And all that water vapor goes into the air! That amount of water would cover the entire state of California 3 meters (m) deep.

What happens to all that water in the air? As long as the air stays warm, the water stays in the air as water vapor. Warmth (heat) indicates the presence of energy. As long as the particles of water vapor have a lot of kinetic energy, they continue to exist as gas.

But if the air cools, things change. As the air cools, the particles lose kinetic energy and slow down. When this happens, particles of water vapor start to come together. Slowing down and coming together is called condensation. Condensation is the change from gas to liquid.

Particles of condensed water vapor form tiny masses (droplets) of liquid water. When invisible water vapor in the atmosphere condenses, the water becomes visible again. Clouds and **fog** are made of these tiny droplets of liquid water.

Condensation usually happens on a cold surface. In class, you observed condensation on the cold surface of a plastic cup filled with ice water. But there are no cups of ice water in the sky. What kind of surface does water vapor condense on?

The clouds in the sky are made of tiny droplets of water.

Most condensation in the air starts with dust particles. Water particles attach to a dust particle. When a tiny mass of water has attached to a dust particle, other water particles will join the liquid mass.

When you look up in the sky and see clouds, you are seeing trillions of droplets of liquid water. Each droplet is made up of billions of water particles, but a single droplet is still too small to see. You can see them when trillions and trillions of them are close together in clouds.

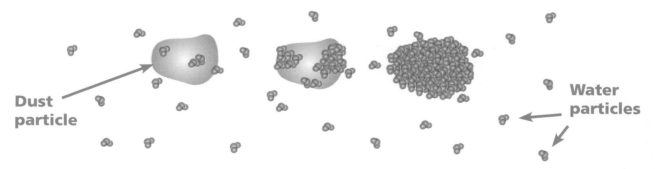

Dust particle

Water particles

The mass of water grows and grows until it forms a tiny droplet of water.

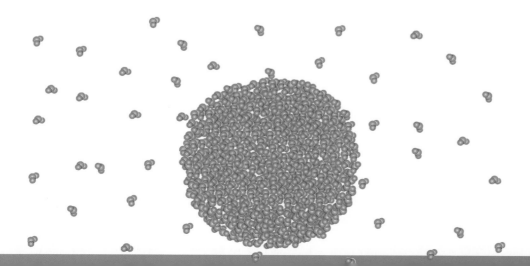

Dew on a spider's web

Where else have you seen condensation other than up in the clouds? Sometimes water vapor condenses close to the ground. This is called fog. Being in fog is really being in a cloud that is at ground level.

Water vapor doesn't always condense in air. If you go out early in the morning after a warm day, you might see condensation called **dew**. In these pictures, dew formed on a spider's web and on a flower.

Water vapor condenses indoors, too. On a cold morning you might see condensation on your kitchen window. Or if you go outside into the cold wearing your glasses, they could get fogged with condensation when you go back inside.

Dew on a flower

Condensation on a window

What happens to the bathroom mirror after you take a shower? The air in the bathroom is warm and full of water vapor. When the air makes contact with the cool mirror, the water vapor condenses on the smooth surface. That's why the mirror is foggy and wet.

When the temperature drops below the freezing point of water (0°C), water vapor will condense and freeze. Frozen condensation is called **frost**. Frost is tiny crystals of ice. Frost might form on a car window on a cold night. You can also see frost on plants early on a winter morning. But you have to get up before the Sun if you want to see the beautiful frost patterns.

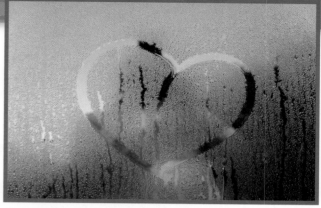

Condensation on a mirror

Frost on a window

Frost on grass and a leaf

Thinking about Condensation

1. What is condensation?

2. What role does temperature play in condensation?

3. What is frost?

4. Why does condensation form on a glass of iced tea?

Where Is Earth's Water?

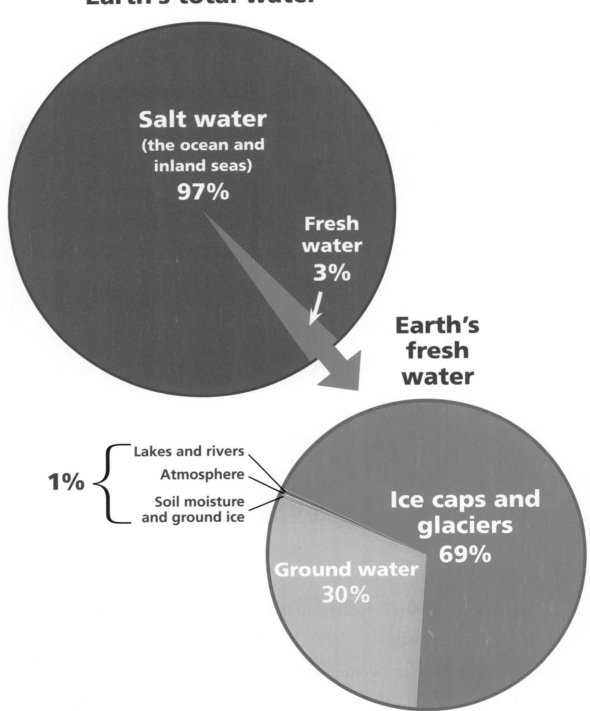

Earth's total water

Salt water
(the ocean and
inland seas)
97%

Fresh
water
3%

Earth's
fresh
water

1% { Lakes and rivers
Atmosphere
Soil moisture
and ground ice

Ice caps and
glaciers
69%

Ground water
30%

The Water Cycle

Water particles in the water you drink today might have once flowed down the Mississippi River. Those same particles might have washed one of George Washington's shirts. They might even have been in a puddle lapped up by a thirsty dinosaur a million years ago!

Water is in constant motion on Earth. You can see water in motion in rushing streams, falling raindrops, and blowing snowflakes. But water is in motion in other places, too. Water is flowing slowly through the soil. Water is drifting across the sky in clouds. Water is rising through the roots and stems of plants. Water is in motion all over the world.

Think about the Mississippi River for a moment. It flows all year long, year after year. Where does the water come from to keep the river flowing?

The water flowing in the river is renewed all the time. Rain and **snow** fall in and near the Mississippi River. Rain falling nearby soaks into the soil and runs into the river. The snow melts in the spring and supplies water for the river during the summer. Rain and snow keep the Mississippi River flowing.

The rain and snow in the Mississippi River are just a tiny part of a global system of water recycling. The system is called the **water cycle**.

The big idea of the water cycle is this. Water evaporates from Earth's surface and goes into the atmosphere. Water in the atmosphere moves to a new location. The water then returns to Earth's surface in the new location. The new location gets a new supply of water.

A simple water-cycle diagram

Water Evaporates from Earth's Surface

The Sun drives the water cycle. Energy from the Sun falls on Earth's surface and changes liquid water into water vapor. The ocean is where most of the evaporation takes place. But water evaporates from lakes, rivers, soil, wet city streets, plants, animals, and wherever there is water. Water evaporates from all parts of Earth's surface, both water and land.

Water evaporates from all of Earth's surfaces.

Water vapor is made of individual water particles. Water vapor enters the air and makes it moist. The moist air moves up in the atmosphere. As moist air rises, it cools. When water vapor cools, it condenses. Water in the atmosphere changes from gas to liquid. Tiny droplets of liquid water form. The condensed water is visible as clouds, fog, and dew.

Water vapor condenses in the atmosphere to form clouds.

Water Falls Back to Earth's Surface

Wind blows clouds around. Clouds end up over mountains, forests, cities, deserts, and the ocean. When clouds are full of condensed water, the water falls back to Earth's surface as rain. If the temperature is really cold, the water will freeze and fall to Earth's surface as snow, **sleet**, or **hail**.

Water falls back to Earth's surface as rain, snow, sleet, or hail.

Water particles move through the water cycle at different speeds. They also follow different paths. For example, rain might soak into the soil. A particle might be taken in by plant roots. It might soon escape into the air through holes in plant leaves during a process called **transpiration**. If the air is cool, water might condense immediately as dew and fall back onto the soil. This is a very small water cycle that **recycles** water back to its starting place quickly.

Rain that lands on the roof of your school might flow to the ground. From there it could enter a stream. After a long journey, it could find its way to the ocean. There the rainwater could reenter the atmosphere as water vapor. By the time it condenses with millions of other particles to form a drop, the rainwater could be hundreds of kilometers (km) away from where it started. When the particle returns to Earth's surface, it could fall on the roof of a school in another state. This is an example of a large water cycle that moves water to a new location.

Rain can sink into the ground or freeze in a glacier. A particle far underground or deep in a mass of ice can take a long time to reenter the water cycle. It might take 100 years for a particle of ground water to come to the surface in a spring, and even longer for a particle to break free from a glacier.

The Sun provides the energy to change liquid water into vapor. Water vapor enters the air, where it is carried around the world. When water condenses, gravity pulls it back to Earth's surface. That's the water cycle, and it goes on endlessly.

Thinking about the Water Cycle

1. What is the water cycle?

2. When water falls from clouds, what forms can it take?

3. Describe a large water cycle that takes a long time to complete.

4. Describe a small water cycle that takes a short time to complete.

Severe Weather

On August 29, 2005, Hurricane Katrina roared across the Gulf of Mexico and onto land. Throughout the country, people watched TV and listened to the radio as Katrina plowed into the states of Louisiana, Mississippi, and Alabama. The wind speed was 250 kilometers (km) per hour. The rain poured down. When the storm had passed, hundreds of people were dead, hundreds of thousands were homeless, and the city of New Orleans was flooded. The cost of the damage was in the billions of dollars.

Hurricane Katrina making landfall on the Gulf Coast

Weather is fairly predictable most of the time. During the summer months in San Francisco, California, mornings and afternoons are often foggy. There might be sunshine in the middle of the day. In the winter months, rain is common. In Los Angeles, California, hot, dry weather is typical in the summer. In Gulf states, summer days are often hot and humid. In the Midwest and East, winters are usually cold, cloudy, and snowy. These are the normal weather conditions that people come to expect where they live.

It's the change from normal to the extreme that catches people's attention. Tornadoes, thunderstorms, windstorms, hurricanes, **droughts**, and floods are examples of **severe weather**. Severe weather brings out-of-the-ordinary conditions. It may cause dangerous situations that can damage property and threaten lives.

Rain is a common type of precipitation.

What Is Weather?

We are surrounded by air. It's a little bit like living on the bottom of an ocean of air. Things are always going on in the air surrounding us. The condition of the air around us is what we call weather.

Weather can be described in terms of four important variables.

A sunny day in Chicago, Illinois

They are temperature, humidity, air pressure, and wind. They are called variables because they change. A day with nice weather might be warm, but not too hot. The sky is clear with just a little bit of moisture in the air. The air is still or moving with a light breeze. That's a perfect day for most people. But not too many days are perfect. Usually it's too hot, too humid, too windy, or too something. But don't worry. Weather always changes.

What Causes Weather to Change?

Energy makes weather happen. Energy makes weather change. The source of energy to create and change weather is the Sun.

When sunlight is intense, the air gets hot. When sunlight is blocked by clouds, or when the Sun goes down, the air cools off.

Moisture in the air takes the form of humidity, clouds, and precipitation. Intense sunlight evaporates more water from the land and ocean of Earth's surface. The result is more humidity, more cloud formation, and more rain. When sunlight is less intense, evaporation slows down.

Movement of air is wind. Uneven heating of Earth's surface results in uneven heating of the air touching Earth's surface. Warm air expands and gets less dense. More-dense, cool air flows under the warm air. This starts a convection current. The air flowing from the cool surface to the warm surface is wind.

When air pressure falls, rain is likely. A storm is possible.

Stormy weather approaching

217

Hurricane
Earl near the
Caribbean
Islands in 2010

Hurricanes and Tropical Storms

Hurricanes are wind systems that rotate around an eye, or center of low air pressure. Hurricanes form over warm tropical seas. They are classified on a scale from 1 to 5, with 5 being the most powerful storm. Katrina was category 4 as it approached the Gulf Coast of the United States.

Most hurricanes that hit the United States start as tropical storms in the Atlantic Ocean. They form during late summer and early fall when the ocean is warmest. As a tropical storm moves west, it draws energy from the warm ocean water. The storm gets larger and stronger, and the wind spins faster and faster.

The spinning wind draws a lot of warm water vapor high in the storm system. When the vapor cools, it condenses. Condensation releases even more energy, which makes the system spin even faster. When the hurricane reaches land, the winds are blowing at deadly speeds, up to 250 km per hour. The rain is very heavy. The wind and rain can cause a lot of destruction.

As soon as a hurricane moves over land, it begins to lose strength. It no longer has warm water to give it energy and water vapor. Within hours, the wind and rain drop to safe levels.

Thunderstorms

Thunderstorms form when an air mass at the ground is much warmer and more humid than the air above. Rapid convection begins. As the warm, humid air rises, the water vapor in it condenses. The condensing water vapor transfers energy to the surrounding air, causing the air to rise even higher. The rapid movement of air also creates a static electric charge in the clouds. When the static electricity discharges, lightning travels from the clouds to the ground, and you hear the sound of thunder. Thunderstorms can cause death, start fires, and destroy communications systems. The powerful winds and heavy rain can cause property damage.

Thunderstorms are most common over land during the afternoon. The Sun heats Earth's surface, and heat transfers to the air. When cold air flows under the warm, moist air, thunderstorms are possible.

Lightning travels from the clouds to the ground.

A tornado spinning through a city

Tornadoes

Tornadoes are powerful forms of wind. They most often happen in late afternoons in spring or summer. When cold air over the land runs into a mass of warm air, the warm air is forced upward violently. At the same time, cooler, more-dense air flows in from the sides and twists the rising warm air. A spinning funnel forms. It "sucks up" everything in its path like a giant vacuum cleaner. The air pressure inside the funnel is very low. The air pressure outside the funnel is much higher. The extreme difference in air pressure can create wind speeds of 400 km per hour or more. Tornadoes can seriously damage everything in their path.

Tornadoes are most common in the south central part of the United States, from Texas to Nebraska. Hundreds of tornadoes occur in this region each year. Warm, moist air from the Gulf of Mexico moves northward. It runs into cooler, drier air flowing down from Canada. This creates perfect conditions for tornadoes. That's why this part of the United States is called Tornado Alley.

A tornado over water is called a waterspout.

220

Hot and Cold

Hot and cold weather are the direct result of solar energy. It gets hot when energy from the Sun is intense. It gets cold when solar energy is low. The ocean also affects temperature. The highest and lowest temperatures are never close to the ocean. Water has the ability to absorb and release large amounts of energy without changing temperature much. This keeps places close to the ocean from getting really hot or really cold.

Death Valley is one of the hottest places on Earth.

Here is a table of temperature extremes for the United States and the world. These temperatures are deadly for most organisms. Only a few tough organisms are able to survive such temperatures.

Area	Location	High Temperature	Low Temperature
United States	Death Valley, California	57°C	
	Prospect Creek, Alaska		−62°C
World	Death Valley, California	57°C	
	Vostok, Antarctica		−89°C

Weather Extremes

The West Coast and Northeast region of North America do not have many hurricanes or tornadoes. But they do have weather extremes. Most of them involve the ocean.

During the winter, it often rains and snows along the East and West Coasts and in the western mountains. When large storms come in from the Atlantic or Pacific Ocean, wind and rain can cause property damage and flooding. In the mountains, the precipitation comes down as snow. Intense snowstorms are called **blizzards**. A single blizzard can drop 4 meters (m) or more of snow. The snow for a whole winter might exceed 10 m.

A blizzard can drop more than 4 meters (m) of snow.

An ice storm can cause a lot of damage.

221

The Pineapple Express is a band of warm, moist air that flows to the West Coast from the warm ocean around the Hawaiian Islands. When the warm, humid Pineapple Express meets cold air flowing down from Alaska, a violent winter storm can develop. High winds and heavy rain can uproot trees, destroy homes, and flood large areas of lowlands.

When seasonal rain and snow fail to develop, droughts can occur. A drought is less-than-normal precipitation. In the Southwest, this means less rain in the deserts and hills, and less snow in the mountains. Less snow means less spring runoff. Less runoff means less flow in rivers and streams. Lakes and ponds shrink and in some cases dry up completely. Soil moisture dries up, and ground water decreases. Reservoirs that people use to store water shrink.

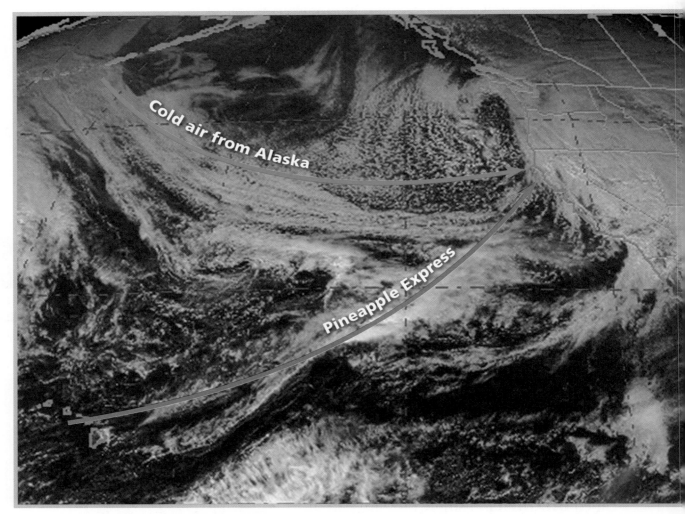

The Pineapple Express carries large amounts of moisture to California.

Water from lakes and rivers dries up during a drought.

Droughts put stress on natural and human communities. Fish and other aquatic organisms might die. Plants that are not adapted for dry environments might die. Reduced water for crops means less food production. People have to conserve water by using less and recycling water when possible.

Serious droughts are not uncommon. During the early 1930s, parts of Colorado, Kansas, New Mexico, Oklahoma, and Texas received little rain. Crops failed. Then came the strong winds. The farms in the area were stripped of their rich topsoil. The farmers had to leave the area because their fields were destroyed. Thousands of families had to leave the area known as the Dust Bowl.

Could it happen again? Many climate scientists think it is happening again now. The precipitation in the Southwest has been declining since the early years of this century. Stream flow and ground water are reduced. Reservoirs are low. The drought that has settled over the Southwest could be part of the overall change in the worldwide **climate**. People in the Southwest should be prepared to use less water. And they should be aware that a general drying of the land could result in more and hotter wildfires.

223

The Role of the Ocean in Weather

The ocean affects weather in the United States in several ways. The ocean is the source of most of the precipitation that falls on the West Coast states. Water evaporates from the ocean, particularly where the Sun has warmed the ocean's surface. Wind carries the water vapor and clouds over the land. As the moist air rises and cools over the coastal mountains, the Sierra Nevada, and the Cascade Range, the water vapor condenses and falls back to Earth's surface. During the spring and summer, the water flows back to the ocean, to complete the water cycle.

The ocean affects the weather.

The ocean creates mild temperatures all year along the West Coast. It rarely gets too hot or too cold. The temperature of the ocean doesn't change quickly. So the ocean keeps the air temperature near the coast even all year.

The ocean creates breezes near the coast. Because water heats up and cools down slowly, there is often a difference in the temperature of the land and the ocean. Uneven heating starts a convection current, which results in wind. The Sun and the ocean are responsible for ocean breezes.

Thinking about Severe Weather

1. What causes hurricanes?

2. What causes tornadoes?

3. How does the water cycle affect weather along the West Coast?

4. How does the ocean influence the weather along the West Coast?

Earth's Climates

What's the weather like today? What was it like last year on this same date? Probably just about the same. We can guess what the weather will be like tomorrow and next year at this time because weather tends to follow predictable patterns over long periods of time. The big patterns of weather define a region's climate. Climate describes the average or typical weather conditions in a region of the world. The climate in Hawaii is quite different from the climate in Wisconsin. The Hawaiian climate is warm, sunny, and pleasant all year long. The Wisconsin climate is freezing cold in the winter, and hot and humid during the summer.

There are about 12 general climate zones in North America. The two variables that are most important for determining a climate zone are the average temperature throughout the year and the amount of precipitation throughout the year.

This climate map shows the distribution of climate types in North America.

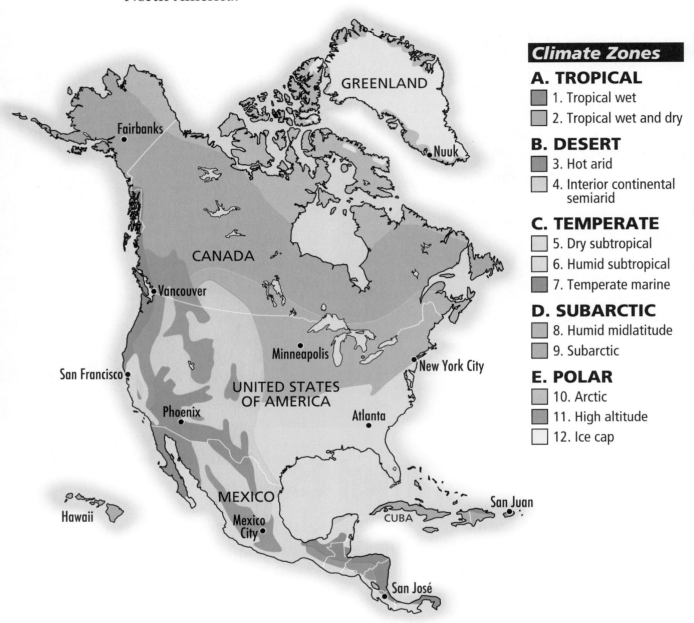

Climate Zones

A. TROPICAL
1. Tropical wet
2. Tropical wet and dry

B. DESERT
3. Hot arid
4. Interior continental semiarid

C. TEMPERATE
5. Dry subtropical
6. Humid subtropical
7. Temperate marine

D. SUBARCTIC
8. Humid midlatitude
9. Subarctic

E. POLAR
10. Arctic
11. High altitude
12. Ice cap

In the Midwest, you can be fairly sure that it will be cold and snowy in January and February and rainy during the summer each year. The same kind of weather will be experienced in Minnesota, Illinois, Connecticut, and Maine. The humid midlatitude climate zone includes the midwestern United States, New England, and the southern part of Canada. This climate zone supports huge diverse forests of deciduous and evergreen trees and all the animals that forests support.

The weather in the southeastern United States is significantly different. Florida, Mississippi, and Louisiana rarely have snow in the winter, and the summers and springs are rainy, hot, and humid. The southern states fall into the humid subtropical climate zone. This zone supports large hardwood forests and many kind of vines.

The hot arid climate zone in the western United States has predictably warm, dry winters and very hot, dry summers. Arizona and parts of Nevada, Utah, and California are sunny and dry all year. Little rain falls during most of the year. During the summer the temperature can be very high, and thunderstorms can deliver heavy rains that can cause flash floods. The hot arid zone supports a wide diversity of drought-resistant plants, including cactus, mesquite, and yucca, and a host of burrowing and sun-loving animals.

Four other climate zones occur in the west (see the climate map). The interior continental semiarid zone is characterized by warm spring and summer weather, cold winters, and summer thunderstorms with the possibility of tornadoes. The semiarid climate supports large expanses of sagebrush and huge grasslands. Land in the interior continental semiarid zone is often used by ranchers to graze livestock.

Humid subtropical zone

Hot arid zone

Interior continental semiarid zone

The high-altitude zone found high in the mountains supports large forests of evergreen trees and provides the right conditions for skiing and other winter sports requiring snow.

Weather in the dry subtropical zone is usually warm and rainy in the winter but hot and dry in the summer. The dry subtropical zone supports oak woodlands, chaparral, and a very diverse community of brush, grasses, and mixed forests. Dry subtropical climates are excellent for farming, fruit orchards, vegetable gardens, and raising livestock.

High-altitude zone

Dry subtropical zone

The temperate marine zone of the Pacific Northwest is cool and wet throughout the year. The climate is strongly influenced by the Pacific Ocean, which keeps the weather cool and moist. This climate zone is characterized by dense forests of large evergreen trees: redwood, fir, pine, and spruce. The moist forests are often home to ferns, mosses, lichens, and fungi. Winters are cool and rainy, while summers are cool and can be foggy and wet.

Two climate zones occur in Alaska. They are the subarctic and the arctic. The climate is extremely cold most of the year, with variable precipitation.

Hawaii has a tropical wet and dry climate, warm and sunny all year long with plenty of tropical rain in many parts of the islands.

Climates vary widely across the country. Many states have only one kind of climate throughout, such as Michigan, Massachusetts, Alabama, and Florida. Other states have two or more kinds of climate. Look at Texas and California. How many climate zones do these states have? So when you are asked what the weather will be like in California, you have to know what part of the state, and what time of year.

Temperate marine zone

Arctic zone

Tropical wet zone

Global Climate Change

Weather is the condition of the atmosphere in a particular place on Earth. Temperature, humidity, and wind describe the weather. The weather is different all over Earth, depending on where you are and the time of year. Climate is the average weather over many years in a region on Earth. The climate in Barrow, Alaska, is very different than the climate in Tahiti. Barrow's climate is extremely cold. The climate on the tropical island of Tahiti is very sunny and warm. Earth's climates are predictable today, but climates have changed many times throughout Earth's history.

Factors Affecting Climate through History

Temperature on Earth is affected by one major energy source, the Sun. The amount of solar energy (heat and light) given off by the Sun is steady day after day, and year after year. But there are many factors that affect the amount of solar energy that transfers to Earth.

An arctic climate

A tropical island climate

Ash from a volcano pollutes the air.

One factor that affects the amount of solar energy transferred to Earth is the amount of pollutants in the air. At times in Earth's history, volcanic eruptions, smoke from forest fires, and major impacts by asteroids and comets have put a lot of dust and many gases into the air. These pollutants act like a shield. They block solar energy from reaching Earth's surface. Smoke and dust that block solar energy can cool the climate in large regions of Earth.

The **greenhouse effect** is another factor that affects the amount of solar energy transferred to Earth. Carbon dioxide, methane, nitrous oxide, and water vapor are greenhouse gases. Greenhouse gases in the air act like a mirror. They let through solar energy, which Earth's surface absorbs. Then Earth's surface transfers the energy to the atmosphere. Once the solar energy is in the atmosphere, the greenhouse gases prevent the energy from easily escaping back into space. Heat builds up and the temperature of the atmosphere rises. The trapping of energy in the atmosphere is the greenhouse effect. It impacts climate worldwide.

The Greenhouse Effect

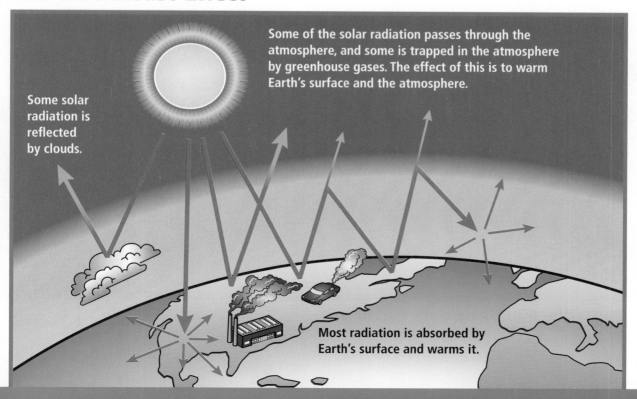

Some of the solar radiation passes through the atmosphere, and some is trapped in the atmosphere by greenhouse gases. The effect of this is to warm Earth's surface and the atmosphere.

Some solar radiation is reflected by clouds.

Most radiation is absorbed by Earth's surface and warms it.

What Is Changing Today?

Today, we are experiencing a period of rapid climate change. The average temperature worldwide has increased about 0.8 degrees Celsius (°C) since 1850. That doesn't sound like much. But think about how much energy it would take to warm all of Earth's atmosphere and the ocean that much. That's a lot of energy.

Scientists have developed climate models that suggest that the global temperature may increase by another 1.5°C–5°C by the year 2100. This temperature change will affect life on Earth and the global climate. Here's how Earth's climate may change.

The Sun rising over Earth

Rising sea level will flood coastal cities.

More farming land will change into desert.

Higher global temperature will cause glaciers and ice sheets to melt worldwide. The arctic polar ice pack will melt completely. Large areas of ice will melt from Greenland and Antarctica. All that melted ice will flow into the ocean and cause the sea level to rise. By 2100, sea level is expected to rise 0.6 meters (m) or more. That is enough to flood many of the low-lying regions of the world. Large parts of Florida, a number of small islands in the Pacific Ocean, and the city of Venice, Italy, would be under water.

As Earth gets warmer, more land will change into desert. Land now used for farming in north central Africa and central Asia will become desert. As a result, the world will produce less food. Food may become more scarce in many parts of the world.

Too much carbon dioxide in the air causes climate change.

What Is Causing Climate Change?

Scientists agree that the major cause of climate change is human activity. The burning of fossil fuels is the number-one human activity affecting climate change. Fossil fuels are the remains of organisms that lived long ago. Over time, those remains changed into oil, coal, and natural gas. When fossil fuels burn, they release carbon dioxide into the air. Humans burn fossil fuels to generate electricity and to power cars.

Carbon dioxide is found naturally in air. In fact, it is essential to life on Earth. Plants use carbon dioxide in the air to produce food by photosynthesis. But since the Industrial Revolution in the 19th century, humans have been releasing more carbon dioxide into the atmosphere than all the plants in the world can absorb. The result is a lot of carbon dioxide in the air. Carbon dioxide is a greenhouse gas. The more carbon dioxide gas we put into the atmosphere, the faster Earth's temperature will rise.

What Can We Do?

So how can we slow climate change? The best way is to stop adding carbon dioxide to the air. But individuals can't make that global decision alone. Governments and big companies need to get involved. For example, the decision to stop burning coal to produce electricity affects many people, because there would be no electricity in their homes. Before we can stop burning fossil fuels to generate electricity, we need to create alternative sources of electricity. Here are some alternative sources for producing electricity.

Wind turbines (windmills) change wind energy into electricity.

Solar energy generates electricity directly with sunlight and solar cells. Solar energy can also produce electricity indirectly by using a large number of curved mirrors as solar collectors. The mirrors focus the Sun's energy on water flowing through a tube. The heated water produces steam that turns electric generators.

A wind farm

A group of solar cells

A system of solar collectors using mirrors

235

Geothermal energy produces electricity with hot water and steam from volcanic vents to turn generators.

Hydroelectric generators use water flowing through turbines to produce electricity.

Thermonuclear reactions in nuclear power plants create heat to produce steam. The steam turns electric generators to produce electricity.

These alternative sources of electricity are carbon-free. They don't release any carbon into the air. But each alternative source of electricity has its own challenges. If we are going to provide alternative energy to large numbers of homes, it needs to be reliable, safe, and accessible to everyone. We need to develop the technology to convert these primary energy sources (wind, moving water, sunlight, and volcanic vents) into electricity that can be used on a large scale.

A geothermal power plant

A hydroelectric power plant

A nuclear power plant

You can help conserve energy by riding a bike instead of riding in a car.

What Can You Do Right Now?

The most important thing you can do to slow climate change is to conserve energy. Energy used in your home and for transportation is where most of the carbon dioxide in the air comes from. So the next time you need to get from one place to another, don't ask for a ride in the car. Instead, maybe you can walk, or ride your bike or skateboard. Use your own energy instead of carbon energy to get around. And you will get some exercise, too!

At home, you can replace burned-out lightbulbs with compact fluorescent lightbulbs. These use a lot less electricity to produce the same amount of light. If your family needs a new appliance, like a refrigerator, freezer, or water heater, suggest an energy-efficient appliance. You can also adjust the thermostat in your home so it is not too cool or too warm. In the winter, put on a sweater instead of turning up the heat. In the summer, wear lightweight clothes, and enjoy the warmth.

What other ways can you conserve energy? Become an energy detective at school. Find ways your school can conserve energy.

A compact fluorescent lightbulb

Life Science

FOSS Science Resources

Living Systems

Table of Contents

Introduction to Systems

Have you heard of the solar system? You probably know that it is the Sun, Earth, Moon, Mars, Venus, and all the other planets and their moons. But why is it called the solar *system*? Solar refers to the Sun, but what is a **system**?

A system is a collection of **interacting** parts. The parts work together to create a structure or produce an action. In the solar system, the parts include the Sun and the planets and their moons. The interactions are the motions of the objects and the force of gravity that holds them together. Gravity and the collection of objects work together as a system.

A pair of scissors is a system. It has two levers with sharp edges. Your hand applies force to the ends of the two levers. The cutting edges apply force to the material between the blades. This system cuts through the material.

The solar system is huge and complex. A pair of scissors is small and simple. Both systems are collections of interacting parts.

A bridge is a system.

A tower is part of a cell phone system.

A bridge is also a system of interacting parts. The parts include steel girders, steel cables, bolts, and concrete supports. The bridge system is a structure that is solid and stable. Bridges don't move much, but they support the weight of the traffic traveling across them.

If you look closely, you can find systems everywhere. Some systems are industrial, like a waste-water treatment plant. Some systems are social, like a hospital or school. Some systems are technological, like the cellular telephone system and the Internet. Some systems are natural, like the migration of monarch butterflies and the cycle of the tides. Some systems are cultural, like baseball. What systems can you think of?

Thinking about Systems

Here is a list of eight systems. Can you think of three or four parts of each system?

1. Refrigerator
2. Skateboard
3. Sunglasses
4. Helium balloon
5. Flashlight
6. Hot dog
7. Sleeping bag
8. Belt

Is Earth a System?

Our planet, Earth, is a really big object, with many interacting parts. Interacting parts! That sounds like Earth might be a system.

Earth has a core made of iron and nickel. Around the core is a thick layer of rock called the mantle. The outside surface of Earth is covered by a thin, hard, rocky crust. The core, mantle, and crust are a system called the **geosphere**. But there is more to Earth than just the geosphere.

Much of Earth is covered by water. Most of the water is in the ocean. A lot of water is in rivers, streams, lakes, ponds, and underground. And more water is stored in huge masses of ice in Greenland, Antarctica, and glaciers. Water is in the air as invisible water vapor and as clouds and fog. The interacting water on, under, and above Earth's surface is a system called the **hydrosphere**.

Above Earth's surface is the **atmosphere**. The atmosphere is a system of interacting gases called air.

Earth's crust, ocean, lakes, ponds, streams, and air are home to millions of plants and animals. This is the **biosphere**. The biosphere is a system of interacting living organisms.

So yes, Earth is a system. The huge Earth system includes the geosphere, hydrosphere, atmosphere, and biosphere. Perhaps the most interesting part of the Earth system is the biosphere. Think about it for a second. What are the parts of the biosphere? What are some of your interacting parts? How do they work together to make the biosphere?

Living organisms in a tide pool are part of the biosphere.

Earth's atmosphere

The Biosphere

The biosphere is all of the organisms living on Earth. Some of the interacting parts live in the North Atlantic Ocean **ecosystem**. The North Atlantic organisms are very different from the organisms living in a coral reef ecosystem or in a desert ecosystem. Everywhere you go, you find different kinds of ecosystems. Each ecosystem has its own kind of organisms.

An ecosystem is part of the biosphere. Every ecosystem has thousands of interacting parts. Each kind of organism is a part of the ecosystem in which it lives. For instance, the Sonoran Desert ecosystem includes saguaro cacti, mesquite trees, Gila woodpeckers, elf owls, horned lizards, sphinx moths, milkweed bugs, harvester ants, kangaroo rats, coyotes, and many other organisms. Organisms interact with one another in many ways.

Food Chains and Food Webs

Food chains and **food webs** are systems of interacting organisms. A food chain simply describes a feeding relationship among a few organisms. A food web is a more complex system showing all the feeding relationships in an ecosystem.

Organisms that make their own food are called **producers**. In **terrestrial** ecosystems, the most important producers are plants. Grasses, trees, and bushes, are producers. In freshwater and ocean ecosystems, algae and **phytoplankton** are the most important producers. Producers make their own food from sunlight, water, **minerals**, and **carbon dioxide** (CO_2).

Animals are **consumers**. Consumers get their food by eating plants or other animals. Plant or animal material that is not eaten is consumed by **bacteria** and **fungi**. Bacteria and fungi are **decomposers**. After decomposition, only minerals are left. The minerals help produce the next generation of plants.

Food Chains

When a spider eats a fly, the matter and **energy** in the fly go to the spider. This feeding relationship can be shown with an arrow. The arrow always points in the direction that the matter and energy flow.

fly   **spider**

If a praying mantis eats a spider, the matter and energy in the spider go to the praying mantis.

fly   **spider**   **praying mantis**

It's possible in a woodland ecosystem for a blue jay to eat the praying mantis, a weasel to eat the blue jay, and a hawk to eat the weasel. Matter and energy pass from one organism to the next when they are eaten. This is called a food chain. And at the beginning of the food chain is a producer. Energy for producers comes from the Sun.

In this case, the producer is a fruit from a tree, a plum. You can draw arrows from one organism to the next to describe a food chain. The arrows show the direction of energy flow. They point from the organism that is eaten to the organism that eats it.

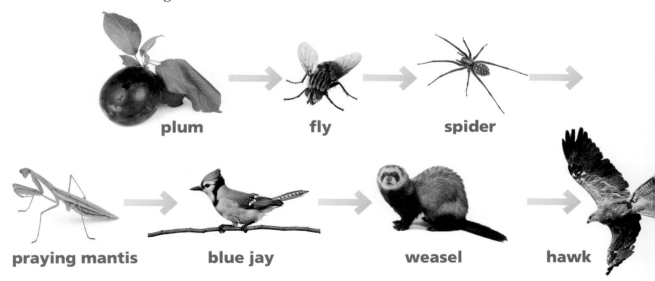

plum   **fly**   **spider**

praying mantis   **blue jay**   **weasel**   **hawk**

Another example of a food chain might have grass as the producer. A chipmunk eats the grass seed. A hawk eats the chipmunk. Bacteria decompose any dead organisms or uneaten parts. You can always draw arrows from dead organisms to the decomposers.

A simple food chain

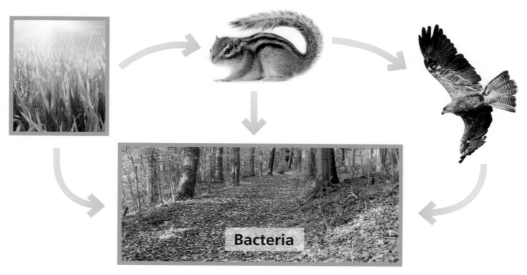

Bacteria

Food Webs

There are many feeding relationships in an ecosystem. If you draw *all* the arrows that show who eats whom, you have a food web, not a food chain. The food web for a freshwater river might look like this.

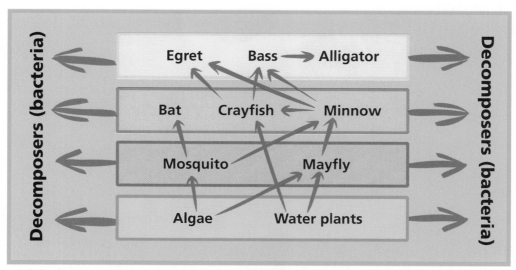

This is an example of a food web for a freshwater river. Bacteria decompose all the organisms when they die.

Locate the crayfish in the example of a food web. Crayfish are food for both egrets and bass. If the river has a lot of crayfish, egrets and bass will both have plenty to eat. But if there are few crayfish, the egrets and bass will have to **compete** with each other for food.

The animal that can get more food is the one that is more likely to survive. In this river ecosystem, egrets and bass compete for crayfish. Are there other competitions for food in the ecosystem?

Organisms in ecosystems depend on one another for the food they need to survive. Herbivores depend on producers to make food. Carnivores depend on consumers for food. Omnivores depend on both producers and consumers for food. Decomposers depend on dead organisms and waste for food. And producers depend on decomposers for raw materials to make food. In a healthy ecosystem, some organisms will be eaten so that other organisms will survive.

Egrets eat crayfish.

Your body has many different systems for different functions.

Your eye is part of the system that helps you see.

Human Systems

You are an organism, living in an ecosystem, interacting with many other organisms in many ways. That means you are part of a system. But are *you* a system?

You do many different functions, including moving, seeing, hearing, eating, smelling, tasting, thinking, talking, and breathing. Each function is performed by a different system in your body.

When you run across the schoolyard, two systems are interacting. Your skeleton is a system of 206 strong, hard bones in many sizes and shapes. Attached to your bones is a system of hundreds of muscles. The bones and muscles work together as you run.

Seeing uses a system that includes your eyes, which convert light into electrical pulses. The electrical pulses travel along nerves into your **brain**. Hearing is a similar system, including an outer ear, inner ear, nerves, and the brain. Smell and taste have systems of **receptors**, nerves, and brain centers.

As you can see, you are a system of subsystems. And you are a subsystem in an ecosystem, which is a subsystem of the Earth system. And Earth is one planet in the solar system, which is one planetary system in the Milky Way Galaxy. The universe is an endless system of subsystems.

Thinking about the Biosphere

1. What is a simple definition of the biosphere on Earth?

2. What is an ecosystem?

3. What is one way that organisms interact in an ecosystem?

4. What is the role of producers in an ecosystem?

5. How might human actions affect the food web in a woodland or a freshwater river?

Monterey Bay

Monterey Bay National Marine Sanctuary

Much of the northern California coast is rocks and cliffs. The ocean water is very cold all year. During the winter and spring, huge waves from the Pacific Ocean crash on the rugged shore. Can anything live in this difficult environment?

The answer is yes. The northern California coast is one of the most diverse and productive ecosystems on Earth. Thousands of different kinds of organisms live and interact in the cold ocean water. This ecosystem is protected in the Monterey Bay National Marine Sanctuary. *Marine* means "ocean" or "sea." A sanctuary is a protected place. This is one place where scientists can study the interactions between ocean organisms and their environment.

The Kelp Forest

Giant kelp grows in most of the 15,783-square-kilometer (km) sanctuary. Kelp looks like a plant, but it is actually algae. Like plants, algae make their own food.

Giant kelp are anchored to the seabed and reach clear to the ocean surface. In some places, the distance is more than 100 meters (m) to the surface. This makes the kelp taller than the tallest trees. For this reason, the California marine ecosystem is often called the kelp forest.

Like the rain forest, the kelp forest has a floor, an understory, and a large canopy. The canopy spreads across the water's surface. But, unlike the rain forest, most of the organisms do not live in the canopy. Most live in the understory and on the floor. Every bit of the rocky bottom has animals clinging to it. These include clams, scallops, mussels, barnacles, limpets, abalones, snails, sponges, sea urchins, sea stars, shrimp, and sea anemones. Every crack and cave shelters a fish, an eel, a crab, or an octopus.

A kelp forest

Fish live in the understory. There are small fish such as anchovies and sardines, medium-sized fish such as sea bass, snappers, and perch, and large fish such as groupers and sharks. The California state marine fish is the bright orange garibaldi. It also lives here. Other animals found in the understory are squids, jellyfish, seals, sea lions, and gray whales.

An orange garibaldi

The canopy provides shelter for a number of small animals that live on and around the kelp. These include snails, crabs, barnacles, and kelp fish. The canopy is a resting and hunting place for sea otters, seabirds, gulls, terns, ospreys, and ducks.

Where do all these animals get the food they need to survive? Like all ecosystems, the kelp forest depends on producers. The giant algae provide matter and energy to the ecosystem, but only a small amount. Microscopic phytoplankton are the most important producers in this ecosystem. These tiny producers (the grass of the sea) are eaten by **zooplankton**. Zooplankton are eaten by baby fish (kelp fish), clams, crabs, and thousands of other organisms. Small fish and crabs are eaten by larger fish (sea bass). The food produced by the phytoplankton eventually feeds the sea lions and sharks at the top of the food web. Marine bacteria decompose all the dead organisms in the ocean ecosystem.

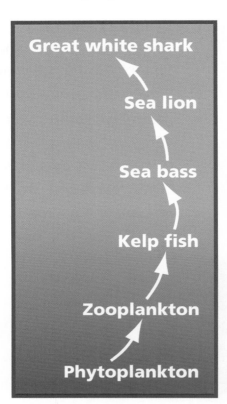

Great white shark
↑
Sea lion
↑
Sea bass
↑
Kelp fish
↑
Zooplankton
↑
Phytoplankton

Monterey Bay food chain

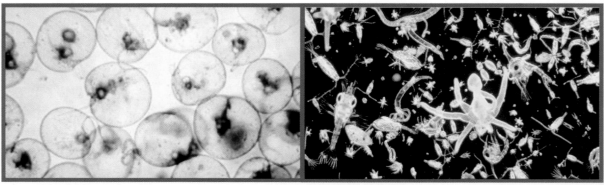

Phytoplankton   **Zooplankton**

Competition for Resources

There is a lot of competition for phytoplankton in the marine ecosystem. The zooplankton that have the best structures for catching phytoplankton will be most successful. This is one example of competition for food.

There is also competition for space. Waves and currents are very strong in the coastal environment. Many organisms must attach firmly to a solid surface or be washed away. The rocky bottom of the ocean is completely covered with organisms.

Kelp forest organisms compete for shelter. Caves, cracks, and old shells are used as hiding places. There is life-or-death competition for places to attach and hide.

This is a hermit crab. Hermit crabs live in empty snail shells. What kind of competition do you think they have in the ecosystem?

Thinking about Marine Ecosystems

1. What do you think happens to waste and dead animals in marine ecosystems?

2. What is the most important producer in both freshwater and marine ecosystems?

3. Identify three ways organisms compete in marine ecosystems.

A terrestrial ecosystem

Comparing Aquatic and Terrestrial Ecosystems

Aquatic and terrestrial ecosystems are very different. But they are the same in some ways. Let's compare.

The **nonliving** factors of the two environments are different. **Aquatic** ecosystems are in water. Terrestrial ecosystems are on land. The temperature in an aquatic ecosystem changes slowly. The temperature in a terrestrial ecosystem can change rapidly over a short period of time. The amount of water in an aquatic ecosystem is predictable. Water in a terrestrial ecosystem can vary widely.

The organisms are different in the two ecosystems. Most aquatic organisms can live only in water. If they were moved to a terrestrial ecosystem, they would die. The same is true for terrestrial organisms moved into aquatic ecosystems.

An aquatic ecosystem

256

A heron is a consumer of crayfish in an aquatic ecosystem.

A fox is a consumer of mice in a terrestrial ecosystem.

Both ecosystems, however, are organized in similar ways. The organisms in aquatic and terrestrial ecosystems all need matter and energy to stay alive.

- Both ecosystems obtain energy from the Sun and matter from the environment.
- Both have food chains and food webs.
- Both have consumers that depend on producers to make food.
- Both have decomposers that break down dead organisms and recycle the raw materials (**nutrients**).
- Herbivores, carnivores, omnivores, and scavengers live in both ecosystems.

In both ecosystems, organisms compete for the resources they need to survive. Plants compete for light. Animals compete for food. Organisms need space and shelter from predators and changes in the nonliving environment. The organism that outcompetes the others is the organism that will survive.

Nature's Recycling System

Think of a tree. Like any organism, the tree will eventually die and fall to the forest floor. What happens to it? Does it pile up with other dead trees, plants, and animals, year after year?

When a tree falls in the forest, it is used for food by decomposers. Organisms that feed on dead trees are called **detritivores**. Some detritivores, such as beetle larvae and worms, dig into the trunks and eat the dead bark and wood. As they eat through the wood, the tree starts to fall apart. Other detritivores, such as termites, dig in and consume more of the wood. As the wood is exposed, fungi and bacteria move in. They consume the last of the wood and the waste left behind by the first decomposers. After several years, all that remains is minerals.

Animal bones, dead leaves, twigs, and fruit are organic matter called detritus.

Let's look more closely at the recycling system. In the deciduous forest of the eastern United States, **detritus** is most visible in fall. Then you are sure to see a layer of dead leaves and twigs, a few large tree limbs, and whole fallen trees. You might see a feather or a clump of fur left behind by a bird or raccoon, or scat (a pile of animal waste). You might find seeds and fallen fruit. You could find a piece of snake skin, or the bones of an animal. All of these bits of organic matter are detritus, and detritus is part of every healthy ecosystem.

You might think that detritus is waste and trash. But decomposers use this accumulation as food. The first decomposers to use the detritus are the detritivores. They concentrate on the largest parts of the detritus layer. Animals like termites, beetle larvae, isopods, and worms start to eat the fallen leaves, and dead wood. As they eat the dead matter, the mass of detritus decreases slowly. The detritivores leave waste of their own, which becomes detritus.

Termites eat wood and other detritus.

Detritus worms are different from earthworms. Detritus worms live in the dead leaf layer. Earthworms burrow into the soil, where they live under the detritus layer. One common detritus worm is called the redworm, or red wiggler. Home composters use redworms to decompose kitchen waste into rich fertilizer for gardens.

After the detritivores have chopped everything up, the real decomposers (bacteria and fungi) get to work. Bacteria and fungi work at the microscopic level. Bacteria don't have **mouths**. Instead, they leak chemicals onto the detritus. The chemicals dissolve nutritious materials from the detritus. The bacteria soak up the dissolved materials. Then they move on to the next bit of organic matter to repeat the process. Fungi get their nutrients the same way. When the fungi and bacteria are finished, the detritus has been reduced to simple minerals. The bacteria soak up the dissolved nutrients. Plants use these minerals to produce food. Then, the system starts again.

Redworms are detritus worms used in composting.

Fungi decompose dead trees.

Mushrooms are fungi.

There's Yeast in My Bread!

If you ever watched someone make bread, you might have noticed that they added a light brown material called yeast to the dough. What is yeast, and why add it to the dough?

Yeast

Yeast is a kind of fungus. You might have heard of some other kinds of fungus. Mildew is a kind of fungus that grows on organic materials like paper and leather. Mushrooms are the visible part of fungi that live on organic matter in the soil. These fungi are distant relatives of the yeast used to make bread.

One baker's yeast organism is a single **cell**. A single yeast cell is way too small to be seen with unaided eyes. With a microscope, you can see that one yeast organism is a tiny round object.

Why put fungus in your bread dough? Yeast eats **sugar**. When a yeast cell takes in a molecule of sugar, it breaks it down to use it for energy. The yeast breaks several carbon atoms off the sugar molecule. The carbon atoms combine with **oxygen**, forming carbon dioxide (CO_2) gas. The carbon dioxide produced by the yeast creates thousands of tiny bubbles in the dough. The dough rises as it fills with gas bubbles. The bubbles make the bread light and soft.

Where does the sugar that feeds the yeast come from? Some bread recipes call for a little sugar, but extra sugar is not necessary. Wheat flour contains a lot of starch and a small amount of a chemical called an enzyme. The enzyme breaks down the starch molecules into simpler molecules. Some of these molecules are sugar. The sugar that the yeast eats is from the starch in the flour. It takes time for the enzyme to act on the starch. So it can take several hours for bread to rise.

Next time you have a slice of bread, look closely at its texture. It is all full of holes, like a sponge. The holes were carbon dioxide bubbles. And remember, when you are eating a piece of bread, you are eating millions of baked yeast cells. Yum!

The holes in bread are the result of carbon dioxide bubbles.

Producers

Plants produce their own food. The food is sugar. The sugar is used by all plant cells. The cells use the energy in the sugar for growth.

Plants use a process called **photosynthesis** to make sugar for growth. The raw materials that plants use to make the sugar are water and carbon dioxide (CO_2). Water from the soil and carbon dioxide from the air combine with light energy from the Sun. Sugar, oxygen, and water are the products.

Most plants are green. Or at least they have a lot of green leaves. Leaves look green because the leaf cells have **chlorophyll**. Chlorophyll can absorb blue and red light. It reflects green light. That's why chlorophyll looks green.

The important part is that chlorophyll absorbs blue and red light. The energy from the absorbed blue and red light is then used to make the sugar molecules during photosynthesis. Sugar is the energy nutrient used by the plant cells to perform their life functions.

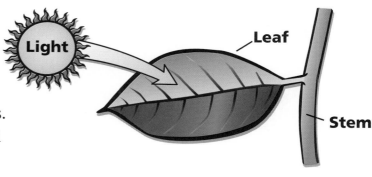

The green leaf cells make sugar out of carbon dioxide (CO_2) and water (H_2O). Carbon dioxide comes from the air. Water comes from the soil, up through the roots. The carbon dioxide and water meet in the green cells.

The carbon dioxide, water, and energy from the Sun combine to make sugar molecules in the plant's cells. The cells also produce oxygen and water molecules. The oxygen is released into the air. The plant reuses water or releases it into the air as water vapor (gas). So where is food produced? Food is produced in the green parts of the plant. Every cell that contains chlorophyll is making sugar.

Water from the roots, carbon dioxide from the air, and light from the Sun enter the cells.

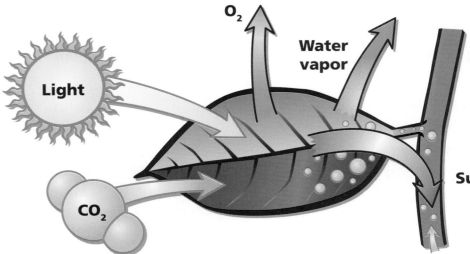

Carbon dioxide, water, and light combine to make sugar. Oxygen (O_2) and water are released into the air.

The Carbon Dioxide-Oxygen Cycle

Through the process of photosynthesis, producers release oxygen to the air. This is very important to the biosphere. Animals and most other living things need oxygen to live. Even plants need oxygen for their life functions. Producers release more oxygen than they use. Carbon dioxide is released as a waste gas by animals and other living things. Producers use that gas to produce more oxygen. This carbon dioxide-oxygen cycle is very important to the health of the biosphere.

Plants

Animals

Food production doesn't stop there. Plants use the sugar to produce a lot of other molecules. They produce other kinds of sugars with names like sucrose, dextrose, and fructose. They produce starches, which store energy in potatoes and grains like wheat. They produce vegetable oils, such as corn oil, sunflower oil, and olive oil.

Plants store energy as sugars, starches, and oils. When the plant needs them, it pulls them out of storage, turns them back into **glucose**, and sends the glucose to the cells. That's how plants survive at night and during winter. They use stored energy to do whatever they need to do.

Other organisms use the energy stored by plants to live and survive. That includes humans. When you eat a slice of bread or a baked potato, you are eating energy stored by a plant. When you eat lettuce and carrots, you are eating sugars, starches, and all the cells made by plants. And when you eat food to nourish your cells, remember where the food came from. It started as carbon dioxide, water, and sunlight. It's really quite amazing when you stop to think about it. You are running on solar energy.

The Sun's energy is used by producers to make their own food. Then, that energy is transferred to you when you eat a plant.

Thinking about Photosynthesis

1. What is sugar?

2. What raw materials do plants need for growth? Where do those materials come from?

3. What is the role played by chlorophyll?

4. What are the products of photosynthesis? Where do they go?

5. Where do plants produce food?

6. Explain how the Sun's energy is transferred through a simple food chain.

Getting Nutrients

All animals, fungi, and many bacteria consume other organisms to get the nutrition they need to live and survive. These organisms are called heterotrophs. Plants, algae, and some bacteria produce their own food, so they do not need to eat other organisms. These producers are called autotrophs. Heterotrophs get their nutrients by eating other organisms or parts of organisms, alive or dead, for food.

Food is important for two reasons. It provides building blocks for growth, development, and system repair. And food is the source of energy that organisms need to live.

Autotrophs produce their own food.

Heterotrophs consume plants and other animals.

267

An adult butterfly

Butterfly Nutrition

Butterflies start life as a tiny egg. When the egg hatches, the tiny larva, called a caterpillar, must eat. Every kind of butterfly has a particular kind of plant that it uses for food. Painted lady larvae feed on mallow plants. The mallow plant is an autotroph. It produces food from carbon dioxide (CO_2), water, and sunlight. The leaves are made of **carbohydrates**, lipids, and proteins, nutrients that the caterpillar needs to live. The caterpillar nibbles off bits of leaf with its biting jaws and swallows them. The caterpillar's gut digests the leaf bits. **Digestion** releases the nutrients that the caterpillar uses to grow. The caterpillar grows and grows, laying in a supply of fat.

When the caterpillar reaches full size, it finds a proper location, attaches itself, hangs down, and pupates. Inside its protective covering, the caterpillar changes into its flying phase. The insect does not eat during this change. It uses energy and matter stored in its body to construct wings, legs, and a new system for feeding.

Butterfly life cycle

After a couple of weeks, the hard outer **membrane** splits. The adult butterfly climbs out and flexes its wings. After pumping fluid into the wing veins, the new painted lady can fly. The adult needs to feed in order to survive. The painted lady's **digestive system** has changed completely. The painted lady no longer has biting jaws for nibbling on leaves. Its mouth has changed into a long, thin tube called a proboscis. The tube is used to suck sweet nectar from flowers. Nectar is a good source of sugar. Sugar provides energy for the butterfly. Flying requires a lot of energy, so access to an energy-rich food source improves the butterfly's chances of survival.

While the butterfly is going about its business, all of the other organisms in the ecosystem are going about their business, too. Animals in the ecosystem are looking for food. The blue jay is always alert for his next meal. If he spots a painted lady larva munching on a mallow leaf, he will likely swoop down and gobble it up.

Blue jays eat butterflies.

Human Nutrition

How do *you* get your food? You are a player at all levels of a food pyramid. When you eat spinach, carrots, apples, or green beans, you are eating producers. Animals that eat producers are primary consumers, like humans and cattle. When you eat a piece of roast beef, you are eating a primary consumer.

When you eat a sardine, you are eating a secondary consumer. Secondary consumers eat primary consumers. Sardines eat little primary consumers called zooplankton such as copepods and fish and crab larvae. Zooplankton eat producers called phytoplankton. If you have a piece of salmon, you are eating a third-level consumer. The salmon eats the sardine (a secondary consumer). So, when you eat the salmon, you are acting as a fourth-level consumer.

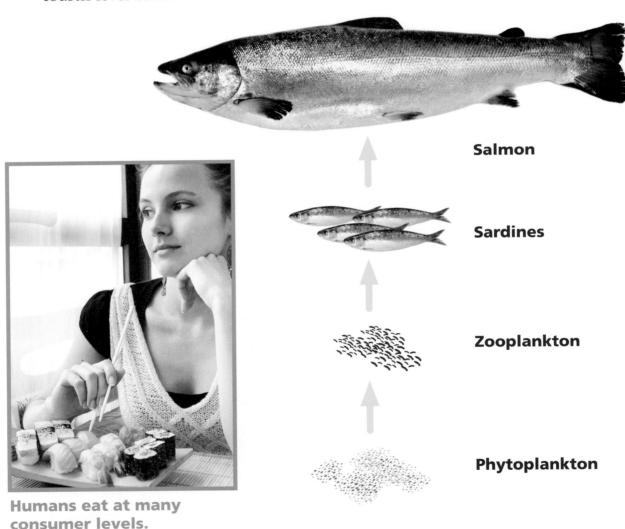

Salmon

Sardines

Zooplankton

Phytoplankton

Humans eat at many consumer levels.

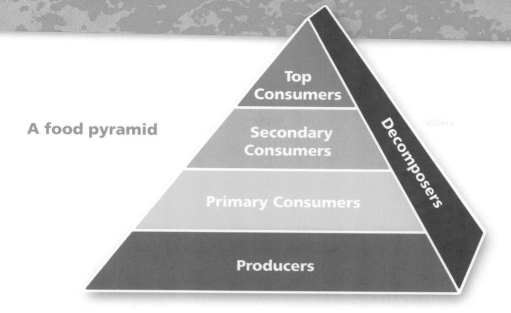

A food pyramid

Humans are aggressive top consumers, like tigers, sharks, orcas, and eagles. But unlike those animals, we can also eat lower on the food pyramid.

How do you extract the nutrients you need from your food? You eat to feed the trillions of living cells that make up your body. The process of breaking human food into nutrients for cells is called digestion. Cells get energy and raw materials from three groups of nutrients. They are carbohydrates, fats, and proteins.

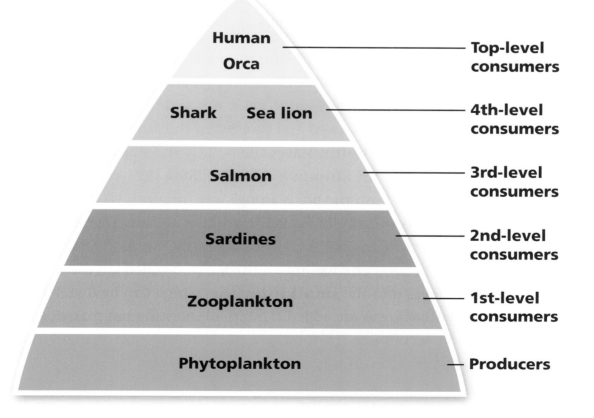

The Human Digestive System

Turning cheese, crackers, meat, vegetables, and fruit juice into nutrients for cells starts in your mouth. Your mouth is the beginning of a disassembly line for food. **Teeth** cut, mash, and grind up large pieces of food. **Saliva** mixes with the food to get it wet and to help break down the food. When you have chewed and moistened the food, you swallow it.

A wad of food, called a **bolus**, leaves the mouth and starts down the **esophagus** toward the **stomach**. Muscles along the length of the esophagus contract to push the bolus along. Your stomach is not just a place where a meal is stored. Things get rough down there. Digestive juices, including acid, are added to the food. Muscles in the stomach squeeze and mash the food. The food changes into a thick liquid called chyme.

The chyme moves into the **small intestine**, which can be 6 meters (m) long. More digestive juices are added. The small intestine has many bacteria. They attack and decompose the food you ate. Here the food changes into nutrients that your cells can use.

The small intestine is lined with millions of **capillaries**. Nutrients pass through the walls of the intestine into the capillaries. The blood carries the nutrients throughout your body, providing building blocks and energy for cells.

The last bits of the food move from the small intestine into the **large intestine** and **colon**. By this time, most nutrients are gone. Bacteria in the colon break down the remaining usable food. Water is extracted also. The remaining material contains fiber, other indigestible material, and dead bacteria. It is called feces. The feces moves into the rectum and is eliminated through the anus.

Because humans are animals, we cannot make our own food. We have to eat food to get our nutrients. Every cell in **multicellular organisms** needs nutrients. The digestive system breaks complex food sources into simple chemicals (nutrients). Those simple chemicals enter the blood and are transported to all the cells.

Food provides the nutrients our bodies need to survive.

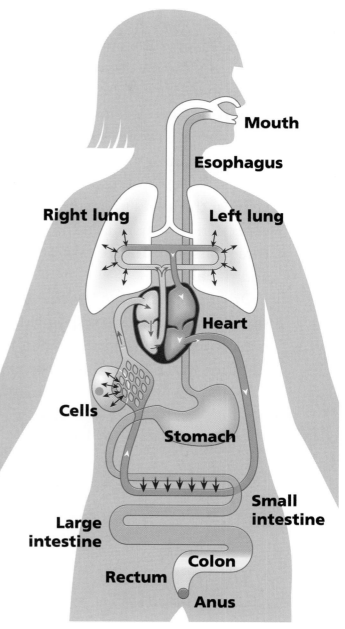

Mouth

Esophagus

Right lung

Left lung

Heart

Cells

Stomach

Small intestine

Large intestine

Colon

Rectum

Anus

Leaf Classification

A Japanese maple tree

Most **vascular plants** have leaves. The leaves on one kind of plant are different from the leaves on other kinds of plants. Scientists can use leaves to identify plants. But with so many different kinds of plants in the world, how do scientists use leaves to identify plants? The answer is **classification** systems.

Leaves have properties that can be used to organize them into groups, or classes. In class, you used the pattern of veins in the leaves to organize your leaf collection. You organized the leaves into three classes, **palmate**, **pinnate**, and **parallel**.

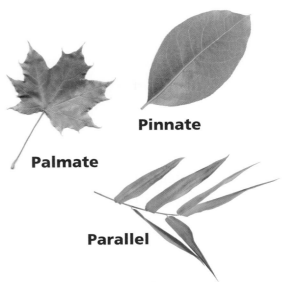

Pinnate

Palmate

Parallel

Other properties can be used to **classify** leaves, too. Leaves have shape. Some are long and pointed. Others are round. Leaves can even be fan shaped, triangular, or heart shaped. You can classify leaves by the shape of the **blade**.

Fan   **Round**   **Heart**   **Compound**

Spear   **Needle**   **Triangle**

The edges of leaves, called **margins**, are different from one another. Margins can be toothed, lobed, scalloped, fuzzy, or smooth. You can classify leaves by their margins.

Toothed   **Lobed**   **Scalloped**

Fuzzy   **Smooth**

Leaves are not the only way to classify plants. Whole plants can be classified. They can be organized into grasses, clovers, cacti, sagebrushes, palms, and so on. Any collection can be classified. Rocks can be classified by the minerals they contain or by form. A collection of rocks can be divided into a set that contains mica, a set that contains calcite, a set that contains quartz, and so on. The same collection of rocks can be classified again into sets of igneous, sedimentary, and metamorphic rocks.

Classification is one way to organize information about the natural world. By putting things together that have the same properties or behaviors, the complex world becomes a little easier to understand.

Thinking about Leaf Classification

1. What is classification?

2. What are three different ways you can classify leaves?

3. If you had a collection of insects, how would you classify them?

Plant Vascular Systems

General Sherman is the biggest living organism in the world. General Sherman is the name of a giant redwood tree living in Sequoia National Park in California. This giant tree stands over 85 meters (m) tall and is 11 m wide at the base.

Like all living organisms, General Sherman is a system made of living cells. Every cell needs water, nutrients, gases, and waste removal. How do all of General Sherman's billions of cells get the resources they need to survive?

General Sherman is a vascular plant. *Vascular* means "containing vessels." You have vessels called **arteries** and **veins**. Many plants have vessels, too. Other vascular plants include wildflowers, sagebrush, cacti, orange trees, lettuce, strawberries, wheat, peas, and celery. All vascular plants have a system of tubes running through them. These **specialized structures transport** nutrients to all the cells.

General Sherman is the world's largest living organism.

276

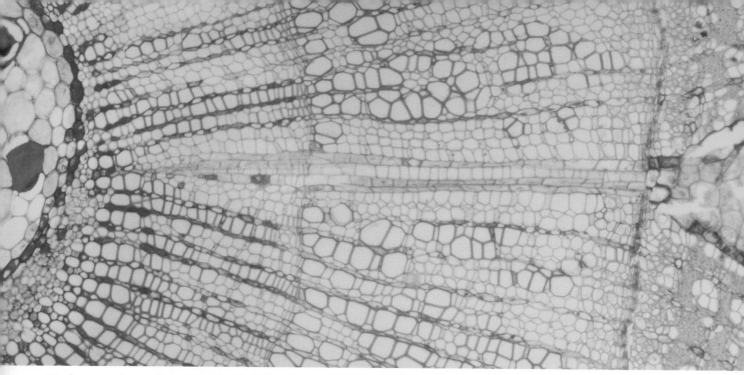

Xylem tubes (stained pink) carry water and minerals from the roots to the cells in the plant.

Xylem

Vascular plants have roots that reach deep into the soil. The roots take up water from the soil. The water enters long, hollow tubes called **xylem**. The xylem tubes start as long cells that are connected end to end. When the tubes are complete, the cells die. The resulting tubes transport water and minerals to the cells at the very top of General Sherman and to all the other living cells as well.

If you cut across the trunk of a tree, you can see the xylem tubes. New xylem cells grow all the time. The old xylem tubes form the main trunk of the tree. We call the old xylem cells wood.

Old xylem cells can be seen as rings in tree trunks.

Phloem

The green leaves of plants produce sugar. The sugar is the food used by all the cells in the plant. Some cells, like root cells and flower cells, do not make sugar. They need to get sugar from the cells that make it.

Vascular plants have a second kind of tube called **phloem**. Phloem tubes transport a sugar-rich liquid called **sap**. The phloem delivers sugar to every living cell that cannot make its own sugar.

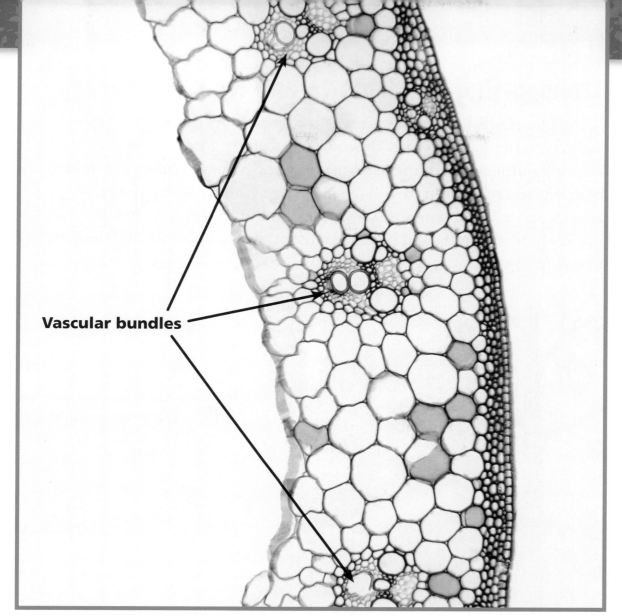

Vascular bundles

A portion of a wheat stem cross section showing
vascular bundles (100X)

Many vascular plants have specialized structures called
vascular bundles. A vascular bundle includes xylem
tubes and phloem tubes. A celery stalk has vascular
bundles you can see in cross section. With a microscope,
you can see the xylem and phloem bundles in other
plants, like wheat.

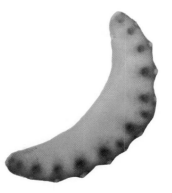

**The dark areas
at the edge of
this celery cross
section are
vascular bundles.**

Transporting Nutrients to and from the Leaves

Vascular plants have two systems of transport tubes that work together. Tubes carrying water up from the roots make up the xylem system. Tubes carrying nutrients down the plant make up the phloem system. The system of xylem and phloem in vascular plants is something like the system of arteries and veins in humans. Take a close look at the illustration below. You can see how the xylem and phloem transport water, minerals, and nutrients to and from cells.

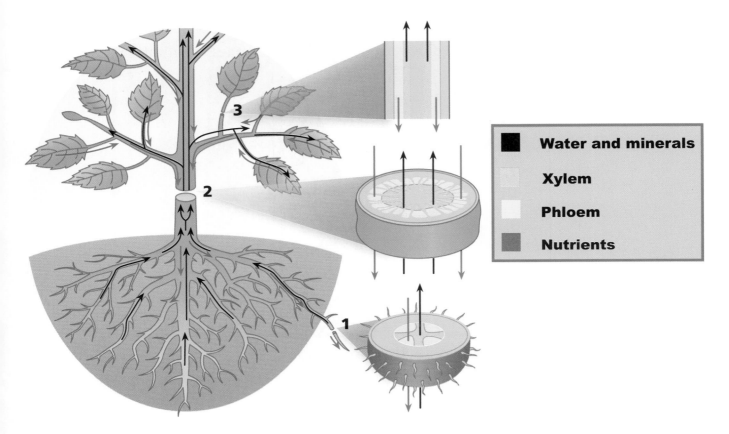

■ Water and minerals

■ Xylem

■ Phloem

■ Nutrients

Water enters the roots underground. At number 1, a short section of root was cut. The section is shown enlarged. The pink tissue is the xylem. Water and minerals dissolved in the water flow up the root toward the stem. The black arrow shows the direction that water and minerals move through the xylem tubes.

At number 2, a section of the main stem was cut. The section has been enlarged. The xylem from all the roots passes through the stem. Often a group of xylem cells is near a group of phloem cells. They form a vascular bundle. You can see a lot of vascular bundles like spokes on a wheel around the outside of the stem.

At number 3, a section of leaf stem was cut. The section was cut again from top to bottom. In the enlarged view, you can see the xylem carrying nutrients and water to the veins in the leaves and from there to the cells in the leaves.

The xylem tubes end in spaces between the cells in the leaves. Minerals and some of the water are taken in by the cells. The rest of the water evaporates through tiny holes in the leaves and passes into the environment. This process is called **transpiration**.

Transporting Sugar to the Cells

Some green plant cells make more sugar than they need for energy. Extra sugar passes out of the cells into the tiny phloem tubes. The sugar mixes with water to make a sweet liquid called sap. The sap flows through the phloem to all the cells that are not green. Cells that are not green can't make their own sugar.

Look at the vascular-plant illustration again. This time follow the red arrows. From the leaf, the sugar flows through the tiny leaf stem (number 3) into the branches. The phloem in all the branches comes together in the main stem (number 2). Finally, the phloem branches out into all the roots, delivering sugar to all the cells in even the tiniest root (number 1). Every cell receives sugar so it can stay alive and do its job.

Xylem and phloem transport water and nutrients to the cells of plants.

Comparing Plants and Animals

Multicellular animals and vascular plants have specialized vascular systems to transport nutrients. In both plants and animals, nutrients flow through systems of vessels. But the systems in animals are different from the systems in plants. Animals have one system of vessels. Blood flows from the **heart** to the cells in arteries. Nutrients transfer to the cells in the capillaries. Then the blood returns to the heart in veins. Blood goes around and around, transporting everything cells need.

Plants have two systems of vessels that are not connected. Water flows from the roots through xylem tubes to all the cells. The water carries minerals as it goes. Extra water then evaporates into the air. Water passes *through* the plant. It does not **circulate** like the blood in animals.

Water and sugar (sap) come out of the green cells and flow to all the other cells in phloem tubes. The phloem carries food and water for cells.

Plants have two "one-way" systems. One system transports water and minerals up, and the other system transports nutrients down. Animals have one system that goes around and around.

Plants like this saguaro cactus have two systems of vessels.

Animals like this frog have one system of vessels.

282

The Story of Maple Syrup

Do you like to eat pancakes or French toast? These treats sure do taste yummy when covered in maple syrup. Real maple syrup comes from maple trees. Do you live in a place that has maple trees? There are more than 30 species of maple trees distributed across the United States. Are they all a source of maple syrup? Let's find out.

Making Maple Syrup

The first step in making maple syrup is to tap a maple tree to collect lots and lots of sap. Sap is basically water with some sugars and a few other substances in it. The sugars are produced during photosynthesis.

In fall, sap can flow into hollow tubes in the vascular system in and near the bark of the tree. There, the sugar in the sap is converted into starch for storage over the winter. As spring approaches, nighttime temperatures still drop below freezing, but daytime temperatures rise above freezing. Then the sap starts to flow. The starch changes into sugar and moves into the sap, which starts to flow down the tree trunk. If you drill a small hole into a tree and insert a small tube, the sap can drip out and into a bucket. The drip stops at night and starts up again as the day warms. The sap will continue to flow until the nighttime temperatures stay above freezing.

How do you turn this slightly sweet sap into very sweet syrup for pancakes? How do you get rid of the extra water? You boil it! Boiling evaporates the water, leaving the sugar behind. In fact, if you boil it too long, you will have a pot filled with solid sugar crystals. A lot of energy is needed to reduce the sap to syrup. Sap with higher sugar content requires less boiling than sap with lower sugar content. Using less energy is better for the environment and for farmers. It takes about 150 liters (L) of sap to produce 4 L of syrup.

The sugar maple tree, which grows in the northeastern United States, has a sugar content of 2–2.5 percent. Maple syrup is mostly made from the sap of sugar maple trees because it is the sweetest. Black maple, red maple, and silver maple also produce sweet sap worthy of boiling down. Other maple trees produce sap but have much lower sugar content, making it more difficult to produce syrup.

Sap has a lower freezing temperature than water: the higher the sugar content, the lower the freezing temperature. So the higher sugar content of the sap in trees in the cold parts of the country helps keep the sap from freezing. Trees in the warm parts of the country do not need sap with really high sugar content.

Sugar maple trees
produce syrup.

The sap is boiled down to remove
extra water to create syrup.

The steps for collecting sap

Trees and Sap

What is going on inside these giant living systems? You have already learned that trees have a vascular system with xylem and phloem. The tree's vascular system is in the sapwood, which is the part of the bark closest to the wood. The vascular system in a tree transports nutrients, carbohydrates, minerals, and water throughout the organism. Xylem transports water and minerals from the roots of the tree to the leaves. Phloem transports nutrients (sugars), produced by photosynthesis in the leaves, down the tree toward the roots. Trees use the sugar for energy to conduct the many activities that keep the tree alive and healthy. Trees produce more sap than they need for their own use, so people can tap some of it to use for maple syrup without injuring the trees.

What technologies do sugar farmers use to get the sap out of the trees? Maple sugar farmers tap their trees by drilling a hole about 5–6.5 centimeters (cm) into the trunk at a slightly upward angle. A spile (rhymes with smile) is tapped into the hole and a bucket is hung from the spile. A spile is kind of like a metal straw. On large farms tree tappers use a network of plastic tubing, often many kilometers long, to bring the sap from hundreds of spiles directly to the sugar shack. This saves a tremendous amount of time and effort collecting sap buckets.

How did the first person discover that maple trees have sweet sap? How did they get it out of the trees before drills were invented? Historians are in agreement that the Native Americans were the first to discover this sweet liquid.

To make sugar, Native Americans made a cut in the maple tree bark and collected the sap as it dripped out. They used hollow logs to store sap. They boiled the sap by dropping very hot stones into it. They eventually shared this technique with the European settlers. Over time, new technologies were invented. The settlers learned to bore holes in the maple trunks and to insert a wooden or metal spile. They used wooden buckets to catch the sap.

Birch and walnut trees can also be tapped for sap. Some Russians drink birch sap. In Ukraine, Japan, China, and South Korea, people drink raw sap for its health benefits.

Can you tap maple trees in your neighborhood and make maple syrup? Remember that to produce sap, the tree has to go through a very cold winter with many months of freezing weather. If your climate doesn't have harsh winters and slow transitions to spring, your trees won't produce lots of high sugar sap. The northeastern part of the United States and the southeastern part of Canada are the regions where most maple syrup is produced.

Many years ago it took 75–115 L of sap to make 4 L of syrup. Now it takes 151–189 L. That's a lot more sap. It also means a lot more boiling. Why is this happening? Scientists are still trying to answer this question. Maybe you'll become a scientist who studies trees. Let us know if you figure out what's going on with the sugar maple tree sap!

Tree sap is a natural resource. Can you find out if people tap other kinds of trees to make things other than syrup?

This family is tapping a maple tree for syrup.

Thinking about Maple Syrup

1. What technologies are used to collect and produce maple syrup?

2. What vascular tissue is tapped to collect the maple sap?

3. How has maple syrup changed in recent years?

4. How is pancake syrup different from maple syrup? Collect labels and promotional information from several brands of both syrups, and evaluate the information.

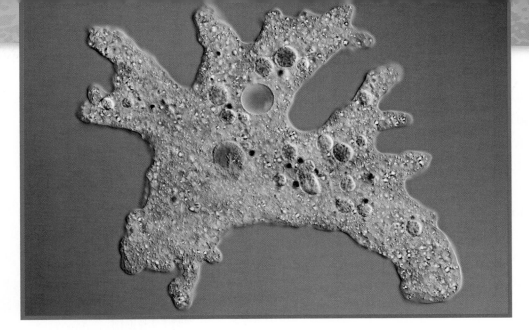

A living amoeba

The Human Circulatory System

The basic unit of life is the cell. All organisms are made of living cells. The simplest organisms, such as the amoeba, are just one cell.

All living cells have something in common. They all have a membrane on the outside. All cells are filled with a liquid called **cytoplasm**, which is mostly water. And all cells need four resources in order to stay alive. They are water, food, gases, and waste disposal.

How Do Cells Get Resources?

Single-celled organisms live in water. The food and gases they need to survive are in the water. The environment brings water, food, and gases to the cells all the time. The cell releases waste products into the water. The environment provides all the resources that single-celled organisms need.

A human is a multicellular organism. A human is made of trillions of cells. Humans don't live in water, and most of the cells are deep inside the body.

Muscles are made of millions of cells. Every cell in a human muscle is alive. That means every cell is getting the resources it needs to survive. How do these muscle cells get the water, food, gases, and waste removal they need to survive?

Multicellular organisms have specialized structures to transport resources to cells. In humans, blood, which is mostly water, is pumped through blood vessels to all the cells. The blood carries food and gases to the cells, and carries away wastes.

The human body is made of many different kinds of cells. There are nerve cells, muscle cells, bone cells, liver cells, lung cells, skin cells, and so on. A group of cells of the same kind, working together to perform a function, is called a tissue. Muscle tissue contracts to produce movement. Bone tissue gives our bodies structure. Nerve tissue sends electric messages. Each tissue is made of its own kinds of cells. But the cells in all tissues need the same basic resources.

Cells break down sugar to get energy. Cells need oxygen to do the job. One of the by-products of the sugar breakdown is the waste gas carbon dioxide (CO_2). If cells don't get oxygen, they will die. If cells don't get rid of the carbon dioxide, they will die.

The human body is made of many different kinds of cells.

Resource Delivery

Blood flows through blood vessels to every cell in the body. The blood is kept flowing with a pump called the heart. The human heart is a four-chambered organ made of powerful muscles. The muscles contract to pump the blood about once every second. You can feel the beat of your pumping heart when you put your hand on your chest. The heart muscle works all the time. It pumps day and night, year after year. Every year your heart beats more than 30 million times!

Blood flows away from the heart in blood vessels called arteries. Blood flows back to the heart in vessels called veins. The smallest blood vessels, the ones that serve the cells, are called capillaries. The system of blood vessels and the heart is called the **circulatory system**. It circulates blood to every cell in your body.

The human circulatory system

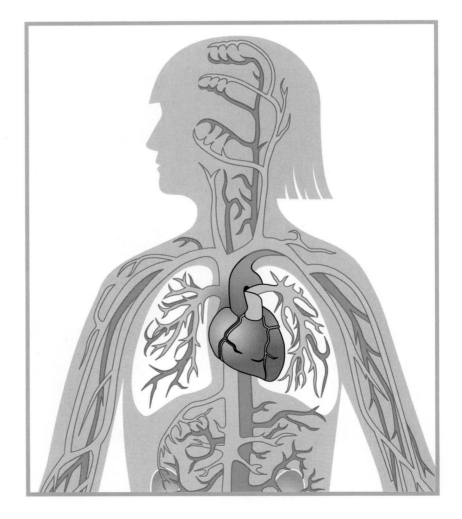

The two most important resources transported to cells are oxygen (a gas) and sugar (food). The most important waste product removed from cells is carbon dioxide (a gas). Oxygen comes from the air we breathe, and sugar comes from the food we eat. In order to get fresh oxygen, dispose of carbon dioxide, and get new sugar for cells, the circulatory system has to connect with the **lungs** and intestines.

To learn how the circulatory system works, let's take an imaginary trip through it. Red blood cells carry oxygen to the cells and carbon dioxide away from the cells. You have about 25 trillion red blood cells in your body. They live only about 4 months, so they are being replaced at the amazing rate of about 3 million per second.

Red blood cells (scanning electron microscope view, about 4,000X)

The Right Side of the Heart

It takes about a minute for a red blood cell to travel once through the circulatory system. Blood returning from the body cells goes to the right side of the heart. The returning red blood cells are carrying carbon dioxide waste. The returning blood enters the upper chamber on the right side of the heart, called the **right atrium**. When the heart beats, the right atrium squeezes blood down into the **right ventricle**.

The next time the heart beats, it pushes blood out of the right ventricle to the lungs. The blood flows through tiny capillaries that are touching the air sacs in the lungs. The red blood cells release carbon dioxide. The carbon dioxide enters the air in the lungs and is exhaled. Then the red blood cells take oxygen from the air you breathe in.

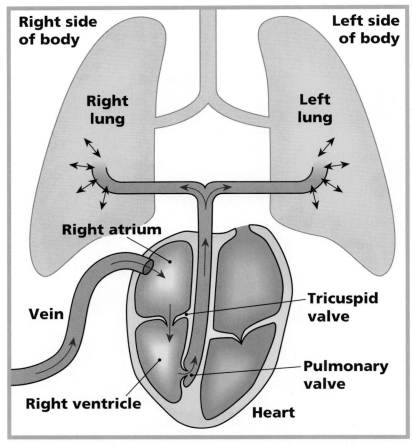

A diagram showing how the right side of the heart works

The Left Side of the Heart

The oxygen-rich red blood cells go back to the left side of the heart. Blood from the lungs flows into the **left atrium**. The next time the heart beats, it squeezes blood into the powerful **left ventricle**. When the left ventricle contracts, it pumps blood through arteries to the body. The red blood cells transport oxygen and pick up waste carbon dioxide. Then the cycle starts over again.

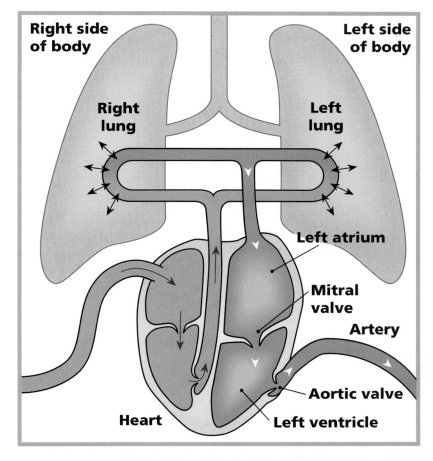

Right side of body

Left side of body

Right lung

Left lung

Left atrium

Mitral valve

Artery

Aortic valve

Heart

Left ventricle

A diagram showing how the left side of the heart works

Thinking about the Human Circulatory System

1. What is the heart and what is its role in the circulatory system?

2. What are heart valves and what do they do?

3. Where are the heart valves?

4. What is the main function of the left side of the human heart?

5. What is the main function of the right side of the human heart?

The Human Respiratory System

The **respiratory system** has three main parts. They are the lungs, the system of tubes that connect the lungs with the outside air, and the diaphragm (an arched muscle). The respiratory system brings oxygen to the red blood cells and gets rid of waste carbon dioxide.

When your arched diaphragm muscle contracts, you breath in. When you inhale (breathe in), oxygen from the air enters your lungs. The air ends up in the 300,000,000 alveoli (air sacs) at the ends of the tiny tubes (bronchioles) in your lungs. The alveoli are surrounded by capillaries. The oxygen passes through the walls of the air sacs into the capillaries. Red blood cells pick up the oxygen. At the same time, the red blood cells release waste carbon dioxide from the body cells into the alveoli. This waste gas goes into the air when you exhale.

Blood flows to the body tissues through arteries. The blood flows through smaller and smaller arteries, ending in networks of capillaries. Capillaries are only 1/100 of a millimeter in diameter. That's just a little bit larger than a red blood cell. Capillaries are so small that red blood cells often travel single file to get through.

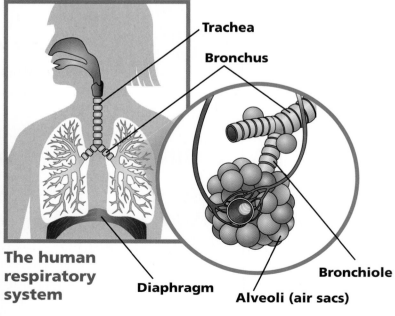

Trachea

Bronchus

The human respiratory system

Diaphragm

Bronchiole

Alveoli (air sacs)

The capillaries touch every cell in the body. Gas exchange takes place while the red blood cell is sliding past a cell. Here, only the thin wall of the capillary is between them. Oxygen passes into the cells, and carbon dioxide passes out. The red blood cell then transports the carbon dioxide to the lungs for disposal.

Red blood cells carry gases. They carry the essential gas, oxygen, to the cells and carry the waste gas, carbon dioxide, away from the cells.

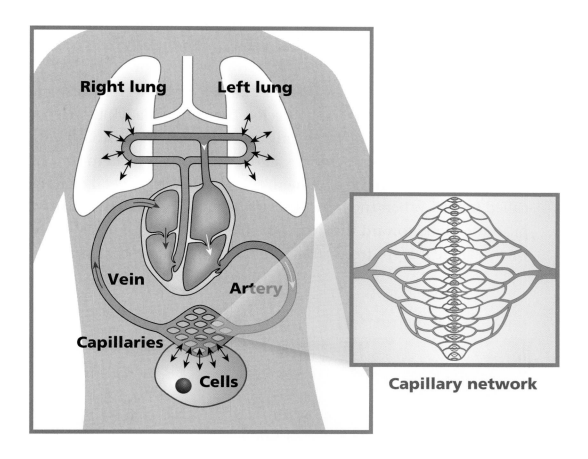

Capillary network

Thinking about the Human Respiratory System

1. What are the parts of the respiratory system? What is the system's function?

2. What are alveoli and what happens there?

Other Circulatory and Respiratory Systems

You have a closed circulatory system. A system of vessels and organs holds your blood, and it stays in there. One of the organs is a muscular heart, which pumps the blood around and around through the system. All vertebrate animals have a similar circulatory system. These animals include mammals, birds, reptiles, fish, and amphibians.

Invertebrate animals have different kinds of systems for distributing food and other nutrients to their cells. The painted lady butterfly is a member of the class of organisms called insects. Insects have an open circulatory system. One vessel runs from their head to the end of their abdomen. In the abdomen, the vessel forms several chambers called hearts. When the insect moves, its muscles make the hearts push the blood toward the head. The blood spills out into the body cavity. There it seeps freely around the organs and other tissues.

A painted lady butterfly

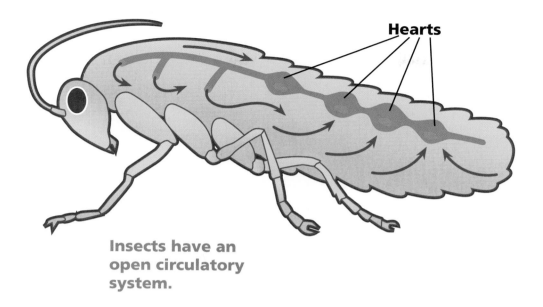

Hearts

Insects have an open circulatory system.

When the blood flows around the gut, nutrients from digested food enter the blood. The nutrient-rich blood nourishes all the cells as it flows through the insect's body cavity. The blood slowly flows toward the abdomen, and when it arrives at the area around the hearts, it enters the vessel through little valves in the hearts. Then the circuit repeats.

Insects don't have blood like you. Insect "blood" is called hemolymph and is yellowish or greenish. Hemolymph does not carry oxygen to the cells or carry waste carbon dioxide (CO_2) away from the cells. Insects have a completely different respiratory system. Air enters the insect's body through a line of holes along its side. The holes are connected to air tubes that branch and branch, eventually reaching all the cells in the insect's body. The cells get their oxygen from these little air tubes, and eliminate their waste carbon dioxide there, too.

Thinking about Other Circulatory and Respiratory Systems

Compare the structures and functions of the human circulatory system with that of the painted lady butterfly.

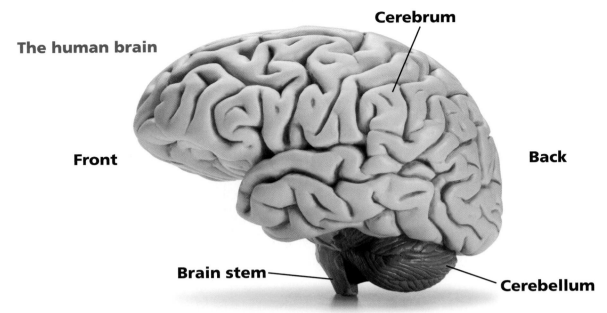

The human brain

Cerebrum

Front

Back

Brain stem

Cerebellum

Stimulus and Response in Humans

Structures of the Brain

The human brain is a compact mass weighing about 1.5 kilograms (kg). The spinal cord extends from the brain down through a hole in the backbone. The brain and spinal cord make up the **central nervous system**. The central nervous system is completely enclosed in bone. The brain is surrounded entirely by the cranium, or skull.

The brain has three major parts, the cerebrum, the cerebellum, and the brain stem. The largest part of the human brain is the large, bumpy, folded cerebrum. It has two halves, the right and left hemispheres. The spheres are symmetrical and are connected to each other. The cerebrum makes up about 70 percent of the mass of the whole human nervous system. The lobes of the cerebrum have areas that have specific functions.

It also has a distinctive set of folds. The fold patterns are similar for all humans. This folded outer surface is called the cerebral cortex. The cerebral cortex processes the signals that come into the brain. Without this thin surface layer, we would not be able to think, recognize faces, or plan ahead.

The more folds a brain has, the more it can process. The cerebrum of a rat, for instance, is smooth, implying that it is not a big thinker. The brain of a dolphin, on the other hand, is more folded than a human's.

The small, roundish structure that lies below and to the back of the brain is the cerebellum. It makes up about 11 percent of the mass of the brain. It processes information from the muscles, tendons, and inner ear. It uses this information to manage and maintain balance and coordination.

At the center of the brain is a small, cordlike structure called the brain stem. It connects the brain and the spinal cord and relays messages to and from the cerebrum and the cerebellum. The brain stem regulates many body functions, such as heartbeat, breathing, and body temperature. You can survive damage to the cerebrum or cerebellum, but damage to the brain stem is usually fatal.

The brain stem also relays information from the body to other parts of the brain. In general, the right hemisphere of the brain receives from and sends messages to the left side of the body, and vice versa. The brain stem coordinates the crossover.

A diagram comparing a human brain with a bird brain

Brain Messages

If an ant is walking on your arm, you know it even if you don't see it. Its feet tickle you, and without even looking, you raise your other arm to brush the ant away. How are you able to do that?

Your arm has touch receptors for the sensation we know as tickle. The ant walking on your arm is a **stimulus**. When a tickle receptor is stimulated, it sends a message to your brain, alerting you to a problem. Your brain decides how to **respond**. It sends a message to your arms, telling them what to do to brush away the ant.

The special cells that make up your brain and the rest of your nervous system are **neurons**. You have several hundreds of billions of neurons throughout your body and brain. Those neurons are constantly sending messages from one place to another.

Your touch receptors, photoreceptors (light sensors), and hearing, taste, and smell receptors are all on the ends of neurons. These **sensory neurons** send messages from the environment to the brain. The brain decides what to do about these messages. If your brain decides that you should act, it sends out messages to your muscles or other systems, telling them to snap into action. This call to action is sent on **motor neurons**.

The receptors on the ends of neurons tell your brain when something tickles.

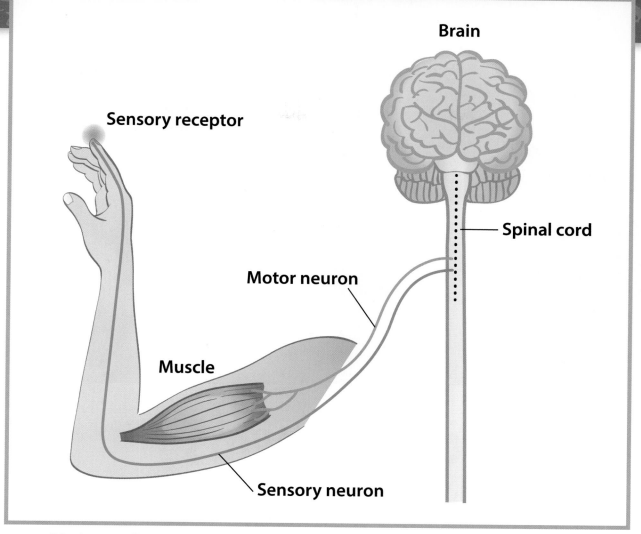

Brain

Sensory receptor

Spinal cord

Motor neuron

Muscle

Sensory neuron

Motor and sensory neurons keep your body in constant communication with your brain.

Sensory neurons and motor neurons are like wires carrying an electric signal. Sensory neurons carry messages to the brain, and motor neurons carry messages away from the brain. Sensory neurons give the brain information, and motor neurons send instructions to the muscles. Your arm responds to the message from the motor neurons by contracting certain muscles. Sensory neurons called stretch receptors give the brain feedback and tell it how much the muscles are stretched or contracted. This communication between the brain and muscles is happening constantly, all over your body.

Sending messages takes time. The longer the pathway, the longer it takes to produce a response. The interval is called response time. You might have noticed this delay when you stub your toe; you can see it being stubbed and hear the sound before you feel the pain! The pathway from your eyes and ears to your brain is much shorter than the pathway from your toes to your brain. So the sensory neurons in your eyes and ears get their messages to the brain before the sensory neurons in your toes can.

Sensory Systems

Awareness of the environment and the ability to respond quickly are absolutely essential for you to stay alive. Fortunately, you have been supplied with an early-warning system to tell you about potential hazards. The system is your senses and your brain, which controls your every action.

Staying Alive

Senses pick up clues from the environment, both far and near, and pass them on to your brain. The brain considers the clues, compares them to your experience, and takes appropriate action.

All our senses have similar systems. Each has one or several types of receptor neurons that receive just one kind of environmental clue. In vision, light of certain wavelengths is converted into electric impulses in neurons in the eye. The other senses respond to vibrations in the air that enter the ear, chemicals in a liquid on the tongue or gas in the nose, or pressure on the skin. In each case, specialized receptor neurons change the environmental clue into a signal that travels to the brain. The brain sorts the signals into our perceptions of vision, sound, taste, smell, and touch.

Sensory Information

All sensory systems collect four types of information from environmental clues, or stimuli. One type of information is sensation. For humans these are vision, touch, taste, hearing, and smell. Each kind of sensation has several parts, such as color and movement in vision.

Another type of information is the amount of sensation. If there is not a large enough stimulus, the system does not detect anything. The amount of sensation that you can sense changes with different conditions.

Another type of information is how long the perception of the sensation lasts. If the stimulus lasts a long time, the amount of sensation decreases. For example, when you first get into a hot bath, the temperature might feel too hot, but this sensation fades quickly.

The last type of information is where the stimulus takes place. This affects the ability to distinguish two closely spaced stimuli. To go back to the ant example, if you have two ants on your arm very close together, can you tell if it is one or two ants? This depends on the number and density of the receptors. The more densely packed the receptors, the closer two ants can be and still be detected by two separate receptors.

Different areas of the brain process messages from different sensory systems. Where the brain receives the message determines whether we see or hear or smell something in response.

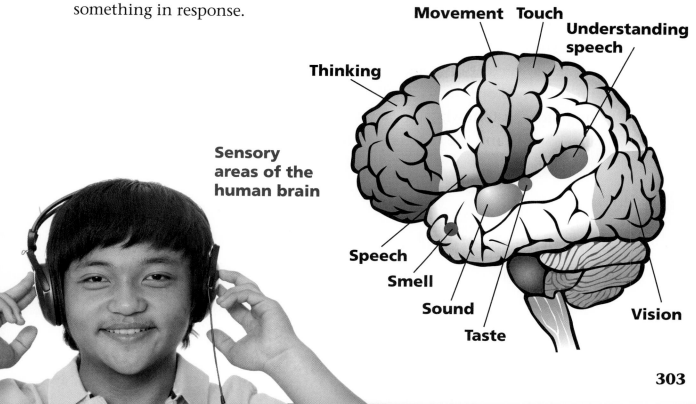

Sensory areas of the human brain

Movement Touch Understanding speech Thinking Speech Smell Sound Taste Vision

**Animals respond
to senses differently
than humans.**

Other animals have different ranges of sensory sensitivity than humans. Eagles see with greater acuity, bees see ultraviolet light, and rattlesnakes detect infrared, or heat. Dogs hear higher sounds and whales lower sounds. Dogs can smell thousands of times better, and great horned owls don't smell at all. And some animals, particularly migratory waterfowl, seem to sense magnetism, although the exact mechanism and the organs are unknown.

Thinking about Sensory Systems

1. How is our sense of vision like our sense of smell? How are they different?

Animal Communication

What is communication? It is passing information from one place to another. When you tell a friend you are thirsty, you are communicating a need for a drink.

Your thirst receptors tell your brain that you are thirsty. Your brain sends an action message to make a sentence. It also sends a message to your mouth to form the words "I am thirsty." If the spoken message enters your friend's ears, her sound receptors produce a signal. A sensory neuron takes the signal to her auditory center. In her brain's speech center, the sounds can be interpreted as a request for water.

A lot has to happen in this simple communication.

Sound

Many animals communicate using sound. Communication to others helps animals survive and reproduce. Wolves and coyotes howl to communicate with each other. Humpback whales make a loud whining sound, called singing. Their songs travel for many kilometers through the ocean. Their songs keep social groups in contact. The distinctive buzzing sound made by a rattlesnake warns potential predators to stay away. Prairie dogs make high-pitched chirps to communicate danger to other prairie dogs.

Other animals that use sound to communicate include crickets, frogs, lions, elephants, alligators, porpoises, owls, red-winged blackbirds—even shrimp. The pistol shrimp can produce one of the loudest sounds in the world.

A wolf and a humpback whale use sound to communicate.

A monarch butterfly and a peacock use the sense of vision to communicate in their environment.

Vision

Animals also use the sense of vision to communicate information to others in their environment. Vision can be used in a couple of ways. An animal might display itself to attract a mate or frighten a predator. The peacock's display is a magnificent fan of tail feathers. Its display is aimed at attracting a mate. The monarch butterfly's bright orange wings communicate to potential predators that it is toxic. Any predator that once tried to eat a monarch remembers the bright colors and avoids attacking a monarch again.

Other animals that use visual signals for communication include fireflies, hummingbirds, skunks, and birds of paradise.

Smell

Smell is a powerful communication tool in much of the animal world. Chemicals called pheromones produce odors that communicate important information. Some moths rely on pheromones to locate a mate. A mature female moth emits a small amount of the pheromone into the night air. When a male moth detects a single molecule of the pheromone, he starts to fly toward the odor. By following the scent, he might find a mate.

Ants use pheromones to mark their trails. Their pheromones can communicate the direction to a food source, the direction home, the presence of an enemy, or other valuable information.

All members of the cat family and dog family use scent markers. Dogs use urine to mark their territory. Chemicals in the urine identify the animal and tell its gender, age, and other information. The main message to outsiders is "Private property! Keep out!" Cats have scent glands at the corners of their mouth. They rub their face against structures that mark the boundary of their territory. They also mark objects within their territory. Does your cat rub its face on a chair leg or your pant leg? It is making sure that other cats know that it has claimed you as personal property.

Ants use pheromones to mark their trails.

A cat rubs its face against a fence to mark its territory.

A skunk uses odor as a weapon.

Odor can also be a weapon. The skunk is famous for its offensive odor. It can fend off most potential predators.

Some flowers have a peculiar odor. The cadaver flower smells like rotting, dead flesh. The odor attracts flies, because it seems like an excellent place to lay eggs. When the eggs hatch, the larvae should have plenty of rotting flesh to eat. But the smell is a false signal used to attract the fly so it will pollinate the flower. Many other plants also communicate with animals.

Humans' sense of smell is not as strong as that of many other animals. Yet it still helps us understand our surroundings. Next time you're walking down your street, pay attention to the odors. What do they tell you about the time of year, where you are, or what you should be cautious of?

Monarch Migration

The monarch butterfly is a migratory animal. It travels from the northern United States and southern Canada to Mexico, and then comes back. But no one butterfly makes the whole round trip. The migration system involves several generations of butterflies.

Let's start with a female monarch butterfly in Ohio. It's August. She hatched farther south, maybe on a farm in Kentucky. After she mates, she looks for a place to lay her eggs. She lays her eggs on milkweed because milkweed is the only food source for monarch larvae.

Soon after laying her eggs, the female butterfly dies. Her eggs hatch in a few weeks. The larvae eat milkweed leaves for several weeks, until they are about the size of your index finger. Then the monarch larvae pupate. They spend a few weeks inside the protective chrysalis. After the change from larvae to adult, each chrysalis splits open. The new adult butterflies climb out and pump up their new wings.

By this time, it is fall. The young monarchs have an adventure ahead. They must fly from Ohio to Mexico. Fall monarch butterflies instinctively start to migrate south all by themselves. The young monarchs head for a place they have never seen before. They take off without a map or a leader. They fly and fly, guided by instinct. Their need to migrate south is an **inherited trait** shared by all the fall monarchs.

Migrating monarchs from all over the eastern half of the United States end up in a small pine-oak forest in the mountains in central Mexico. Here the butterflies settle down with millions of other monarchs from the north. It is a safe place to spend the winter. The millions of monarchs crowd together for protection from predators and weather. They are inactive throughout the winter.

In spring, the days get longer and warmer. The butterflies become active, drink water, and start flying north. But the butterflies that migrated from Ohio do not fly back to Ohio. They fly as far as Texas, Louisiana, or Mississippi. They look for fields of milkweed and lay their eggs. The monarchs that made the long migration to Mexico die. Their offspring, generation 1, continue the northward migration.

When the weather gets cold, monarchs migrate from the eastern United States to central Mexico. They cluster in the pine-oak forest.

These first generation (Gen. 1) spring monarchs grow to be adults and fly a short distance north. They find milkweed, mate, lay eggs, and die. Their offspring, the second generation (Gen. 2), continue the northward migration. They find milkweed, mate, lay eggs, and die. Their offspring, generation 3, continue the journey.

The third generation (Gen. 3) monarchs fly north. They reach the limit of the monarch's range. By now, it is well into the summer. Some adult monarchs make it to Ohio, completing the Ohio monarch cycle. Others end up in Wisconsin, Michigan, or Maine. Some continue north into Canada. These third generation migrants find milkweed, mate, lay eggs, and die. By the time the fourth generation (Gen. 4) hatches, it is fall.

The adults in generation 4 live much longer than their parents or grandparents. They live for 6 to 7 months. They start to migrate south, responding to the shorter, cooler days of fall.

Look at the map of the monarch migration. Can you trace the northern migration, generation by generation?

The monarch butterfly migration system

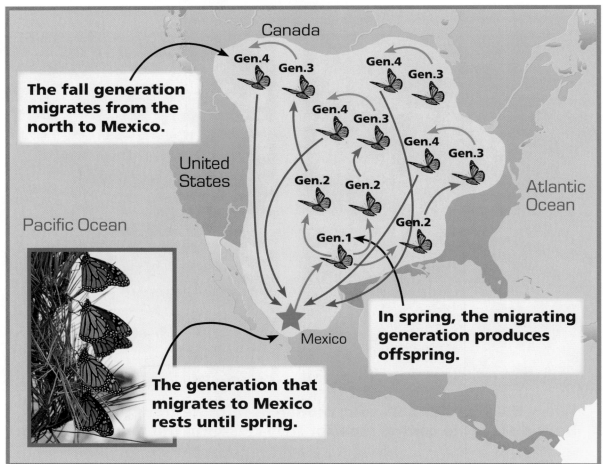

Canada

Gen.4 Gen.3   Gen.4 Gen.3

The fall generation migrates from the north to Mexico.

Gen.4 Gen.3

United States   Gen.4 Gen.3

Gen.2 Gen.2

Pacific Ocean   Gen.2

Gen.1

Atlantic Ocean

In spring, the migrating generation produces offspring.

Mexico

The generation that migrates to Mexico rests until spring.

Monarch observers have recently seen many fewer monarch butterflies arriving in Mexico. The reasons for the decrease are not fully understood. One reason is a decrease in milkweed plants along the monarch's migratory path. Milkweed used to grow as a weed on farmland. Now farmers have better ways to prevent milkweed from growing. So monarchs have a harder time finding safe locations to lay eggs. The monarch larva depends on the milkweed plant for food. Any change in milkweed growth affects the survival of monarch populations.

How can you help the monarch populations? You can help teach people in your community about the migration system of monarchs and their need for milkweed. You can find out what native milkweed plants grow in your state and plant milkweed seeds. You can work with others to make sure milkweed plants thrive.

Thinking about Monarchs

1. Think about the monarch migration system. What are the parts?

2. What natural causes might affect the growth of milkweed plants? How might humans affect milkweed growth?

3. Predict the effect of logging in the pine-oak forest of central Mexico where monarchs spend the winter.

4. What are communities doing to protect monarchs?

North Atlantic Ocean Ecosystem

The largest ecosystems on Earth are the ocean ecosystems. Fish, crustaceans, mollusks, birds, and mammals of all sizes live and interact there. Like all ecosystems, ocean ecosystems have large populations of producers and consumers. Primary consumers feed on producers. Secondary consumers feed on primary consumers, and so on.

Where are the producers? You can see some of them on the ocean shores. Plant-like organisms called kelp and other seaweeds live in shallow water and near the ocean's surface. Seaweed cells contain chlorophyll, so they can make food from carbon dioxide (CO_2) during photosynthesis. Some shallow areas have sea grass, which also turns carbon dioxide into sugar during photosynthesis. Kelp and sea grass are two producers. But you probably have never seen the most important producers in the ocean. The base of the ocean food pyramid is microscopic organisms called phytoplankton.

There are thousands of species of phytoplankton. They are photosynthetic. They all need water, carbon dioxide, sunlight, and minerals. Water is all around organisms living in the ocean. Carbon dioxide from the atmosphere gets dissolved in the seawater. Sunlight can shine into the top few meters of the ocean (the photic zone).

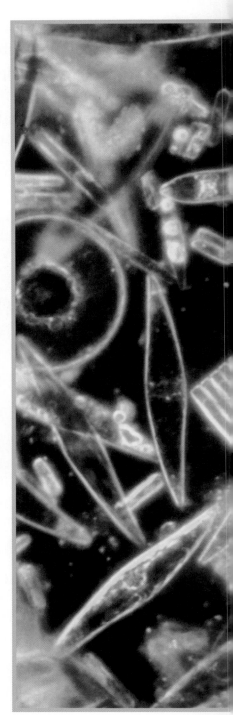

The research vessel, Knorr, went on a 3-week expedition.

Phytoplankton Blooms

In spring, the number of hours of daylight increases. Conditions are right for large increases in the number of microscopic producers. These population growth spurts are called blooms. A bloom occurs when many phytoplankton reproduce and live and fewer die.

Scientists are studying the phytoplankton bloom in the North Atlantic Ocean. This bloom is important for two reasons. First, it produces the food that supports the North Atlantic ecosystem. This ecosystem produces fish that help feed people all over the world. Second, the phytoplankton remove tons of carbon dioxide from the atmosphere.

Researchers wanted to know what **variables** drive the annual phytoplankton bloom. They observed that the bloom starts weeks before the days start to get longer. But they didn't know why. The research team put robotic instruments into the North Atlantic early in the spring. The instruments collected data. The data showed that rough seas push cold northern water under warmer nutrient-rich water. As the cold and warm layers interact, eddies (whirlpools) form. The eddies bring phytoplankton up into the photic zone. These conditions encourage rapid reproduction of the phytoplankton. The eddies get the bloom started several weeks before the longer days of spring.

The North Atlantic bloom generates a huge amount of food for a diverse food web. How does the food web work? Zooplankton feed on the phytoplankton producers. Zooplankton are tiny (microscopic) animals. These include the larvae of crustaceans (such as crabs and shrimp), larvae of fish, larvae of jellyfish, marine copepods, and a host of other tiny animals. Zooplankton are eaten by larger animals, including fish, jellyfish, krill, seabirds, and whales. Just as terrestrial ecosystems depend on green producers such as grass and trees, ocean ecosystems depend on green phytoplankton.

A tiny marine copepod

A storm in the North Atlantic stirs up a large amount of food for seabirds.

The Carbon Cycle

Carbon is essential for plants and animals to survive. Terrestrial plants get carbon from carbon dioxide gas during photosynthesis. Phytoplankton get dissolved carbon dioxide from seawater. The carbon stays in organisms until it is digested for energy. Digestion breaks down the food and releases carbon dioxide into the environment. The carbon dioxide circulates in the atmosphere until an autotroph uses it or it dissolves into a body of water. The movement of carbon dioxide from the environment to organisms and back into the environment is the carbon cycle.

The carbon cycle

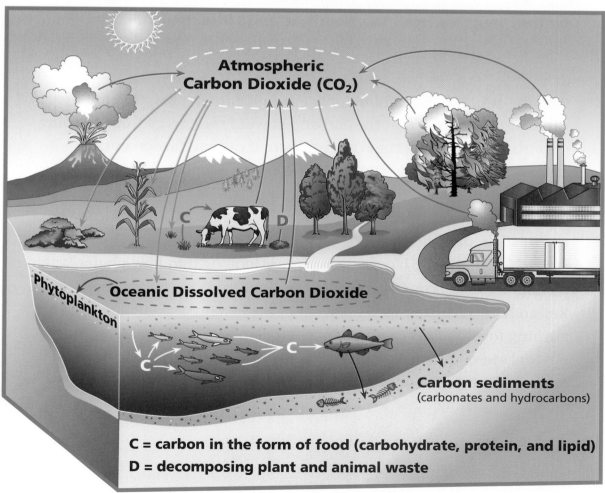

C = carbon in the form of food (carbohydrate, protein, and lipid)
D = decomposing plant and animal waste

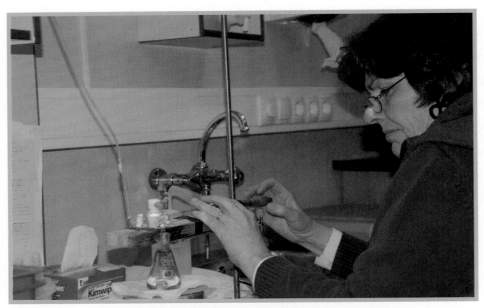

Testing samples from the North Atlantic bloom

In the atmosphere, carbon dioxide is a greenhouse gas. Greenhouse gases absorb energy from the Sun and prevent the energy from escaping into space. The greater the concentration of carbon dioxide in the atmosphere, the warmer the atmosphere gets. Scientists are concerned that an increase of carbon dioxide in the atmosphere is raising the temperature of Earth. Global warming might stress ecosystems and cause the sea level to rise all around the planet.

The North Atlantic bloom scientists are looking into how phytoplankton blooms affect the concentration of carbon dioxide in the atmosphere. Researchers calculate that 33 percent of the carbon dioxide produced by burning fossil fuels is captured by phytoplankton. The North Atlantic phytoplankton bloom captures 20 percent of that. Some of the carbon drifts down into the deep ocean, so it stays out of the atmosphere.

Oceanic Research Instrumentation

The North Atlantic bloom research was a collaboration of many science specialists and engineers. To understand what was going on in the ecosystem, they needed to decide what data to collect and how to collect the data. Because the sea is so stormy and rough in the early spring, they could not simply lower their instruments into the water over the side of a ship. They needed to release instruments to float unattended for a period of time.

Two robotic instruments were designed to obtain data. One was a buoy that floats freely in the ocean. It collected data on current speed and direction, and temperature at and near the surface. The buoy stays at a planned depth not far beneath the surface. From anywhere in the ocean, communication antennae transfer data to a satellite that researchers on land can check any time. The buoy can make observations for weeks at a time before being retrieved.

Scientists prepare to lower the robotic buoy into the North Atlantic.

Knorr recovers the buoy.

Engineers prepare the seaglider for launch.

Scientists collect the glider from the North Atlantic

This scientist pulls the water sampler back on the vessel to study.

The second instrument was a robotic probe that swims. It is like a tiny submarine that carries instruments, not people. This robot can dive down to 1,000 meters (m) and then glide back to the surface. On each glide, instruments can monitor plankton, nutrients, temperature, and currents. The glider sends data to researchers on land via satellite.

Researchers on ships used other instruments to make observations. Special devices collected samples of seawater at different depths. These samples showed how many phytoplankton and zooplankton were at different depths.

In this research, data on two variables, time and place, are necessary. These data tell when the bloom starts, where it occurs, and when and where it ends. When researchers observe many phytoplankton dying, they know that the dead phytoplankton drift to the bottom of the sea. When this happens, the carbon in the phytoplankton can no longer cycle back into the atmosphere.

This kind of scientific discovery requires close collaboration. Scientists design the experiments, and engineers invent and build the amazing instruments that make observations and deliver data.

References

References

Science Safety Rules

1. Listen carefully to your teacher's instructions. Follow all directions. Ask questions if you don't know what to do.

2. Tell your teacher if you have any allergies.

3. Never put any materials in your mouth. Do not taste anything unless your teacher tells you to do so.

4. Never smell any unknown material. If your teacher tells you to smell something, wave your hand over the material to bring the smell toward your nose.

5. Do not touch your face, mouth, ears, eyes, or nose while working with chemicals, plants, or animals.

6. Always protect your eyes. Wear safety goggles when necessary. Tell your teacher if you wear contact lenses.

7. Always wash your hands with soap and warm water after handling chemicals, plants, or animals.

8. Never mix any chemicals unless your teacher tells you to do so.

9. Report all spills, accidents, and injuries to your teacher.

10. Treat animals with respect, caution, and consideration.

11. Clean up your work space after each investigation.

12. Act responsibly during all science activities.

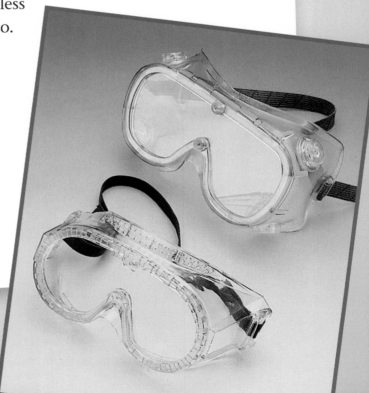

Glossary

absorb to soak in (170)

air the mixture of gases surrounding Earth (106)

air pressure the force exerted on a surface by the mass of the air around or in contact with it (173)

anemometer a weather instrument that measures wind speed with wind-catching cups (179)

aquatic referring to water (256)

artery a blood vessel that carries blood from the heart to the body (276)

asteroid a small, solid object that orbits the Sun (133)

astronomer a scientist who studies objects in the universe, including stars, planets, and moons (106)

astronomy the study of the universe and the objects in it (158)

atmosphere the layer of gases surrounding Earth. The layers include the troposphere, stratosphere, mesosphere, thermosphere, and exosphere. (36, 107, 246)

axis an imaginary line around which a mass, like a planet, rotates (154)

bacteria microorganisms that act as decomposers (247)

barometer a weather instrument that measures air pressure (179)

bends a condition that causes pain in deep-sea divers' arms and legs after they return to the surface (44)

Big Dipper a group of seven bright stars in the shape of a dipper (153)

biosphere a system of interacting living organisms on Earth (246)

black hole a region in space without light that has a strong gravitational pull (157)

blade the flat part of a leaf (274)

blizzard a severe storm with low temperatures, strong winds, and large quantities of snow (221)

boiling point the temperature at which liquid turns to gas. The boiling point of water is 100°C. (49)

bolus a wad of food (272)

brain part of the central nervous system protected by the skull (251)

caisson a large box with no bottom used as a working environment underwater. (46)

capillary the smallest blood vessel. Gases, nutrients, and wastes are exchanged between capillaries and cells. (273)

carbohydrate a nutrient, such as sugar and starch, that provides energy (268)

carbon dioxide (CO₂) a compound made from carbon and oxygen; a waste gas produced during cellular respiration. Plants use carbon dioxide during photosynthesis to make food. **(7, 247)**

cell the basic unit of life **(261)**

central nervous system where sensory impulses pass through the brain and spinal cord **(298)**

change to make different **(12)**

chemical reaction the process in which substances change to make one or more new substances that have different properties from the original ones **(38)**

chemist a person trained in chemistry **(70)**

chlorophyll a molecule that absorbs red and blue light and reflects green light **(263)**

circulate to move in a circle **(282)**

circulatory system the system of blood vessels and organs that transports blood to all the cells in the body **(290)**

citric acid a white, crystalline solid acid found in citrus fruits **(51)**

classification the process by which scientists identify and organize objects and organisms, such as plants **(274)**

classify to identify and organize according to similar properties or other criteria **(274)**

climate the average or typical weather conditions in a region of the world **(42, 223)**

cloud a large accumulation of tiny droplets of water, usually high in the air **(100)**

colon the large intestine where solid waste is compacted in preparation for elimination **(273)**

comet a mass of ice, rock, and gas orbiting the Sun **(145)**

compete to rely on or need the same resource as another organism **(250)**

compress to reduce in volume by applying pressure **(37)**

concentrated a solution containing a lot of solute **(30)**

concentration the ratio of solute to solvent in a solution **(32)**

condensation the change of state from gas to liquid **(26, 169)**

conduction the transfer of energy from one object to another by contact **(189)**

conserve to stay constant during an interaction. Matter can change, but it's always conserved. To use wisely and protect carefully **(13)**

constellation a group of stars in a pattern given a name by people **(153)**

constraint a restriction or limitation **(61)**

consumer an organism that cannot make its own food. Consumers eat other organisms. **(247)**

convection current a circular movement of fluid (such as air) that is the result of uneven heating of the fluid **(193)**

crater a hole formed by an object hitting a surface **(105)**

crescent Moon the curved shape of the visible part of the Moon before and after a new Moon **(100)**

criteria a set of standards for evaluation or testing something **(61)**

crystal the natural form of some solid substances. Crystal shape is also a physical property that helps to identify a substance. **(12)**

cycle a set of events or actions that repeat in a predictable pattern **(119)**

cytoplasm the liquid that fills living cells **(288)**

day the time between sunrise and sunset on Earth **(89)**

decomposer an organism that breaks down plant and animal material into simple chemicals **(247)**

decompression the change from higher pressure to lower pressure **(45)**

Degree Celsius (°C) the unit of temperature in the metric system. Water freezes at 0°C and boils at 100°C **(49)**

density mass per unit volume **(11)**

desalination the process of separating the water from the salt in ocean water **(56)**

detritivore an organism that feeds on broken down materials from dead organisms **(258)**

detritus organic litter made up of dead organisms, their parts, and waste **(258)**

dew water that condenses outdoors on a surface when the temperature drops at night **(208)**

diameter the straight-line distance through the center of an object, one side to the other side **(118)**

diatomaceous earth the shell-like remains of microscopic aquatic organisms (diatoms) **(10)**

digestion the process of breaking down food into nutrients that can be used by cells **(268)**

digestive system the organs and structures that digest food. The digestive system includes the teeth, mouth, esophagus, stomach, small intestine, large intestine, and colon. **(269)**

dilute a solution containing little solute **(33)**

dissolve the process of a substance becoming incorporated uniformly into another **(9)**

drought a less-than-normal amount of rain or snow over a period of time **(216)**

dwarf planet a round object that orbits the Sun and does not orbit a planet **(102)**

Earth the third planet from the Sun, known as the water planet **(94)**

ecosystem a community of organisms interacting with each other and with the nonliving environment **(247)**

energy the ability to make things happen. Energy can take many forms, such as heat and light. **(14, 248)**

energy transfer the movement of energy from one place to another **(187)**

engineer a scientist who designs and builds systems that result in new products or solve problems **(58)**

esophagus the tube connecting the mouth and the stomach **(272)**

evaporate when water in a material dries up or goes into the air or the change of state from liquid to gas **(12)**

evaporation the process by which liquid water changes into water vapor **(12, 169)**

exosphere the layer of the atmosphere above the thermosphere. The exosphere is the transition from the atmosphere to space. **(177)**

explosion a fast reaction that produces heat, light, and sound energies, and a lot of gas **(80)**

extract a solution of substances dissolved out of organic material **(18)**

extraterrestrial beyond Earth **(116)**

first-quarter Moon a phase of the Moon in the lunar cycle halfway between a new Moon and a full Moon **(123)**

fog a large accumulation of water droplets close to the ground **(207)**

food chain a description of the feeding relationships between organisms in an environment **(247)**

food web the feeding relationships among all the organisms in an ecosystem. Arrows show the flow of matter and energy from one organism to another. **(247)**

force a push or a pull that acts on an object or a system **(148)**

fossil fuel the preserved remains of organisms that lived long ago and changed into oil, coal, or natural gas **(41, 197)**

freeze the change of state from liquid to solid as a result of cooling **(24)**

freezing point the temperature at which a liquid becomes a solid. The freezing point of water is 0°C. **(83)**

frost frozen condensation on a surface **(209)**

full Moon the phase of the Moon when all of the sunlit side of the Moon is visible from Earth **(100)**

fungus (plural **fungi**) an organism that lacks chlorophyll and gets nutrients from dead or living organisms **(247)**

galaxy a group of billions of stars. Earth is in the Milky Way galaxy. **(109)**

gas a state of matter that is shapeless, usually visible, and expands to fill any closed container it is placed in **(6, 117)**

gas giant planet one of the four planets that are made of gas. These are Jupiter, Saturn, Uranus, and Neptune. **(133)**

gaseous existing in the gas state (not a solid or liquid) **(6)**

geosphere the solid, rocky part of Earth's crust **(190, 245)**

gibbous Moon the shape of the Moon when it appears to be more than a quarter but not yet full and when it is less than full but not quite a third quarter. **(125)**

glucose a sugar found in food; the sugar broken down in cells to release energy **(266)**

gravitational attraction the mutual force pulling together all objects that have mass **(151)**

gravity the force of attraction between masses **(117)**

greenhouse effect the trapping of heat in the atmosphere causing Earth's temperature to rise **(231)**

greenhouse gas a gas, such as carbon dioxide, that contributes to the warming of the atmosphere **(42)**

hail precipitation in the form of balls or pellets of ice **(214)**

heart a muscular organ that pumps blood **(282)**

herbicide a poison intended to kill plants **(43)**

humidity water vapor in the air **(173)**

hurricane a severe cyclonic tropical storm that produces high winds and heavy rainfall **(162)**

hydrosphere all of the water on Earth in solid (ice), liquid (water), and gas (water vapor) phase **(190, 245)**

hygrometer a weather instrument that measures humidity **(179)**

impermeable not allowing substances to pass through **(58)**

inherited trait a characteristic that is passed down from generation to generation **(311)**

interact to act upon one another **(243)**

kinetic energy energy of motion **(186)**

Kuiper Belt a huge region beyond the gas giant planets, made up of different-sized icy chunks of matter **(133)**

large intestine the part of the digestive system between the small intestine and the rectum where water is removed from the solid waste **(273)**

left atrium the upper chamber on the left side of the heart **(293)**

left ventricle the lower chamber on the left side of the heart **(293)**

liquid a fluid state of matter with no definite shape but definite volume; and takes the shape of the container it is in **(6, 137)**

lunar cycle the 4-week period during which the Moon orbits Earth one time and is visible in all of its phases **(121)**

lunar eclipse the effect observed when Earth passes exactly between the Moon and the Sun, casting its shadow on the full Moon **(129)**

lung the organ in animals where gases, such as oxygen and carbon dioxide, pass between the atmosphere and the blood **(291)**

magnetism the ability to attract iron **(11)**

magnify to make an object appear larger **(105, 163)**

margin the edge of a leaf **(275)**

mass a quantity of matter; the amount of material in something **(6, 135)**

matter anything that has mass and takes up space **(6, 118)**

melt to change state from a solid to a liquid state as a result of warming **(15)**

membrane the outside of a living cell **(269)**

mesosphere the region of the atmosphere above the stratosphere **(176)**

meteorologist a scientist who studies the weather **(173)**

methane the main ingredient in natural gas **(79)**

Milky Way the galaxy in which the solar system resides **(134)**

mineral a nutrient that xylem transports to the cells in a vascular plant **(247)**

mixture two or more materials together **(5)**

model an explanation or representation of an object, system, or process that cannot be easily studied **(20)**

Moon Earth's natural satellite **(100)**

motor neuron the cells that send information to the muscles **(300)**

mouth a body opening where an animal takes in food **(260)**

multicellular organism an organism composed of many cells **(273)**

neuron a communication cell found in the brain and nervous system **(300)**

new Moon the phase of the Moon when the sunlit side of the Moon is not visible from Earth **(122)**

night the time between sunset and sunrise on Earth **(97)**

nitrogen a colorless, odorless gas that makes up about 78 percent of Earth's atmosphere (air) **(26)**

nonliving referring to something that has never been alive or to things that were once alive and are no longer alive **(256)**

nutrient a chemical in food that helps keep an organism alive and active **(257)**

observatory a building that houses a telescope **(106)**

oceanographer a scientist who studies the chemistry and geology of the ocean **(20)**

opaque matter through which light cannot travel **(89)**

orbit to move or travel around an object in a curved path (can also be a noun, the path traveled) **(102)**

osmosis the movement of water through a semipermeable membrane in a solution with a higher solute concentration until the concentration on both sides of the membrane is equal **(59)**

osmotic pressure a force that drives water molecules through a semipermeable membrane **(59)**

oxygen a waste gas produced by plants during photosynthesis. Oxygen is used by all plants and animals during cellular respiration. A colorless, odorless gas that makes up about 21 percent of Earth's atmosphere (air) **(26, 262)**

ozone a form of oxygen that forms a thin protective layer in the stratosphere **(168)**

palmate describing a leaf in which several veins start at one point near the base. The veins look like the fingers of a hand. **(274)**

parallel describing a leaf in which the veins are straight lines all running in the same direction **(274)**

particle a very small piece or part **(10)**

permeable allowing liquid and gas substances to pass through **(58)**

phase the shape of the visible part of the Moon **(122)**

phloem the long cells through which nutrients, such as sugars, are distributed in a plant **(278)**

photosynthesis a process used by plants and algae to make sugar (food) out of light, carbon dioxide, and water **(170, 263)**

physical property a characteristic that describes a substance, such as color, size, shape, or texture **(10)**

phytoplankton microscopic plantlike organisms in aquatic environments that produce their own food **(247)**

pinnate describing a leaf that has one main vein with smaller veins branching off sideways from it **(274)**

planet a large, round object orbiting a star **(102)**

planetarium a theater with a dome-shaped ceiling that represents the sky **(158)**

precipitation rain, snow, sleet, or hail that falls from clouds **(169)**

predict to estimate accurately in advance based on a pattern or previous knowledge **(100)**

pressure the force exerted by an object or fluid on something else **(37)**

producer an organism, such as a plant or algae, that makes its own food **(247)**

product the substance(s) created or resulting from a chemical reaction **(78)**

radiant energy energy that travels through air and space as waves **(188)**

radiation energy that travels through air and space as waves **(175)**

radioactivity the process by which certain elements emit radiation **(39)**

rain liquid water that is condensed from water vapor in clouds and falls to Earth in drops **(25, 179)**

ratio the comparison of two (or more) parts of a whole **(32)**

reactant one of the starting substances in a chemical reaction **(78)**

receptor cells that send messages to the brain when it receives stimuli **(251)**

recycle to use again **(214)**

reflect to bounce off an object or surface **(119)**

renewable resource a natural resource that can replenish itself naturally over time. Air, plants, water, sunlight, and animals are renewable resources. **(205)**

respiratory system the system of lungs and connecting tubes that transports oxygen to the red blood cells and gets rid of carbon dioxide **(294)**

respond to react or to answer **(300)**

reverse osmosis the process of using pressure to push pure water out of a salt solution using a semipermeable membrane **(60)**

right atrium the upper chamber on the right side of the heart **(292)**

right ventricle the lower chamber on the right side of the heart **(292)**

room temperature the temperature of a comfortable indoor space. Room temperature is about 22°C. **(49)**

rotate to turn on an axis **(97)**

saliva the liquid produced in the mouth that aids digestion **(272)**

salt table salt. A white crystalline solid that dissolves in water. Its chemical name is sodium chloride. **(7)**

sap a sugar-rich liquid transported by phloem **(278)**

satellite an object, such as a moon, that orbits another object, such as a planet **(117)**

saturated a solution in which the solvent cannot dissolve any more solute **(44)**

scale something divided into regular parts to use as a tool for measuring. Rulers and thermometers both use scales. **(83)**

season a time of year that brings predictable weather conditions to a region on Earth **(92)**

semipermeable membrane a filter that allows water to pass through it but does not let dissolved materials pass through it **(58)**

sensory neuron a nerve cell that sends information from sense organs to the brain **(300)**

severe weather out-of-the-ordinary and extreme weather conditions **(216)**

shadow the dark area behind an object that blocks light **(89)**

sleet precipitation in the form of ice pellets created when rain freezes as it falls to Earth from the atmosphere **(214)**

small intestine the part of the digestive system between the stomach and large intestine, where nutrients are absorbed from digested food **(272)**

snow precipitation in the form of ice crystals (snowflakes) **(212)**

sodium chloride the chemical name for table salt **(15)**

solar eclipse the visual effects created when the Moon passes exactly between Earth and the Sun **(129)**

solar energy heat and light from sunshine **(179)**

solar system the Sun and the eight planets and other objects that orbit the Sun **(106)**

solar wind the steady flow of particles from the Sun **(162)**

solid a state of matter that has a definite shape **(6)**

soluble capable of being dissolved. Table salt is soluble in water. **(51)**

solute a substance that dissolves in a solvent to form a solution **(9)**

solution a mixture of one or more substances dissolved in solvent **(9)**

solvent a substance in which a solute dissolves to form a solution **(9)**

specialized structure a structure used primarily for one purpose **(276)**

star a huge sphere of hydrogen and helium gas that radiates heat and light **(101)**

stimulus something that causes an action or response **(300)**

stomach the organ where food is reduced to mush by acid and muscle activity **(272)**

stratosphere the region of the atmosphere beyond the troposphere. The ozone layer is in the stratosphere. **(175)**

substance a pure material that is not a mixture **(6)**

sugar the nutrient that cells use for energy **(262)**

Sun the star at the center of the solar system around which all of the solar system objects orbit **(89)**

sunrise a time in the morning when the Sun appears over the horizon. The Sun always rises in the east. **(91)**

sunset a time in the evening when the Sun disappears under the horizon. The Sun always sets in the west. **(91)**

supersaturated a solution that contains more solute than it normally would at a given temperature or pressure **(45)**

system a collection of interacting parts **(243)**

teeth hard structures in the mouth used for cutting, biting, and chewing food **(272)**

telescope an optical instrument that makes distant objects appear closer and larger **(105)**

temperature a measure of how hot or cold matter is **(24, 114)**

terrestrial planet the four small, rocky planets closest to the Sun. These are Mercury, Venus, Earth, and Mars. **(133)**

terrestrial referring to land **(247)**

thermometer a weather instrument that measures temperature **(178)**

thermonuclear reaction a change in atomic structure that creates huge amounts of heat and light energy, such as the reactions that occur in the Sun **(135)**

thermosphere the region of the atmosphere above the mesosphere **(176)**

third-quarter Moon a phase of the Moon in the lunar cycle halfway between the full Moon and the new Moon **(123)**

thunderstorm severe weather that produces heavy rainfall and powerful static electric discharges **(195)**

tornado a rapidly rotating column of air that extends from a thunderstorm to the ground. Wind speeds can reach 400 kilometers (km) per hour or more in a tornado. **(195)**

transfer to pass from one place to another. Heat energy transfers to make solids melt. **(23)**

transparent clear; describes something through which you can see an image clearly **(6)**

transpiration the process in which water is removed from the cells and passes into the environment **(214, 281)**

transport to move or carry **(276)**

troposphere the region of the atmosphere that begins at Earth's surface and extends upward for 9 to 20 km. Weather happens in the troposphere. **(173)**

unaided eyes looking at something without the use of a telescope or microscope **(101)**

variable anything you can change in an experiment that might affect the outcome **(316)**

vascular bundle the group of xylem tubes and phloem tubes in a vascular plant **(279)**

vascular plant a plant with an internal system of tubes for transporting nutrients to its roots, stems, and leaves **(274)**

vein a blood vessel that carries blood from the body to the heart **(276)**

volume three-dimensional space **(6)**

waning getting smaller **(126)**

water cycle the global water-recycling system. Water evaporates from Earth's surface, goes into the atmosphere, and condenses and returns to Earth's surface as precipitation in a new location **(212)**

water vapor the gaseous state of water **(25, 167)**

waxing getting larger **(124)**

weather the condition of the air around us. Heat, moisture, pressure, and movement are three important variables that determine weather. **(162)**

weather variables data that meteorologists measure. These include temperature, wind speed and direction, air pressure, cloud cover, and precipitation. **(173)**

wind air in motion **(173)**

wind meter a weather instrument that measures wind speed **(179)**

wind turbine a modern windmill **(196)**

wind vane a weather instrument that indicates wind direction **(179)**

xylem the hollow cells of a plant that transport water and minerals to plant cells **(277)**

zooplankton microscopic animals in aquatic environments **(254)**

Photo Credits

Cover/Title page: © Tatiana Ivkovich/Shutterstock; Page 1: © Tobik/Shutterstock; Page 5: © PaulPaladin/Shutterstock (top); © iStockphoto/Leonid Nyshko (middle); © R.Filip/Shutterstock (bottom left); © iStockphoto/Rob Belknap (bottom right); Page 6: © Dave Bradley Photography, Inc.; Page 7: © iStockphoto/bravobravo (top); © matka_Wariatka/Shutterstock (bottom left); © Jesus Cervantes/Shutterstock (bottom right); Page 8: © Dave Bradley Photography, Inc.; © iStockphoto/Michael Czosnek (top); Page 9: © Steve Holderfield/Shutterstock (top); © Galyna Andrushko/Shutterstock (bottom); Pages 10-11: © Dave Bradley Photography, Inc.; Page 12: © Lawrence Hall of Science; Page 13: © Dave Bradley Photography, Inc./Delta Education (top left, top right, bottom left, bottom right); © xpixel/Shutterstock (sand); © Deyan Georgiev/Shutterstock (salt); Page 14: © Dutourdumonde Photography/Shutterstock (left); © Vladislav Kireychev/Shutterstock (right); Page 15: © iStockphoto/mddphoto; Page 16: © Darrin Henry/Shutterstock; Page 17: © Valerii Ivashchenko/Shutterstock; Page 18: © iStockphoto/carefullychosen (left); © Mettus/Shutterstock (left inset); © iStockphoto/MoniqueRodriguez (right); © iStockphoto/ALEAIMAGE (right inset); Page 19: © Jaroslaw Grudzinski/Shutterstock (top); © iStockphoto/Harald Richter (bottom left); © iStockphoto/AtWaG (bottom right); Page 20: © Studio 37/Shutterstock; Page 21: © iStockphoto/gillesd (top); © iStockphoto/Joy Prescott (bottom); Page 22: © iStockphoto/ftwitty; Page 23: © iStockphoto/esemelwe; Page 24: ©iStockphoto/sandsun (top); © iStockphoto/JulienGrondin (bottom left); © iStockphoto/Huriye AKINCI IRIYARI (bottom right); Page 25: © David Young Wolff/PhotoEdit (top); © Lawrence Hall of Science (bottom left, bottom right); Page 26: © psamtik/Shutterstock; Page 27: © iStockphoto/christie & cole studio inc. (left); © PhotoAlto/Fotosearch (right); Pages 28-29: © Dinardo Design (background); © Lawrence Hall of Science (illustrations); Page 30: © tkemot/Shutterstock (top); © Lawrence Hall of Science (bottom); Pages 31-34: © Lawrence Hall of Science; Page 35: © Scott MacNeill (top); © Samuel Acosta/Shutterstock (bottom left); © ssuaphotos/Shutterstock (bottom right); Page 36: NASA; Page 37: © frantisekhojdysz/Shutterstock; Page 38: Ellen Sharples (top); Louis Jean Desire Delaistre and Julien Leopold Boilly (bottom); Page 39: © Photo Researchers, Inc.; Page 40: © Scripps Institution of Oceanography, UC; Page 41: © iStockphoto/mikeuk (top); © iStockphoto/David Parsons (bottom left); © iStockphoto/Kimberly Deprey (bottom right); Page 43: © justal/SXC.hu (background); © Peg Skorpinski; Page 44: © Farferros/Shutterstock; Page 45: © Scott MacNeill; Page 46: © iStockphoto/Jody Menard (top); © Scott MacNeill (bottom); Page 47: © Scott MacNeill; Page 48: © Charles D. Winters/Photo Researchers, Inc.; Page 49: © iStockphoto/Ann Cady (top); © Lawrence Hall of Science (bottom); Page 50: © Lawrence Hall of Science; Page 51: © iStockphoto/Mike Grindley; Pages 52-55: © Mario Wyon; Page 56: © Planetary Visions LTD/Science Photo Library; Page 57: © Longjourneys/Shutterstock (top); © Lawrence Hall of Science (bottom) Pages 58- 59: © Lawrence Hall of Science; Page 60: © iStockphoto/Terry J Alcorn; Page 61: © shao weiwei/Shutterstock; Page 62: © Yuriy Chertok/Shutterstock; Page 63: © Lledo/Shutterstock (top left); © Arthur Hidden/Shutterstock (top right); © Tatiana Popova/Shutterstock (bottom left); © Ruth Peterkin/Shutterstock (bottom right); Page 64: © Blend Images/Shutterstock (top); Courtesy of the Flying Monkeys (bottom); Page 65: Courtesy of Arthur Fry; Page 66: © Morgan Lane Photography/Shutterstock (left); © Eduard Stelmakh/Shutterstock (right); Page 67: © stocksnapp/Shutterstock (left); © Olha Ukhal/Shutterstock (right); Page 68: Graphic Arts Collection, National Museum of American History, Smithsonian Institution, Photograph number: 86-6161; Page 69: © Fotoline/Shutterstock; Page 70: Courtesy of the Hagley Museum & Library, Kwolek05; Page 71: © Elena Elisseeva/Shutterstock; Pages 72-75: © Pedro Salaverría/Shutterstock (background); Page 72: © Lawrence Hall of Science; Page 74: © Darren Baker/Shutterstock; Page 75: © iStockphoto/Laurence Gough; Page 76: © Dave Bradley Photography, Inc.; Page 77: © iStockphoto/Brane Bozic; Page 78: Library of Congress (top); © iStockphoto/Steve Snyder (bottom); Page 79: © iStockphoto/wsfurlan (top); © iStockphoto/JC photography (second from top); © iStockphoto/Felix Alim (third from top); © Lawrence Hall of Science (bottom); Page 80: © iStockphoto/Michael Smith; Page 81: © David Woods/Corbis; Page 82: © Sony Ho/Veer; Page 83: © iStockphoto/Jamie Farrant (background); © iStockphoto/Joachim Angeltun; Page 84: © Delta Education; Page 85: © iStockphoto/Baris Simsek; Page 88: © iStockphoto/parameter ; Page 89: © Ekaterina Pokrovsky/Shutterstock (top); © Cheryl E. Davis/Shutterstock (bottom); Pages 90–92: © Scott MacNeill; Page 93: © Mi.Ti./Shutterstock (top); © Rafal Olechowski/Shutterstock (bottom); Page 94: © vovan/Shutterstock (top); © Alex Ciopata/Shutterstock (bottom); Page 95: © Stephen Finn/Shutterstock; Page 96: © Jeff R. Clow/Shutterstock (top); © iStockphoto/PeskyMonkey (bottom); Page 97: © Scott MacNeill; Page 98: © Frank Zullo/Photo Researchers, Inc. (top); © Scott MacNeill (bottom); Page 99: © Scott MacNeill; Page 100: © gary yim/Shutterstock (left); © Danshutter/Shutterstock (top right); © Natalia Macheda/Shutterstock (bottom right); Page 101: © MarcelClemens/Shutterstock; Page 102: © Babak Tafreshi (TWAN); Page 103: © Scott MacNeill; Page 104: © Tobias Machhaus/Shutterstock; Page 105: © Stock Montage/Getty Images (top); © Scala/Art Resource, NY (bottom left); © iStockphoto/Paul LeFevre (bottom right); Page 106: © UC Regents/Lick Observatory (top); © Scott Kardel (bottom left); © iStockphoto/mikeuk (bottom right); Page 107: © iStockphoto/jamesbenet (top); NASA, ESA, The Hubble Heritage Team (STScI/AURA), J. Bell (Cornell Univ.) and M. Wolff (Space Sci Inst.) (bottom); Page 108: © Rick Whitacre/Shutterstock (left); © Konstantin Mironov/Shutterstock (right); Page 109: NASA; Page 24: NASA, ESA, The Hubble Heritage Team (STScI/AURA); Page 110: NASA (Earth); © ravl/Shutterstock (Moon); © patrimonio designs limited/Shutterstock (U.S. map); Pages 112–116: NASA; Page 117: © Ozerov Alexander/Shutterstock; Page 118: © Scott MacNeill; Page 119: © Philipe Ancheta/Shutterstock (top); © Vasyl Helevachuk/Shutterstock (lightbulb); © Rose Craig/Lawrence Hall of Science (bottom); Page 120: © Rose Craig/Lawrence Hall of Science (top); © Scott MacNeill; Pages 121–123: © Scott MacNeill; Page 124: © Rose Craig/Lawrence Hall of Science (top); © Larry Landolfi/Photo Researchers, Inc.; Page 125: © Larry Landolfi/Photo Researchers, Inc.; Page 126: © Larry Landolfi/Photo Researchers, Inc.; © Rose Craig/Lawrence Hall of Science (bottom); Page 127: © Konstantin Sutyagin/Shutterstock (top); © Scott MacNeill (bottom); Page 128: © Scott MacNeill; Page 129: © Igor Kovalchuk/Shutterstock (top); © FloridaStock/Shutterstock (bottom); Page 130: © Maksim Nikalayenka/Shutterstock (top); © Scott MacNeill; Page 131: © Primož Cigler/Shutterstock (top); © Scott MacNeill; Page 132: © iStockphoto/Dan Wood (top); © Todd Taulman/Shutterstock (middle); © Scott MacNeill (bottom); Page 133: © Jurgen Ziewe/Shutterstock; Page 134: © Sebastian Kaulitzki/Shutterstock (top); © Vibrant Image Studio/Shutterstock (bottom); Page 135: SOHO (ESA & NASA); Page 136: NASA/Lunar and Planetary Institute (top); © oorka/Shutterstock (middle); NASA/JPL (bottom); Page 137: NASA/JPL; Page 138: © iStockphoto/pjmorley; Page 139: NASA/JPL-Caltech (top left); © James Steidl/Shutterstock (bottom left); © iStockphoto/parameter (right); Page 140: NASA, JPL/Lunar and Planetary Institute (top); © iofoto/Shutterstock (bottom); Page 141: NASA/JPL (top); © Stephen Girimont/Shutterstock (bottom); Page 142: NASA/JPL/USGS (top); © Tomislav Stajduhar/Shutterstock (bottom); NASA/JPL (bottom inset); Page 143: © 2001 Calvin J. Hamilton (top); NASA/JPL (bottom left); © Diego Barucco/Shutterstock (bottom right); Page 144: Dr. R. Albrecht, ESA/ESO Space Telescope European Coordinating Facility; NASA /NASA Planetary Photojournal (top); NASA/JPL-Caltech (bottom); Page 145: © Martin Ezequiel Gardeazabal/Shutterstock (left); © Giovanni Benintende/Shutterstock (right); Page 146: NASA, ESA, and H. Weaver and E. Smith (STScI) (top); JPL/NASA/STScI (bottom); Page 147: © Jurgen Ziewe/Shutterstock (Sun & inset); © iofoto/Shutterstock (planets); Page 148: © Rose Craig/Lawrence Hall of Science; Page 149: © Lawrence Hall of Science (table); © Artpose Adam Borkowski/Shutterstock (ball); Page 150: © Lawrence Hall of Science (table); © Artpose Adam Borkowski/Shutterstock (ball); Page 151: © iStockphoto/Christian Miller; Page 152: © Konstantin Mironov/Shutterstock (top); NASA/JPL-Caltech/R. Hurt (SSC/Caltech) (bottom); Pages 153–155: © Scott MacNeill; Page 156: © iStockphoto/Pere Sanz; Pages 157–162: © clearviewstock/Shutterstock (background); Page 157: © Paul. E. Alers/NASA via Getty Images; Page 158: Courtesy of Dr. Seth Shostak, SETI Institute (top); © iStockphoto/cbpix (bottom); Page 159: © Bryan Bedder/Getty Images (top); © STAN HONDA/AFP/Getty Images (bottom); Page 160: NASA (top); © Time Life Pictures/NASA/Time Life Pictures/Getty Images (bottom); Page 161: NASA; Page 162: Courtesy of Ellen Lopez (top); © siloto/Shutterstock (bottom); Page 163: © Noel Powell, Schaumburg/Shutterstock (top); © Scala/Art Resource, NY (bottom left); public image (bottom right); Page 164: © kesipun/Shutterstock (left); © alexkar08/Shutterstock (right); Page 165: © Scott MacNeill; Page 166: © Sergey Mikhaylov/Shutterstock (top); © iStockphoto/leona barratt (bottom); Page 167: © nadiya_sergey/Shutterstock; Page 168: © Katharina Wittfeld/Shutterstock; Page 169: © Pakhnyushcha/Shutterstock (top); © Dainis Derics/Shutterstock (bottom); Page 170: © Andrejs Pidjass/Shutterstock (top); © Mikhail Malyshev/Shutterstock (bottom); Page 171: NASA; Page 172: © iStockphoto/Lars Lentz (top); © Scott MacNeill (right); Page 173: © Lomaney/Shutterstock; Page 174: © Galyna Andrushko/Shutterstock; Page 175: © Ivan Cholakov Gostock-dotnet/Shutterstock; © Efremova Irina/Shutterstock (inset); Page 176: © William Attard McCarthy/Shutterstock (top); © iStockphoto/Snaprender (middle); NASA (bottom); Page 177: NASA; Page 178: © Ivaschenko Roman/Shutterstock (bottom left); © Sofron/Shutterstock (top right); © iStockphoto/Prill Mediendesign & Fotografie (middle right); © Lawrence Hall of Science (bottom right); Page 179: © Laurie Meyer; © iStockphoto/Arturo Limon (anemometer); Page 180: © Jean Frooms/Shutterstock (top); © Laurie Meyer (inset); © Mariusz Gwizdon/Shutterstock (bottom); Page 181: © Newton Page/Shutterstock; Page 182: © silver-john/Shutterstock; Page 183: © Amanda Hsu Perkins/Shutterstock; © mikeledray/Shutterstock (inset); Page 184: © iStockphoto/Michelle Milliman (top); © Scott MacNeill (bottom); Page 185: © Timothy R. Nichols/Shutterstock; Page 186: © Rose Craig/Lawrence Hall of Science; Page 187: © Scott MacNeill (top); © Liz Van Steenburgh/Shutterstock (bottom); Page 188: © Marian Weyo/Shutterstock (top); © STILLFX/Shutterstock (bottom); Page 189: © iStockphoto/Juanmonino (top); © Scott MacNeill (bottom); Page 190: © Caitlin Mirra/Shutterstock; Page 191: © Michael William/Shutterstock (top); © Scott MacNeill (bottom); Pages 192–194: © Scott MacNeill; Page 195: © Robert Fullerton/Shutterstock (left); © iStockphoto/Jim Lopes (right); Page 196: © RCPPHOTO/Shutterstock (top); © TOMO/Shutterstock (bottom); Page 197: © Stephen Bures/Shutterstock; Page 198: © Shi Yali/Shutterstock; Page 199: © Aleksander Bolbot/Shutterstock (top); © iStockphoto/Ralph125 (bottom); Page 200: © Falk Kienas/Shutterstock; © Cordelia Molloy/Photo Researchers, Inc. (inset); Page 201: CORBIS (top); © iStockphoto/Dvougao (bottom); Page 202: © Johannes Kornelius/Shutterstock (top); © iStockphoto/Jeremy Davies (bottom); Page 203: © Time & Life Pictures/Getty Images (top); CORBIS (bottom); Page 204: © riekephotos/Shutterstock; Page 205: © luchschen/Shutterstock (left); © Olena Mykhaylova/Shutterstock (right); Page 206: © Yuriy Kulyk/Shutterstock; © iStockphoto/Eduardo Jose Bernardino (inset); Page 207: © Jorge Salcedo/Shutterstock (top); © Rose Craig/Lawrence Hall of Science (bottom); Page 208: © Andrejs Zavadskis/Shutterstock (top); © Stephen Clarke (TheClarkester)/Shutterstock (spider web); © Gary Paul Lewis/Shutterstock (flower); © Cyprian/Shutterstock (bottom); Page 209: © Anna Jurkovska/Shutterstock (top); © Andrey.tiyk/Shutterstock (frost); © Ruta Saulyte-Laurinaviciene/Shutterstock (leaf); © Evgeny Karandaev/Shutterstock (bottom); Page 210: © Rose Craig/Lawrence Hall of Science; Page 211: © iofoto/Shutterstock; Pages 212–214: © Scott MacNeill; Page 215: © Beata Becla/Shutterstock; Page 216: NOAA (top); © iStockphoto/Lars Christensen (bottom); Page 217: © Boykov/Shutterstock (top); © Rudy Lopez Photography/Shutterstock (bottom); Page 218: NOAA (top); © Ramon Berk/Shutterstock (bottom); Page 219: © valdezrl/Shutterstock; Page 220: © lafoto/Shutterstock (top); © Dark o/Shutterstock (bottom); Page 221: © Galyna Andrushko/Shutterstock (top); © iStockphoto/Nicole K Cioe (middle); © iStockphoto/Denis Jr. Tangney (bottom); Page 222: GOES image/NOAA; Page 223: © Jack schiffer/Shutterstock (top); © Andrejs Jegorovs/Shutterstock (right); Page 224: © Glen Jones/Shutterstock (top); © Dwight Smith/Shutterstock (inset); Page 225: © Andy Z./Shutterstock; © Jeff Oien/Shutterstock (inset); Page 226: © Scott MacNeill; Page 227: © Darryl Brooks/Shutterstock (top); © Scott Prokop/Shutterstock (middle); © peresanz/Shutterstock (bottom); © Jeffrey T. Kreulen/Shutterstock (bottom inset); Page 228: © Kapu/Shutterstock (top); © Elnur/Shutterstock (middle); © David Brimm/Shutterstock (bottom left inset); © kompasstudio/Shutterstock (bottom right inset); Page 229: © Barbara Jablonska/Shutterstock (top); © Ramunas Bruzas/Shutterstock (middle); © Mike Brake/Shutterstock (bottom); Page 230: © Gary Whitton/Shutterstock (left); © Sebastien Burel/Shutterstock (right); Page 231: © Johann Helgason/Shutterstock (top); Scott MacNeill (bottom); Page 232: © Hunor Focze/Shutterstock; Page 233: © Jan Kaliciak/Shutterstock (top); © Anthon Jackson/Shutterstock (bottom); Page 234: © Laurin Rinder/Shutterstock; Page 235: © Larry Malone/Lawrence Hall of Science (top right); © airphoto.gr/Shutterstock (left); © Tom Brakefield/Getty Images (bottom right); Page 236: © Laurence Gough/Shutterstock (top left); © Peter38/Shutterstock (bottom left); © Zeljko Radojko/Shutterstock (top right); © James L. Davidson/Shutterstock (bottom right inset); Page 237: © Kivrins Anatolijs/Shutterstock (top); © Feng Yu/Shutterstock (bottom); Page 239: © ningii/Shutterstock; Page 243: © Jurgen Ziewe/Shutterstock; Page 244: © gilya/Shutterstock (left); © domdeen/Shutterstock (right); Page 245: NASA; Page 246: © Cary Kalscheuer/Shutterstock (top); © MarcelClemens/Shutterstock (bottom); © Mikhail hoboton Popov/Shutterstock (inset); Page 247: © Harry B. Lamb/Shutterstock; Page 248: © Le Do/Shutterstock (fly); © Smit/Shutterstock (spider); © JIANG HONGYAN/Shutterstock (praying mantis); © Mageon/Shutterstock (plum); © Mike Truchon/Shutterstock (blue jay); © IrinaK/Shutterstock (weasel); © iStockphoto/rusm (hawk); Page 249: © Maksym Protsenko/Shutterstock (grass); © Eric Isselée/Shutterstock (chipmunk); © iStockphoto/rusm (hawk); © Michael Schneidmiller/Shutterstock (bacteria); © Rose Craig/Lawrence Hall of Science (bottom); Page 250: © Ivaschenko Roman/Shutterstock (top); © Chris Twine/Shutterstock (bottom); Page 251: © oliveromg/Shutterstock (left); © Andrey Armyagov/Shutterstock (right); Page 252: © Dorn1530/Shutterstock; Page 253: © iStockphoto/Island Effects (bottom); © worldswildlifewonders/Shutterstock (inset); Page 254: © Darren J. Bradley/Shutterstock (top); © William C. Jorgensen/Visuals Unlimited (bottom left); © D.P. Wilson/Photo Researchers, Inc. (bottom right); Page 255: © iStockphoto/Nancy Nehring (top); © Jonathan Lenz/Shutterstock (bottom); Page 256: © Caitlin Mirra/Shutterstock (top); © Tim Mainiero/Shutterstock (bottom); Page 257: © FloridaStock/Shutterstock (left); © Kirsanov/Shutterstock (right); Page 258: © Aleksander Bolbot/Shutterstock (top); © Dewitt/Shutterstock (inset); Page 259: © Tom Grundy/Shutterstock (left); © David Lade/Shutterstock (right); © Dr. Morley Read/Shutterstock (bottom); Page 260: © Kokhanchikov/Shutterstock (top); © Kenneth Sponsler/Shutterstock (left); © iStockphoto/Helena Lovincic (right); Page 261: © AVAVA/Shutterstock (top); © phloen/Shutterstock (bottom); Page 262: © tomer turjeman/Shutterstock (left); © manzrussali/Shutterstock (right); Page 263: © LiliGraphie/Shutterstock (top); © Scott MacNeill (bottom); Page 264: © Elenamiv/Shutterstock (top); © Scott MacNeill; Page 265: © Vladitto/Shutterstock (clouds); © Elenamiv/Shutterstock (leaves); © Monkey Business Images/Shutterstock (kids); Page 266: © Jacek Chabraszewski/Shutterstock; Page 267: © Triff/Shutterstock (top); © Manamana/Shutterstock (bottom); Page 268: © Palis Michalis/Shutterstock (top); © iStockphoto/Alasdair Thomson (bottom); Page 269: © iStockphoto/Lee Pettet (top); © Gerald A. DeBoer/Shutterstock (bottom); Page 270: © Vibrant Image Studio/Shutterstock (left); © saiko3p/Shutterstock (top); © Filipe B. Varela/Shutterstock (bottom); Page 271: © Scott MacNeill; Page 272: © MSPhotographic/Shutterstock (top); © Anton Albert/Shutterstock (inset); Page 273: © Nayashkova Olga/Shutterstock (left); © Scott MacNeill (right); Page 274: © Martin Fowler/Shutterstock (top); © Zoom Team/Shutterstock (palmate); © Vasilius/Shutterstock (pinnate); © Madlen/Shutterstock (parallel); © Anne Kitzman/Shutterstock (fan); © Triff/Shutterstock (round, heart, triangle); © Sally Scott/Shutterstock (compound); © Chad Zuber/Shutterstock (spear); © Kuttelvaserova/Shutterstock (needle); Page 275: © filmfoto/Shutterstock (toothed, lobed); © vipman/Shutterstock (scalloped); © Valentyn Volkov/Shutterstock (fuzzy, smooth); Page 276: © Rebecca Connolly/Shutterstock; Page 277: © Brian Maudsley/Shutterstock (top); © Federico Rostagno/Shutterstock (bottom); Page 278: © OlegD/Shutterstock (top); © iStockphoto/Kyprianos Elisseou (bottom); Page 279: © Jubal Harshaw/Shutterstock (top); © Jose Gil/Shutterstock (bottom); Page 280: © Scott MacNeill; Page 281: © Konkolas/Shutterstock; Page 282: © Hintau Aliaksei/Shutterstock (left); © spirit of america/Shutterstock (right); Page 283: © Danny E Hooks/Shutterstock; Page 284: © BONNIE WATTON/Shutterstock (left); © Kim D. French/Shutterstock (right); Page 285: © intoit/Shutterstock (left); © GoodMood Photo/Shutterstock (right); Page 286: © James A Boardman/Shutterstock (left); © Henk Jacobs/Shutterstock (right); Page 287: © sianc/Shutterstock; Page 288: © Lebendkulturen.de/Shutterstock; Page 289: © Andy Dean Photography/Shutterstock; Page 290: © Scott MacNeill; Page 291: © iStockphoto/virusowy; Pages 292–293: © Scott MacNeill; Page 294: © Vladitto/Shutterstock (left); © Scott MacNeill (right); Page 295: © Scott MacNeill; Page 296: © iStockphoto/Marek Mnich; Page 297: © Scott MacNeill; Page 298: © iStockphoto/DNY59; Page 299: © Scott MacNeill; Page 300: © iStockphoto/Dori Oconnell; Page 301: © Scott MacNeill; Page 302: © Petrenko Andriy/Shutterstock; Page 303: © naluwan/Shutterstock (left); © Scott MacNeill (right); Page 304: © AnetaPics/Shutterstock (left, bottom); © Peter Wey/Shutterstock (right); Page 305: © Andi Berger/Shutterstock; Page 306: © carlosdelacalle/Shutterstock (bottom); © Sean Donohue Photo/Shutterstock (inset); Page 307: © Jason Patrick Ross/Shutterstock (top); © Eky Studio/Shutterstock (inset); Page 308: © noolwlee/Shutterstock (left); © iStockphoto/Aleksandar Nakic (right); Page 309: © Heiko Kiera/Shutterstock; Page 310: © Butterfly Hunter/Shutterstock (top); © dcwcreations/Shutterstock (bottom left); © StevenRussellSmithPhotos/Shutterstock (bottom right); Page 311: © NCG/Shutterstock; Page 312: © Olinchuk/Shutterstock (map); © Cathy Kovarik/Shutterstock (butterflies); © Marco Uliana/Shutterstock (butterfly); Page 313: © Maxal Tamor/Shutterstock; © Butterfly Hunter/Shutterstock (butterfly); Page 314: © NSF Polar Programs/NOAA; Page 315: © Craig Lee, APL-UW/NSF; Page 316: © Eric Rehm, APL-UW/NSF; Page 317: © Scott MacNeill; Pages 318–320: © Eric Rehm, APL-UW/NSF; Page 324: © Delta Education; Page 327: © Elenamiv/Shutterstock; Page 335: © Mny-Jhee/Shutterstock.